# Justice as Fairness

## A RESTATEMENT

# John Rawls

*Edited by Erin Kelly*

THE BELKNAP PRESS OF
HARVARD UNIVERSITY PRESS
*Cambridge, Massachusetts*
*London, England*

Third printing, 2003

*Library of Congress Cataloging-in-Publication Data*

Rawls, John, 1921–
  Justice as fairness : a restatement / John Rawls ; edited by Erin Kelly.
    p.  cm.
  Includes bibliographical references and index.
  ISBN 0-674-00510-4 (cloth : alk. paper)—ISBN 0-674-00511-2 (pbk. : alk. paper)
  1. Justice.  2. Fairness.  I. Kelly, Erin.  II. Title.
JC578 .R3693 2001
320'.01'1—dc21
00-065034

For my cherished friend and valued colleague,
Burton Dreben, to whom I owe so much

# Contents

Editor's Foreword                                                    *xi*

Preface                                                             *xv*

**PART I**   *Fundamental Ideas*                                    *1*

§1. Four Roles of Political Philosophy                              *1*
§2. Society as a Fair System of Cooperation                        *5*
§3. The Idea of a Well-Ordered Society                             *8*
§4. The Idea of the Basic Structure                                *10*
§5. Limits to Our Inquiry                                          *12*
§6. The Idea of the Original Position                              *14*
§7. The Idea of Free and Equal Persons                             *18*
§8. Relations between the Fundamental Ideas                        *24*
§9. The Idea of Public Justification                               *26*
§10. The Idea of Reflective Equilibrium                            *29*
§11. The Idea of an Overlapping Consensus                          *32*

**PART II**   *Principles of Justice*                              *39*

§12. Three Basic Points                                            *39*
§13. Two Principles of Justice                                     *42*
§14. The Problem of Distributive Justice                           *50*
§15. The Basic Structure as Subject: First Kind of Reason          *52*
§16. The Basic Structure as Subject: Second Kind of Reason         *55*

§17. Who Are the Least Advantaged?                                        57

§18. The Difference Principle: Its Meaning                                 61

§19. Objections via Counterexamples                                        66

§20. Legitimate Expectations, Entitlement, and Desert                      72

§21. On Viewing Native Endowments as a Common Asset                        74

§22. Summary Comments on Distributive Justice and Desert                   77


PART III    *The Argument from the Original Position*                      80

§23. The Original Position: The Set-Up                                     80

§24. The Circumstances of Justice                                          84

§25. Formal Constraints and the Veil of Ignorance                         85

§26. The Idea of Public Reason                                            89

§27. First Fundamental Comparison                                          94

§28. The Structure of the Argument and the Maximin Rule                    97

§29. The Argument Stressing the Third Condition                           101

§30. The Priority of the Basic Liberties                                  104

§31. An Objection about Aversion to Uncertainty                           106

§32. The Equal Basic Liberties Revisited                                  111

§33. The Argument Stressing the Second Condition                          115

§34. Second Fundamental Comparison: Introduction                          119

§35. Grounds Falling under Publicity                                       120

§36. Grounds Falling under Reciprocity                                     122

§37. Grounds Falling under Stability                                       124

§38. Grounds against the Principle of Restricted Utility                  126

§39. Comments on Equality                                                  130

§40. Concluding Remarks                                                    132


PART IV    *Institutions of a Just Basic Structure*                       135

§41. Property-Owning Democracy: Introductory Remarks                      135

§42. Some Basic Contrasts between Regimes                                 138

§43. Ideas of the Good in Justice as Fairness                             140

§44. Constitutional versus Procedural Democracy                           145

§45. The Fair Value of the Equal Political Liberties                      148

§46. Denial of the Fair Value for Other Basic Liberties                   150

§47. Political and Comprehensive Liberalism: A Contrast                    153

§48. A Note on Head Taxes and the Priority of Liberty                      157

§49. Economic Institutions of a Property-Owning Democracy                 158

§50. The Family as a Basic Institution                                    *162*
§51. The Flexibility of an Index of Primary Goods                   *168*
§52. Addressing Marx's Critique of Liberalism                         *176*
§53. Brief Comments on Leisure Time                                    *179*

**PART V**    *The Question of Stability*                                  *180*

§54. The Domain of the Political                                            *180*
§55. The Question of Stability                                              *184*
§56. Is Justice as Fairness Political in the Wrong Way?            *188*
§57. How Is Political Liberalism Possible?                             *189*
§58. An Overlapping Consensus Not Utopian                        *192*
§59. A Reasonable Moral Psychology                                    *195*
§60. The Good of Political Society                                         *198*

Index                                                                              *203*

# Editor's Foreword

In *A Theory of Justice* (1971), John Rawls proposed a conception of justice that he called "justice as fairness."[1] According to justice as fairness, the most reasonable principles of justice are those that would be the object of mutual agreement by persons under fair conditions. Justice as fairness thus develops a theory of justice from the idea of a social contract. The principles it articulates affirm a broadly liberal conception of basic rights and liberties, and only permit inequalities in wealth and income that would be to the advantage of the least well off.

In "Justice as Fairness: Political Not Metaphysical" (1985), Rawls began to develop the idea that an account of justice with liberal content is best understood as a *political* conception.[2] A political conception of justice is justified by reference to political values and should not be presented as part of a more "comprehensive" moral, religious, or philosophical doctrine. This idea is central to *Political Liberalism* (1993).[3] Under the political and social conditions of free institutions, we encounter a plurality of distinct and incompatible doctrines, many of which are not unreasonable. Political liberalism acknowledges and responds to this "fact of reasonable pluralism" by showing how a political conception can fit into various and even conflicting comprehensive doctrines: it is a possible object of an overlapping consensus between them.

1. *A Theory of Justice* (Cambridge, Mass.: Harvard University Press, 1971; rev. ed., 1999).
2. "Justice as Fairness: Political Not Metaphysical," *Philosophy and Public Affairs* 14 (Summer 1985): 223–252.
3. *Political Liberalism* (New York: Columbia University Press, 1993).

Developing the idea of political liberalism has led Rawls to reformulate his presentation and defense of justice as fairness. Whereas *A Theory of Justice* presented justice as fairness as part of a comprehensive liberal outlook, this restatement shows how it can be understood as a form of political liberalism. Indeed, Rawls presents justice as fairness as the most reasonable form of political liberalism. In doing so, he recasts the basic arguments for the two principles of justice that are central to a conception of justice as fairness.

This book originated as lectures for a course on political philosophy that Rawls taught regularly at Harvard in the 1980s. The course included a study of the works of historically important figures (Hobbes, Locke, Rousseau, Kant, Hegel, Mill, and Marx) and also presented the fundamentals of Rawls's own view. The lectures on justice as fairness were distributed to the class in written form, at first to supplement reading assignments from *A Theory of Justice.* They addressed questions not taken up in *Theory,* and corrected what Rawls had come to see as mistakes in some of *Theory*'s arguments. Later the lectures were presented on their own, as a more or less complete restatement of the theory of justice as fairness. By 1989 the manuscript had evolved into something close to its current form.

Rawls did revise the manuscript again in the early 1990s as he completed *Political Liberalism.* It is not, however, substantially different from the 1989 version, except for the addition of §50 on the family. After the publication of *Political Liberalism,* Rawls turned his attention to a number of other works, including *The Law of Peoples,*[4] which was originally to be Part VI of this restatement. The rest, now published, are "Reply to Habermas," an introduction to the paperback edition of *Political Liberalism,* and "The Idea of Public Reason Revisited."[5] Ideas from those works are found here, though not always as fully developed as in their already published form.

Because of illness, Rawls has been unable to rework the manuscript in its final state, as he had planned. Still, most of the manuscript was nearly complete. Parts IV and V are the most unfinished, and with more time, surely Rawls would have filled out those sections and integrated them more fully with the first three parts. Part IV reads as addenda to the more detailed and

4. *The Law of Peoples* (Cambridge, Mass.: Harvard University Press, 1999).

5. "Reply to Habermas," *Journal of Philosophy* 92 (March 1995): 132–180, reprinted in the paperback edition of *Political Liberalism* (1996); "The Idea of Public Reason Revisited," *University of Chicago Law Review* 64 (Summer 1997): 765–807, reprinted in *Collected Papers,* ed. Samuel Freeman (Cambridge, Mass.: Harvard University Press, 1999), and in *The Law of Peoples.*

free-standing Parts I–III. Part V is a preliminary effort to reformulate the arguments for the stability of justice as fairness that were presented in Part Three of *A Theory of Justice*. Using the notion of an overlapping consensus, Part V argues for the stability of justice as fairness as a political conception of justice, an idea pursued in *Political Liberalism* and the more recent works. Although they are unfinished, Parts IV and V present important pieces of the overall argument for justice as fairness. The editorial decision has been to leave them, as well as the other parts of the book, mostly untouched. Some sections were reordered so as to introduce basic distinctions earlier. What is now §42 originally followed §50, §47 followed §44, §§55 and 57 were reversed, and §56, which had been the last section of Part V, has been inserted between them.

Additional changes involved the following. References to Part VI, "The Law of Peoples," have been removed. Some exposition of basic concepts, such as the veil of ignorance, has been added. Where this was done, the wording was drawn from *A Theory of Justice* and *Political Liberalism,* and footnotes to those works have been added accordingly and bracketed. Throughout, the approach to making changes has been conservative. Revisions were kept to a minimum and care has been taken not to alter the substance of what Rawls wrote. All changes were made with the author's knowledge.

I am grateful for the help I received in preparing this manuscript. I would especially like to acknowledge Joshua Cohen and Mard Rawls, both of whom worked through the text with me in detail. Their critical judgment and numerous suggestions were extremely valuable. For their useful advice, I would also like to thank Arnold Davidson, Barbara Herman, Percy Lehning, Lionel McPherson, and T. M. Scanlon.

# *Preface*

In this work I have two aims. One is to rectify the more serious faults in *A Theory of Justice*[1] that have obscured the main ideas of justice as fairness, as I called the conception of justice presented in that book. Since I still have confidence in those ideas and think the more important difficulties can be met, I have undertaken this reformulation. I try to improve the exposition, to correct a number of mistakes, to include some useful revisions, and to indicate replies to a few of the more common objections. I also recast the argument at many points.

The other aim is to connect into one unified statement the conception of justice presented in *Theory* and the main ideas found in my essays beginning with 1974. *Theory* itself was nearly six hundred pages and the more relevant essays (of which there are about ten) bring the total close to a thousand pages.[2] Moreover, the essays are not fully compatible, and ambiguities

---

1. In 1975 I made revisions for the first foreign translation of *A Theory of Justice* (1971, rev. ed. 1999). These have appeared in many subsequent foreign translations but never, before 1999, in English. The revised edition rectifies that situation (it contains no further revisions). When these lectures were given, the revisions, some of which address problems discussed in the lectures, were not available in English, and it was assumed the students had only the original text. Therefore, some references to *Theory* in this restatement may be to discussions that do not appear in the revised edition. In these cases, pages in the first edition are indicated. All other page references are to the revised edition. References will always include the section number, which is the same in both editions.

2. Here I list the more relevant essays for reference: "Reply to Alexander and Musgrave," *Quarterly Journal of Economics* 88 (November 1974): 633–655; "A Kantian Conception of

in stating various ideas—for example, that of an overlapping consensus—make it difficult to find a clear and consistent view. The interested reader is entitled to assistance in seeing how these essays and *Theory* might fit together, where the revisions go and what difference they make. This assistance I try to provide by presenting in one place an account of justice as fairness as I now see it, drawing on all those works. I have tried to make this reformulation more or less self-contained.

For those who have some acquaintance with *Theory*, the main changes are of three kinds: first, changes in the formulation and content of the two principles of justice used in justice as fairness; second, changes in how the argument for those principles from the original position is organized; and third, changes in how justice as fairness itself is to be understood: namely, as a political conception of justice rather than as part of a comprehensive moral doctrine.

To explain: two examples of changes of the first kind are these: one is a quite different characterization of the equal basic liberties and their priority, a change required to meet the forceful criticisms raised by H. L. A. Hart (§13); another is a revised account of primary goods which connects them with the political and normative conception of citizens as free and equal persons, so that these goods no longer appear (as many pointed out to me, including Joshua Cohen and Joshua Rabinowitz) to be specified solely on the basis of psychology and human needs (§17). I also try to meet objections raised by Amartya Sen (§51).

---

Equality," *Cambridge Review* 96 (1975): 94–99, and reprinted as "A Well-Ordered Society" in *Philosophy, Politics, and Society,* 5th ser., ed. Peter Laslett and James Fishkin (New Haven: Yale University Press, 1979); "Fairness to Goodness," *Philosophical Review* 84 (October 1975): 536–555; "The Basic Structure as Subject," *Values and Morals,* ed. Alan Goldman and Jaegwon Kim (Dordrecht: D. Reidel, 1978); "Kantian Constructivism in Moral Theory," *Journal of Philosophy* 77 (September 1980): 515–572; "Social Unity and Primary Goods," in *Utilitarianism and Beyond,* ed. Amartya Sen and Bernard Williams (Cambridge: Cambridge University Press, 1982); "The Basic Liberties and Their Priority," *Tanner Lectures on Human Values,* vol. 3, ed. Sterling McMurrin (Salt Lake City: University of Utah Press, 1982); "Justice as Fairness: Political Not Metaphysical," *Philosophy and Public Affairs* 14 (Summer 1985): 223–252; "On the Idea of an Overlapping Consensus," *Oxford Journal of Legal Studies* 7 (February 1987): 1–25; "On the Priority of Right and Ideas of the Good," *Philosophy and Public Affairs* 17 (Fall 1988): 251–276; "The Domain of the Political and Overlapping Consensus," *New York Law Review* 64 (June 1989): 233–255. These essays are occasionally noted in the footnotes of the text, sometimes by an obvious abbreviation. Excepting "The Basic Structure as Subject" and "The Basic Liberties and Their Priority," these all appear in John Rawls, *Collected Papers,* ed. Samuel Freeman (Cambridge, Mass.: Harvard University Press, 1999).

The main change of the second kind is a division of the argument from the original position for the two principles of justice into two fundamental comparisons. In one comparison the two principles are compared with the principle of (average) utility. In the other comparison the two principles are compared with a modification of themselves formed by substituting for the difference principle the principle of (average) utility constrained by a minimum. These two comparisons enable us to separate the reasons for the first principle of justice, covering the basic liberties, and for the first part of the second, that of fair equality of opportunity, from the reasons for the other part of the second principle, the difference principle. In contrast to what the exposition in *Theory* may suggest, this division of the argument shows that the reasons for the difference principle do not rest (as K. J. Arrow and J. C. Harsanyi and others have not unreasonably thought) on a great aversion to uncertainty viewed as a psychological attitude (§§34–39). That would be a very weak argument. Rather, the appropriate reasons rest on such ideas as publicity and reciprocity.

Changes of the third kind arise in clarifying how justice as fairness is to be understood. *Theory* never discusses whether justice as fairness is a comprehensive moral doctrine or a political conception of justice. In one place it says (*Theory*, §3: 15) that if justice as fairness succeeds reasonably well, the next step would be to study the more general view suggested by the name "rightness as fairness." Even though the problems examined in *Theory* in any detail are always the traditional and familiar ones of political and social justice, the reader can reasonably conclude that justice as fairness was set out as part of a comprehensive moral doctrine that might be developed later should success encourage the attempt.

This restatement removes that ambiguity: justice as fairness is now presented as a political conception of justice. To carry out this change in how justice as fairness is to be understood forces many other changes and requires a family of further ideas not found in *Theory*, or at least not with the same meaning or significance. Besides the introduction of the idea of a political conception of justice itself, we need the idea of an overlapping consensus of comprehensive, or partially comprehensive, religious, philosophical, and moral doctrines in order to formulate a more realistic conception of a well-ordered society, given the fact of pluralism of such doctrines in a liberal democracy. We also need the ideas of a public basis of justification and of public reason, as well as certain general facts of commonsense political sociology, some of which are accounted for by what I call the burdens of judgment, again an idea not used in *Theory*.

Offhand, it may seem surprising that viewing justice as fairness as a political conception, and not as part of a comprehensive doctrine, should require a family of further ideas. The explanation is that now we must always distinguish between the political conception and various comprehensive doctrines, religious, philosophical, and moral. These doctrines usually have their own ideas of reason and justification. So likewise does justice as fairness as a political conception, namely, the ideas of public reason and of a public basis of justification. The latter ideas must be specified in a way that is appropriately political and hence distinct from the parallel ideas of comprehensive doctrines. Given the fact of reasonable pluralism (as I shall call it), we must keep track of different points of view if justice as fairness (or any political conception) is to have any chance of gaining the support of an overlapping consensus.

The meaning of these remarks will not be clear at this point. Their aim is simply to give an indication, to those already familiar with *Theory,* of the kinds of changes they will find in this brief restatement.

As always, I am grateful to many of my colleagues and students for their thoughtful and helpful commentaries and criticisms over the years. They are too numerous to mention here, but to all of them I am deeply indebted. I also wish to thank Maud Wilcox for her sensitive editing of the 1989 version of the text. Finally, I must express my deepest appreciation to Erin Kelly and my wife, Mardy, who made completion of the book possible despite my declining health.

October 2000

**JUSTICE AS FAIRNESS**

*A Restatement*

# PART I

# *Fundamental Ideas*

## §1. Four Roles of Political Philosophy

1.1. We begin by distinguishing four roles that political philosophy may have as part of a society's public political culture. Consider first its practical role arising from divisive political conflict and the need to settle the problem of order.

There are long periods in the history of any society during which certain basic questions lead to deep and sharp conflict and it seems difficult if not impossible to find any reasoned common ground for political agreement. To illustrate, one historical origin of liberalism is the Wars of Religion in the sixteenth and seventeenth centuries following the Reformation; these divisions opened a long controversy about the right of resistance and liberty of conscience, which eventually led to the formulation and often reluctant acceptance of some form of the principle of toleration. The views in Locke's *Letter on Toleration* (1689) and Montesquieu's *The Spirit of Laws* (1748) have a long prehistory. Hobbes's *Leviathan* (1652)—surely the greatest work of political philosophy in English—is concerned with the problem of order during the turmoil of the English civil war; and so also is Locke's *Second Treatise* (also 1689). To illustrate in our own case how divisive conflict may lead to political philosophy, recall the extensive debates between Federalists and Anti-Federalists in 1787–88 over ratification of the Constitution, and how the question of the extension of slavery in the years before the Civil War called forth fundamental discussions of that institution and of the nature of the union between the states.

We suppose, then, that one task of political philosophy—its practical role, let's say—is to focus on deeply disputed questions and to see whether, despite appearances, some underlying basis of philosophical and moral agreement can be uncovered. Or if such a basis of agreement cannot be found, perhaps the divergence of philosophical and moral opinion at the root of divisive political differences can at least be narrowed so that social cooperation on a footing of mutual respect among citizens can still be maintained.

To fix ideas, consider the conflict between the claims of liberty and the claims of equality in the tradition of democratic thought. Debates over the last two centuries or so make plain that there is no public agreement on how basic institutions are to be arranged so as to be most appropriate to the freedom and equality of democratic citizenship. There is a divide between the tradition derived from Locke, which stresses what Constant called "the liberties of the moderns"—freedom of thought and liberty of conscience, certain basic rights of the person and of property, and the rule of law—and the tradition derived from Rousseau, which stresses what Constant called "the liberties of the ancients"—the equal political liberties and the values of public life.[1] This overstylized contrast brings out the depth of the conflict.

This conflict is rooted not only in differences of social and economic interests but also in differences between general political, economic, and social theories about how institutions work, as well as in different views about the probable consequences of public policies. Here we focus on another root of the conflict: the different philosophical and moral doctrines that deal with how the competing claims of liberty and equality are to be understood, how they are to be ordered and weighed against each other, and how any particular way of ordering them is to be justified.

1.2. I note briefly three other roles of political philosophy which we consider further as we proceed. One is that political philosophy may contribute to how a people think of their political and social institutions as a whole, and their basic aims and purposes as a society with a history—a nation—as opposed to their aims and purposes as individuals, or as members of families and associations. Moreover, the members of any civilized society

---

1. See "Liberty of the Ancients Compared with That of the Moderns" (1819), in Benjamin Constant, *Political Writings,* trans. and ed. Biancamaria Fontana (New York: Cambridge University Press, 1988). Constant's dates: 1767–1830. The phrase "liberties of the ancients" refers to the liberties of native-born male citizens specified by the rights of political participation in the Athenian democracy at, say, the time of Pericles.

need a conception that enables them to understand themselves as members having a certain political status—in a democracy, that of equal citizenship—and how this status affects their relation to their social world.

This need political philosophy may try to answer, and this role I call that of orientation.[2] The idea is that it belongs to reason and reflection (both theoretical and practical) to orient us in the (conceptual) space, say, of all possible ends, individual and associational, political and social. Political philosophy, as a work of reason, does this by specifying principles to identify reasonable and rational ends of those various kinds, and by showing how those ends can cohere within a well-articulated conception of a just and reasonable society. Such a conception may offer a unified framework within which proposed answers to divisive questions can be made consistent and the insights gained from different kinds of cases can be brought to bear on one another and extended to other cases.

1.3. A third role, stressed by Hegel in his *Philosophy of Right* (1821), is that of reconciliation: political philosophy may try to calm our frustration and rage against our society and its history by showing us the way in which its institutions, when properly understood from a philosophical point of view, are rational, and developed over time as they did to attain their present, rational form. This fits one of Hegel's well-known sayings: "When we look at the world rationally, the world looks rationally back." He seeks for us reconciliation—*Versöhnung*—that is, we are to accept and affirm our social world positively, not merely to be resigned to it.

We shall be concerned with this role of political philosophy in several respects. Thus I believe that a democratic society is not and cannot be a community, where by a community I mean a body of persons united in affirming the same comprehensive, or partially comprehensive, doctrine. The fact of reasonable pluralism which characterizes a society with free institutions makes this impossible.[3] This is the fact of profound and irreconcilable differences in citizens' reasonable comprehensive religious and philosophical conceptions of the world, and in their views of the moral and aesthetic values to be sought in human life. But this fact is not always easy to accept,

---

2. The term and its meaning is suggested by Kant's use of it in his essay "Was Heisst: Sich im Denken orientieren?" *Kant's gesammelte Schriften,* Preußischen Akademie der Wissenschaften, vol. 8 (Berlin, 1912). For him, reason is similarly the faculty of orientation as very briefly characterized in the text.

3. For the meaning of "reasonable" as used in the text, see §§2, 11, 23.

and political philosophy may try to reconcile us to it by showing us the reason and indeed the political good and benefits of it.

Again, political society is not, and cannot be, an association. We do not enter it voluntarily. Rather we simply find ourselves in a particular political society at a certain moment of historical time. We might think our presence in it, our being here, is not free. In what sense, then, can citizens of a democracy be free? Or as we shall ask eventually, what is the outer limit of our freedom (§26)?

One can try to deal with this question by viewing political society in a certain way, namely, as a fair system of cooperation over time from one generation to the next, where those engaged in cooperation are viewed as free and equal citizens and normal cooperating members of society over a complete life. We then try to formulate principles of political justice such that if the basic structure of society—the main political and social institutions and the way they fit together as one scheme of cooperation—satisfies those principles, then we can say without pretense and fakery that citizens are indeed free and equal.[4]

1.4. The fourth role is a variation of the previous one. We view political philosophy as realistically utopian: that is, as probing the limits of practicable political possibility. Our hope for the future of our society rests on the belief that the social world allows at least a decent political order, so that a reasonably just, though not perfect, democratic regime is possible. So we ask: What would a just democratic society be like under reasonably favorable but still possible historical conditions, conditions allowed by the laws and tendencies of the social world? What ideals and principles would such a society try to realize given the circumstances of justice in a democratic culture as we know them? These circumstances include the fact of reasonable pluralism. This condition is permanent as it persists indefinitely under free democratic institutions.

The fact of reasonable pluralism limits what is practicably possible under the conditions of our social world, as opposed to conditions in other historical ages when people are often said to have been united (though perhaps they never have been) in affirming one comprehensive conception.

---

4. The idea of political philosophy as reconciliation must be invoked with care. For political philosophy is always in danger of being used corruptly as a defense of an unjust and unworthy status quo, and thus of being ideological in Marx's sense. From time to time we must ask whether justice as fairness, or any other view, is ideological in this way; and if not, why not? Are the very basic ideas it uses ideological? How can we show they are not?

Eventually we want to ask whether the fact of reasonable pluralism is a historical fate we should lament. To show that it is not, or that it has its very considerable benefits, would be to reconcile us in part to our condition. Of course, there is a question about how the limits of the practicable are discerned and what the conditions of our social world in fact are; the problem here is that the limits of the possible are not given by the actual, for we can to a greater or lesser extent change political and social institutions, and much else. However, I shall not pursue this deep question here.

## §2. Society as a Fair System of Cooperation

2.1. As I said above, one practicable aim of justice as fairness is to provide an acceptable philosophical and moral basis for democratic institutions and thus to address the question of how the claims of liberty and equality are to be understood. To this end we look to the public political culture of a democratic society, and to the traditions of interpretation of its constitution and basic laws, for certain familiar ideas that can be worked up into a conception of political justice. It is assumed that citizens in a democratic society have at least an implicit understanding of these ideas as shown in everyday political discussion, in debates about the meaning and ground of constitutional rights and liberties, and the like.[5]

Some of these familiar ideas are more basic than others. Those we use to organize and to give structure to justice as fairness as a whole I count as fundamental ideas. The most fundamental idea in this conception of justice is the idea of society as a fair system of social cooperation over time from one generation to the next (*Theory*, §1: 4). We use this idea as the central organizing idea in trying to develop a political conception of justice for a democratic regime.

This central idea is worked out in conjunction with two companion fundamental ideas. These are: the idea of citizens (those engaged in cooperation) as free and equal persons (§7); and the idea of a well-ordered society, that is, a society effectively regulated by a public conception of justice (§3).

As indicated above, these fundamental intuitive ideas are viewed as being

5. The exposition of justice as fairness starts with these familiar ideas. In this way we connect it with the common sense of everyday life. But because the exposition begins with these ideas does not mean that the argument for justice as fairness simply assumes them as a basis. Everything depends on how the exposition works out as a whole and whether the ideas and principles of this conception of justice, as well as its conclusions, prove acceptable on due reflection. See §10.

familiar from the public political culture of a democratic society. Even though such ideas are not often expressly formulated, nor their meanings clearly marked out, they may play a fundamental role in society's political thought and in how its institutions are interpreted, for example, by courts and in historical or other texts regarded as being of enduring significance. That a democratic society is often viewed as a system of social cooperation is suggested by the fact that from a political point of view, and in the context of the public discussion of basic questions of political right, its citizens do not regard their social order as a fixed natural order, or as an institutional structure justified by religious doctrines or hierarchical principles expressing aristocratic values. Nor do they think a political party may properly, as a matter of its declared program, work to deny any recognized class or group its basic rights and liberties.

2.2. The central organizing idea of social cooperation has at least three essential features:

(a) Social cooperation is distinct from merely socially coordinated activity—for example, activity coordinated by orders issued by an absolute central authority. Rather, social cooperation is guided by publicly recognized rules and procedures which those cooperating accept as appropriate to regulate their conduct.

(b) The idea of cooperation includes the idea of fair terms of cooperation: these are terms each participant may reasonably accept, and sometimes should accept, provided that everyone else likewise accepts them. Fair terms of cooperation specify an idea of reciprocity, or mutuality: all who do their part as the recognized rules require are to benefit as specified by a public and agreed-upon standard.

(c) The idea of cooperation also includes the idea of each participant's rational advantage, or good. The idea of rational advantage specifies what it is that those engaged in cooperation are seeking to advance from the standpoint of their own good.

Throughout I shall make a distinction between the reasonable and the rational, as I shall refer to them. These are basic and complementary ideas entering into the fundamental idea of society as a fair system of social cooperation. As applied to the simplest case, namely to persons engaged in cooperation and situated as equals in relevant respects (or symmetrically, for short), reasonable persons are ready to propose, or to acknowledge when proposed by others, the principles needed to specify what can be seen by all as fair terms of cooperation. Reasonable persons also understand that they are to honor these principles, even at the expense of their own interests as circumstances may require, provided others likewise may be expected to honor them. It is unreasonable not to be ready to propose such principles, or not to honor fair terms of cooperation that others may reasonably be expected to accept; it is worse than unreasonable if one merely seems, or pretends, to propose or honor them but is ready to violate them to one's advantage as the occasion permits.

Yet while it is unreasonable, it is not, in general, not rational. For it may be that some have a superior political power or are placed in more fortunate circumstances; and though these conditions are irrelevant, let us assume, in distinguishing between the persons in question as equals, it may be rational for those so placed to take advantage of their situation. In everyday life we imply this distinction, as when we say of certain people that, given their superior bargaining position, their proposal is perfectly rational, but unreasonable all the same. Common sense views the reasonable but not, in general, the rational as a moral idea involving moral sensibility.[6]

2.3. The role of the principles of justice (as part of a political conception of justice) is to specify the fair terms of social cooperation (*Theory*, §1). These principles specify the basic rights and duties to be assigned by the main political and social institutions, and they regulate the division of benefits arising from social cooperation and allot the burdens necessary to sustain it. Since in a democratic society citizens are regarded from the point of view of the political conception as free and equal persons, the principles of a democratic conception of justice may be viewed as specifying the fair terms of cooperation between citizens so conceived.

By way of these specifications, the principles of justice provide a response to the fundamental question of political philosophy for a constitutional democratic regime. That question is: what is the most acceptable po-

6. This kind of distinction between the reasonable and the rational was made by W. M. Sibley in "The Rational versus the Reasonable," *Philosophical Review* 62 (October 1953): 554–560. The text connects the distinction closely with the idea of cooperation among equals and specifies it accordingly for this more definite idea. From time to time we come back to the distinction between the reasonable and the rational. See §23.2 and §23.3. It is of central importance in understanding the structure of justice as fairness, as well as T. M. Scanlon's general contractualist moral theory. See his "Contractualism and Utilitarianism," in *Utilitarianism and Beyond*, ed. Amartya Sen and Bernard Williams (Cambridge: Cambridge University Press, 1982).

litical conception of justice for specifying the fair terms of cooperation between citizens regarded as free and equal and as both reasonable and rational, and (we add) as normal and fully cooperating members of society over a complete life, from one generation to the next? This question is fundamental because it has been the focus of the liberal critique of monarchy and aristocracy and of the socialist critique of liberal constitutional democracy. It is also the focus of the present conflict between liberalism and conservative views over the claims of private property and the legitimacy (as opposed to the effectiveness) of social policies associated with the so-called welfare state.[7]

In using the conception of citizens as free and equal persons we abstract from various features of the social world and idealize in certain ways. This brings out one role of abstract conceptions: they are used to gain a clear and uncluttered view of a question seen as fundamental by focusing on the more significant elements that we think are most relevant in determining its most appropriate answer. Unless explicitly stated otherwise, we do not try to answer any question except the fundamental question stated above.

## §3. The Idea of a Well-Ordered Society

3.1. As stated in §2.1, the fundamental idea of a well-ordered society—a society effectively regulated by a public conception of justice—is a companion idea used to specify the central organizing idea of society as a fair system of cooperation. Now to say that a political society is well ordered conveys three things:

First, and implied by the idea of a public conception of justice, it is a society in which everyone accepts, and knows that everyone else accepts, the very same political conception of justice (and so the same principles of political justice). Moreover, this knowledge is mutually recognized: that is, people know everything they would know if their acceptance of those principles were a matter of public agreement.

Second, and implied by the idea of effective regulation by a public conception of justice, society's basic structure—that is, its main political and social institutions and the way they hang together as one system of coopera-

---

7. I say "so-called welfare state" because Part IV distinguishes between a property-owning democracy and a capitalist welfare state and maintains that the latter conflicts with justice as fairness.

tion—is publicly known, or with good reason believed, to satisfy those principles of justice.

Third, and also implied by the idea of effective regulation, citizens have a normally effective sense of justice, that is, one that enables them to understand and apply the publicly recognized principles of justice, and for the most part to act accordingly as their position in society, with its duties and obligations, requires.

In a well-ordered society, then, the public conception of justice provides a mutually recognized point of view from which citizens can adjudicate their claims of political right on their political institutions or against one another.

3.2. The idea of a well-ordered society is plainly a very considerable idealization. One reason we form this idea is that an important question about a conception of justice for a democratic society is whether, and how well, it can serve as the publicly recognized and mutually acknowledged conception of justice when society is viewed as a system of cooperation between free and equal citizens from one generation to the next. A political conception of justice that could not fulfill this public role must be, it seems, in some way seriously defective. The suitability of a conception of justice for a well-ordered society provides an important criterion for comparing political conceptions of justice. The idea of a well-ordered society helps to formulate that criterion and to specify further the central organizing idea of social cooperation.

The idea of a well-ordered society has two meanings. Its general meaning is given above in §3.1: a well-ordered society is a society effectively regulated by some public (political) conception of justice, whatever that conception may be. But the idea has a particular meaning when we refer to the well-ordered society of a particular conception of justice, as when we say that all members of society accept and know that all the others accept the same political conception of justice, for example, a particular natural rights doctrine, or a form of utilitarianism, or justice as fairness. Note that, given the fact of reasonable pluralism, a well-ordered society in which all its members accept the same comprehensive doctrine is impossible. But democratic citizens holding different comprehensive doctrines may agree on political conceptions of justice. Political liberalism holds that this provides a sufficient as well as the most reasonable basis of social unity available to us as citizens of a democratic society.

## §4. The Idea of the Basic Structure

4.1. Another fundamental idea is the idea of the basic structure (of a well-ordered society). This idea is introduced so as to formulate and present justice as fairness as having an appropriate unity. Along with the idea of the original position (§6), it is needed to complete other ideas and to order them into a perspicuous whole. The idea of the basic structure may be seen in that light.

As indicated above in §3, the basic structure of society is the way in which the main political and social institutions of society fit together into one system of social cooperation, and the way they assign basic rights and duties and regulate the division of advantages that arises from social cooperation over time (*Theory*, §2: 6). The political constitution with an independent judiciary, the legally recognized forms of property, and the structure of the economy (for example, as a system of competitive markets with private property in the means of production), as well as the family in some form, all belong to the basic structure. The basic structure is the background social framework within which the activities of associations and individuals take place. A just basic structure secures what we may call background justice.

4.2. One main feature of justice as fairness is that it takes the basic structure as the primary subject of political justice (*Theory*, §2). It does so in part because the effects of the basic structure on citizens' aims, aspirations, and character, as well as on their opportunities and their ability to take advantage of them, are pervasive and present from the beginning of life (§§15–16). Our focus is almost entirely on the basic structure as the subject of political and social justice.

Since justice as fairness starts with the special case of the basic structure, its principles regulate this structure and do not apply directly to or regulate internally institutions and associations within society.[8] Firms and labor unions, churches, universities, and the family are bound by constraints arising from the principles of justice, but these constraints arise indirectly from just background institutions within which associations and groups exist, and by which the conduct of their members is restricted.

8. This seems obvious in most cases. Clearly the two principles of justice (§13) with their political liberties are not supposed to regulate the internal organization of churches and universities. Nor is the difference principle to govern how parents are to treat their children or to allocate the family's wealth among them. See Part IV, §50, on the family.

For example, while churches can excommunicate heretics, they cannot burn them; this constraint is to secure liberty of conscience. Universities cannot discriminate in certain ways: this constraint is to help to establish fair equality of opportunity. Parents (women equally with men) are equal citizens and have equal basic rights including the right of property; they must respect the rights of their children (which the latter have as prospective citizens) and cannot, for instance, deprive them of essential medical care. Moreover, to establish equality between men and women in sharing the work of society, in preserving its culture and in reproducing itself over time, special provisions are needed in family law (and no doubt elsewhere) so that the burden of bearing, raising, and educating children does not fall more heavily on women, thereby undermining their fair equality of opportunity.

One should not assume in advance that principles that are reasonable and just for the basic structure are also reasonable and just for institutions, associations, and social practices generally. While the principles of justice as fairness impose limits on these social arrangements within the basic structure, the basic structure and the associations and social forms within it are each governed by distinct principles in view of their different aims and purposes and their peculiar nature and special requirements. Justice as fairness is a political, not a general, conception of justice: it applies first to the basic structure and sees these other questions of local justice and also questions of global justice (what I call the law of peoples) as calling for separate consideration on their merits.

The principles of justice to be followed directly by associations and institutions within the basic structure we may call principles of local justice.[9] Altogether then we have three levels of justice, moving from inside outward: first, local justice (principles applying directly to institutions and associations); second, domestic justice (principles applying to the basic structure of society); and finally, global justice (principles applying to international law). Justice as fairness starts with domestic justice—the justice of the basic structure. From there it works outward to the law of peoples and inward to local justice. The law of peoples has been discussed elsewhere.[10] No attempt will be made here to deal systematically with local justice. In general, principles for the basic structure constrain (or

9. I follow here Jon Elster's illuminating work, *Local Justice* (New York: Russell Sage Foundation, 1992).

10. See Rawls, *The Law of Peoples* (Cambridge, Mass.: Harvard University Press, 1999).

limit), but do not determine uniquely, the suitable principles of local justice.

4.3. Note that our characterization of the basic structure does not provide a sharp definition, or criterion, from which we can tell what social arrangements, or aspects thereof, belong to it. Rather, we start with a loose characterization of what is initially a rough idea. As indicated above, we must specify the idea more exactly as seems best after considering a variety of particular questions. With this done, we then check how the more definite characterization coheres with our considered convictions on due reflection.

The role of a political conception of justice, however, is not to say exactly how these questions are to be settled, but to set out a framework of thought within which they can be approached. Were we to lay down a definition of the basic structure that draws sharp boundaries, not only would we go beyond what that rough idea could reasonably contain but we would also risk wrongly prejudging what more specific or future conditions may call for, thus making justice as fairness unable to adjust to different social circumstances. For our judgments to be reasonable, they must usually be informed by an awareness of those more specific circumstances.[11]

Finally, to anticipate, since justice as fairness presents itself as a possible focus of a reasonable overlapping consensus (§11), and since the basic structure is the primary subject of justice, the boundaries and aspects of this structure must eventually be drawn and specified in ways that, if possible, at least permit, if not encourage, such a consensus. So generally stated, it is not evident what this condition requires; but these matters we try to answer as we take up a wider range of questions.

## §5. Limits to Our Inquiry

5.1. Before discussing the other fundamental ideas of justice as fairness, let us note some limits to our inquiry. The first limit, as has been indicated, is that we must fix on the basic structure as the primary subject of political justice and leave aside questions of local justice. We view justice as fairness not as a comprehensive moral doctrine but as a political conception to apply to that structure of political and social institutions.

11. I am indebted to Erin Kelly for discussion on the points in this and the preceding paragraph.

The second limit is that we are concerned for the most part with the nature and content of justice for a well-ordered society. Discussion of this case is referred to in justice as fairness as ideal, or strict compliance, theory. Strict compliance means that (nearly) everyone strictly complies with, and so abides by, the principles of justice. We ask in effect what a perfectly just, or nearly just, constitutional regime might be like, and whether it may come about and be made stable under the circumstances of justice (*Theory*, §22), and so under realistic, though reasonably favorable, conditions. In this way, justice as fairness is realistically utopian: it probes the limits of the realistically practicable, that is, how far in our world (given its laws and tendencies) a democratic regime can attain complete realization of its appropriate political values—democratic perfection, if you like.

We focus on ideal theory because the current conflict in democratic thought is in good part a conflict about what conception of justice is most appropriate for a democratic society under reasonably favorable conditions. This is clear from what, for our purposes, we called the fundamental question of political philosophy (§2.3). Nevertheless, the idea of a well-ordered society should also provide some guidance in thinking about nonideal theory, and so about difficult cases of how to deal with existing injustices. It should also help to clarify the goal of reform and to identify which wrongs are more grievous and hence more urgent to correct.

A third limit to our inquiry, mentioned before, is that we shall not here discuss the important question of the just relations between peoples, nor how the extension of justice as fairness to these relations illustrates the way in which it is suitably universal. I assume Kant's view ("Perpetual Peace" (1795)) is correct and that a world government would be either an oppressive global despotism or a fragile empire torn by frequent civil wars as separate regions and cultures tried to win their political autonomy.[12] A just world order is perhaps best seen as a society of peoples, each people maintaining a well-ordered and decent political (domestic) regime, not necessarily democratic but fully respecting basic human rights.[13]

In justice as fairness the question of justice between peoples is postponed until we have an account of political justice for a well-ordered democratic society. Observe, though, that beginning with the justice of the basic

---

12. As Robert A. Dahl puts it in *Dilemmas of Pluralist Democracy* (New Haven: Yale University Press, 1982), p. 16: "today no unit smaller than a country can provide the conditions necessary for a good life, while no unit larger than a country is likely to be as democratically governed as a modern polyarchy."

13. This larger topic is discussed at length in *The Law of Peoples*.

structure does not imply that we cannot revise our account for a democratic society (domestic justice) in view of what justice between peoples turns out to require. The two parts of a more complete political conception—the justice of domestic society as well as of the relations between societies—can be adjusted to each other in the course of working them out.

5.2. Finally, I stress a point implicit in what we have said: namely, that justice as fairness is not a comprehensive religious, philosophical, or moral doctrine—one that applies to all subjects and covers all values. Nor is it to be regarded as the application of such a doctrine to the basic structure of society, as if this structure were merely another subject to which that comprehensive view is to be applied. Neither political philosophy nor justice as fairness is, in that way, applied moral philosophy. Political philosophy has its own distinctive features and problems. Justice as fairness is a political conception of justice for the special case of the basic structure of a modern democratic society. In this respect it is much narrower in scope than comprehensive philosophical moral doctrines such as utilitarianism, perfectionism, and intuitionism, among others. It focuses on the political (in the form of the basic structure), which is but a part of the domain of the moral.

## §6. The Idea of the Original Position

6.1. So far we have discussed three fundamental ideas introduced in *Theory*, §§1–2, the idea of a society as a fair system of cooperation and the idea of a well-ordered society, and the idea of the basic structure of society. Next we discuss two other fundamental ideas, introduced in *Theory*, §§3–4. One is the idea of the original position; the other is the idea of citizens as free and equal persons. The sixth fundamental idea, that of public justification, is discussed in §§9–10.

Let us begin with how we might be led to the original position and the reasons for using it. The following line of thought might lead us to it: we start with the organizing idea of society as a fair system of cooperation between free and equal persons. Immediately the question arises as to how the fair terms of cooperation are specified. For example: Are they specified by an authority distinct from the persons cooperating, say, by God's law? Or are these terms recognized by everyone as fair by reference to a moral order of values,[14] say, by rational intuition, or by reference to what some

14. This order I assume to be viewed as objective as in some form of moral realism.

have viewed as "natural law"? Or are they settled by an agreement reached by free and equal citizens engaged in cooperation, and made in view of what they regard as their reciprocal advantage, or good?

Justice as fairness adopts a form of the last answer: the fair terms of social cooperation are to be given by an agreement entered into by those engaged in it. One reason it does this is that, given the assumption of reasonable pluralism, citizens cannot agree on any moral authority, say a sacred text or a religious institution or tradition. Nor can they agree about a moral order of values or the dictates of what some view as natural law. So what better alternative is there than an agreement between citizens themselves reached under conditions that are fair for all?

6.2. Now this agreement, like any other, must be entered into under certain conditions if it is to be a valid agreement from the point of view of political justice. In particular, these conditions must situate free and equal persons fairly and must not permit some to have unfair bargaining advantages over others. Further, threats of force and coercion, deception and fraud, and so on must be ruled out. So far, so good. These considerations are familiar from everyday life. But agreements in everyday life are made in determinate situations within the background institutions of the basic structure; and the particular features of these situations affect the terms of the agreements reached. Clearly, unless those situations satisfy the conditions for valid and fair agreements, the terms agreed to will not be regarded as fair.

Justice as fairness hopes to extend the idea of a fair agreement to the basic structure itself. Here we face a serious difficulty for any political conception of justice that uses the idea of contract, whether or not the contract is social. The difficulty is this: we must specify a point of view from which a fair agreement between free and equal persons can be reached; but this point of view must be removed from and not distorted by the particular features and circumstances of the existing basic structure. The original position, with the feature I have called the "veil of ignorance" (*Theory*, §24), specifies this point of view. In the original position, the parties are not allowed to know the social positions or the particular comprehensive doctrines of the persons they represent. They also do not know persons' race and ethnic group, sex, or various native endowments such as strength and intelligence, all within the normal range. We express these limits on information figuratively by saying the parties are behind a veil of ignorance.[15]

---

15. [See Rawls, *Political Liberalism* (New York: Columbia University Press, 1993), pp. 24–25.]

One reason why the original position must abstract from the contingencies—the particular features and circumstances of persons—within the basic structure is that the conditions for a fair agreement between free and equal persons on the first principles of justice for that structure must eliminate the bargaining advantages that inevitably arise over time within any society as a result of cumulative social and historical tendencies. "To persons according to their threat advantage" (or their de facto political power, or wealth, or native endowments) is not the basis of political justice. Contingent historical advantages and accidental influences from the past should not affect an agreement on principles that are to regulate the basic structure from the present into the future.[16]

6.3. The idea of the original position is proposed, then, as the answer to the question of how to extend the idea of a fair agreement to an agreement on principles of political justice for the basic structure. That position is set up as a situation that is fair to the parties as free and equal, and as properly informed and rational. Thus any agreement made by the parties as citizens' representatives is fair. Since the content of the agreement concerns the principles of justice for the basic structure, the agreement in the original position specifies the fair terms of social cooperation between citizens regarded as such persons. Hence the name: justice as fairness.

Observe that, as stated in *Theory*, the original position generalizes the familiar idea of the social contract (*Theory*, §3). It does so by making the object of agreement the first principles of justice for the basic structure, rather than a particular form of government, as in Locke. The original position is also more abstract: the agreement must be regarded as both hypothetical and nonhistorical.

(i) It is hypothetical, since we ask what the parties (as described) could, or would, agree to, not what they have agreed to.

(ii) It is nonhistorical, since we do not suppose the agreement has ever,

16. This is an essential feature of justice as fairness as a form of the contract doctrine. It differs from Locke's view in this respect, and also from the contract views of Robert Nozick in *Anarchy, State, and Utopia* (New York: Basic Books, 1974), of James Buchanan in *The Limits of Liberty* (Chicago: University of Chicago Press, 1975), and of David Gauthier in *Morals by Agreement* (Oxford: Oxford University Press, 1986). In these three works citizens' basic rights, liberties, and opportunities, as secured by the basic structure, depend on contingencies of history, and social circumstance and native endowment, in ways excluded by justice as fairness. We come back to this in §16.1.

or indeed ever could actually be entered into. And even if it could, that would make no difference.

The second point (ii) means that what principles the parties would agree to is to be decided by analysis. We characterize the original position by various stipulations—each with its own reasoned backing—so that the agreement that would be reached can be worked out deductively by reasoning from how the parties are situated and described, the alternatives open to them, and from what the parties count as reasons and the information available to them. We return to this in Part III.

6.4. Here there may seem to be a serious objection: since hypothetical agreements are not binding at all, the agreement of the parties in the original position would appear to be of no significance.[17] In reply, the significance of the original position lies in the fact that it is a device of representation or, alternatively, a thought-experiment for the purpose of public- and self-clarification. We are to think of it as modeling two things:

First, it models what we regard—here and now—as fair conditions under which the representatives of citizens, viewed solely as free and equal persons, are to agree to the fair terms of cooperation whereby the basic structure is to be regulated.

Second, it models what we regard—here and now—as acceptable restrictions on the reasons on the basis of which the parties, situated in fair conditions, may properly put forward certain principles of political justice and reject others.

Thus if the original position suitably models our convictions about these two things (namely, fair conditions of agreement between citizens as free and equal, and appropriate restrictions on reasons), we conjecture that the principles of justice the parties would agree to (could we properly work them out) would specify the terms of cooperation that we regard—here and now—as fair and supported by the best reasons. This is because, in that case, the original position would have succeeded in modeling in a suitable

17. This question is discussed by Ronald Dworkin in §1 of his critical review entitled "Justice and Rights," *University of Chicago Law Review* (1973), reprinted in *Taking Rights Seriously* (Cambridge, Mass.: Harvard University Press, 1977), as chap. 6. I have discussed his interpretation briefly in "Justice as Fairness: Political Not Metaphysical," *Philosophy and Public Affairs* 14 (Summer 1985): 236f., n. 19; reprinted in Rawls, *Collected Papers,* ed. Samuel Freeman (Cambridge, Mass.: Harvard University Press, 1999), 400f., n. 19.

manner what we think on due reflection are the reasonable considerations to ground the principles of a political conception of justice.

6.5. To illustrate regarding fair conditions: the parties are symmetrically situated in the original position. This models our considered conviction that in matters of basic political justice citizens are equal in all relevant respects: that is, that they possess to a sufficient degree the requisite powers of moral personality and the other capacities that enable them to be normal and fully cooperating members of society over a complete life (§7). Thus, in accordance with the precept of formal equality that those equal (similar) in all relevant respects are to be treated equally (similarly), citizens' representatives are to be situated symmetrically in the original position. Otherwise we would not think that position fair to citizens as free and equal.

To illustrate regarding appropriate restrictions on reasons: if we are reasonable, it is one of our considered convictions that the fact that we occupy a particular social position, say, is not a good reason for us to accept, or to expect others to accept, a conception of justice that favors those in that position. If we are wealthy, or poor, we do not expect everyone else to accept a basic structure favoring the wealthy, or the poor, simply for that reason. To model this and other similar convictions, we do not let the parties know the social position of the persons they represent. The same idea is extended to other features of persons by the veil of ignorance.

In short, the original position is to be understood as a device of representation. As such it models our considered convictions as reasonable persons by describing the parties (each of whom is responsible for the fundamental interests of a free and equal citizen) as fairly situated and as reaching an agreement subject to appropriate restrictions on reasons for favoring principles of political justice.

## §7. The Idea of Free and Equal Persons

7.1. To this point we have simply used the idea of free and equal persons; we must now explain its meaning and role. Justice as fairness regards citizens as engaged in social cooperation, and hence as fully capable of doing so, and this over a complete life. Persons so regarded have what we may call "the two moral powers," explained as follows:

(i) One such power is the capacity for a sense of justice: it is the capacity to understand, to apply, and to act from (and not merely in accordance with) the principles of political justice that specify the fair terms of social cooperation.

(ii) The other moral power is a capacity for a conception of the good: it is the capacity to have, to revise, and rationally to pursue a conception of the good. Such a conception is an ordered family of final ends and aims which specifies a person's conception of what is of value in human life or, alternatively, of what is regarded as a fully worthwhile life. The elements of such a conception are normally set within, and interpreted by, certain comprehensive religious, philosophical, or moral doctrines in the light of which the various ends and aims are ordered and understood.

7.2. In saying that persons are regarded as having the two moral powers, we are saying that they have the requisite capacities not only to engage in mutually beneficial social cooperation over a complete life but also to be moved to honor its fair terms for their own sake. In *Theory,* these two powers are taken as defining "moral persons" and "moral personality" (*Theory,* §§3–4). What is meant, though, by saying that persons are free and equal?

Here it is important to keep in mind that justice as fairness is a political conception of justice: that is, it is designed for the special case of the basic structure of society and is not intended as a comprehensive moral doctrine. Therefore, the idea of the person, when specified into a conception of the person, belongs to a political conception. (A fundamental idea becomes a conception if we specify its elements in a particular way.) This means that the conception of the person is not taken from metaphysics or the philosophy of mind, or from psychology; it may have little relation to conceptions of the self discussed in those disciplines. It must of course be compatible with (one or more) such philosophical or psychological conceptions (so far as they are sound), but that is another story. The conception of the person itself is meant as both normative and political, not metaphysical or psychological.

As noted earlier (§2.1–2), the conception of the person is worked up from the way citizens are regarded in the public political culture of a democratic society, in its basic political texts (constitutions and declarations of human rights), and in the historical tradition of the interpretation of those texts. For these interpretations we look not only to courts, political parties, and statesmen, but also to writers on constitutional law and jurisprudence, and to the more enduring writings of all kinds that bear on a society's political philosophy.

7.3. In what sense are citizens regarded as equal persons? Let's say they are regarded as equal in that they are all regarded as having to the essential minimum degree the moral powers necessary to engage in social cooperation over a complete life and to take part in society as equal citizens. Having these powers to this degree we take as the basis of equality among citizens as persons (*Theory*, §77): that is, since we view society as a fair system of cooperation, the basis of equality is having to the requisite minimum degree the moral and other capacities that enable us to take part fully in the cooperative life of society. Thus the equality of citizens is modeled in the original position by the equality of their representatives: that is, by the fact that these representatives are symmetrically situated in that position and have equal rights in its procedure for reaching agreement.

I note that in taking the moral powers as the basis of equality we in effect distinguish between a political society and the many associations within it and across it. The latter are associations that cross political boundaries, such as churches and scientific societies. Some of these associations are communities: churches and scientific societies again illustrate this; but universities and other cultural institutions are also communities. The members of a community are united in pursuing certain shared values and ends (other than economic) that lead them to support the association and in part bind them to it. In justice as fairness a democratic political society has no such shared values and ends apart from those falling under or connected with the political conception of justice itself. The citizens of a well-ordered society affirm the constitution and its political values as realized in their institutions, and they share the end of giving one another justice, as society's arrangements require.

The significance of this distinction between a democratic society and the communities within it will become evident later and rests on a number of its special features. For example, we are born into society, and while we may be born into communities also, into religions and their distinctive cultures, only society with its political form of government and its law exercises coercive power. While we can leave communities voluntarily (the constitutional liberties guarantee this: apostasy is not a crime), there is a sense in which we cannot leave our political society voluntarily (§26). Also a community can reward or single out its members in proportion to their contribution to its shared values and ends; but a democratic society has no such shared values and ends (falling under the good) by which its citizens can be distin-guished.[18] All who can be fully cooperating members of political society count as equals and can be treated differently only as the public political conception of justice allows.

It is a serious error not to distinguish between the idea of a democratic political society and the idea of community. Of course, a democratic society is hospitable to many communities within it, and indeed tries to be a social world within which diversity can flourish in amity and concord; but it is not itself a community, nor can it be in view of the fact of reasonable plural-ism. For that would require the oppressive use of government power which is incompatible with basic democratic liberties. From the start, then, we view a democratic society as a political society that excludes a confessional or an aristocratic state, not to mention a caste, slave, or a racist one. This exclusion is a consequence of taking the moral powers as the basis of politi-cal equality.

7.4. In what sense are citizens free? Here again we must keep in mind that justice as fairness is a political conception of justice for a democratic society. The relevant meaning of free persons is to be drawn from the politi-cal culture of such a society and may have little or no connection, for exam-ple, with freedom of the will as discussed in the philosophy of mind. Fol-lowing up this idea, we say that citizens are regarded as free persons in two respects.

First, citizens are free in that they conceive of themselves and of one an-other as having the moral power to have a conception of the good. This is not to say that, as part of their political conception, they view themselves as inevitably tied to the pursuit of the particular conception of the good which they affirm at any given time. Rather, as citizens, they are seen as capable of revising and changing this conception on reasonable and rational grounds, and they may do this if they so desire. As free persons, citizens claim the right to view their persons as independent from and not identified with any particular conception of the good, or scheme of final ends. Given their moral power to form, to revise, and rationally to pursue a conception of the good, their public or legal identity as free persons is not affected by changes over time in their determinate conception of the good.

For example, when citizens convert from one religion to another, or no

18. On this point see "The Basic Structure as Subject," in Rawls, *Political Liberalism*, lect. VII, §8, pp. 279ff.

longer affirm an established religious faith, they do not cease to be, for questions of political justice, the same persons they were before. There is no loss of what we may call their public, or legal, identity—their identity as a matter of basic law. In general, they still have the same basic rights and duties, they own the same property and can make the same claims as before, except insofar as these claims were connected with their previous religious affiliation. We can imagine a society (indeed history offers numerous examples) in which basic rights and recognized claims depend on religious affiliation and social class. Such a society has a different political conception of the person. It may not have a conception of citizenship at all; for this conception, as we are using it, goes with the conception of society as a fair system of cooperation for reciprocal advantage between free and equal citizens.

There is another sense of identity specified by reference to citizens' deeper aims and commitments. Let's call it their nonlegal or moral identity.[19] Now citizens usually have both political and nonpolitical aims and commitments. Thus they affirm the values of political justice and want to see them embodied in political institutions and social policies. They also work for the other nonpolitical values and ends of the associations to which they belong. These two aspects of their moral identity citizens must adjust and reconcile. It can happen that in their personal affairs, or in the internal life of their associations, citizens may regard their final ends and attachments very differently from the way the political conception supposes. They may have, and often do have at any given time, affections, devotions, and loyalties that they believe they would not, indeed could and should not, stand apart from and evaluate objectively. They may regard it as simply unthinkable to view themselves apart from certain religious, philosophical, and moral convictions, or from certain enduring attachments and loyalties.

These two kinds of commitments and attachments—political and nonpolitical—specify moral identity and give shape to a person's way of life, what one sees oneself as doing and trying to accomplish in the social world. If we suddenly lost them, we would be disoriented and unable to carry on. In fact, there would be, we might think, no point in carrying on. Our conceptions of the good may and often do change over time, however, usually slowly but sometimes rather suddenly. When these changes are sudden, we are particularly likely to say that we are no longer the same person. We

19. I am indebted to Erin Kelly for the distinction between the two kinds of aims that characterize citizens' moral identities as described in this and the next paragraph.

know what this means: we refer to a profound and pervasive shift, or reversal, in our final ends and commitments; we refer to our different moral (which includes our religious) identity. On the road to Damascus Saul of Tarsus becomes Paul the Apostle. Yet such a conversion implies no change in our public or legal identity, nor in our personal identity as this concept is understood by some writers in the philosophy of mind. And in a well-ordered society supported by an overlapping consensus, citizens' (more general) political values and commitments, as part of their noninstitutional, or moral, identity are roughly the same.

7.5. A second respect in which citizens view themselves as free is that they regard themselves as self-authenticating sources of valid claims. That is, they regard themselves as being entitled to make claims on their institutions so as to advance their conceptions of the good (provided these conceptions fall within the range permitted by the public conception of justice). These claims citizens regard as having weight of their own apart from being derived from duties and obligations specified by a political conception of justice, for example, from duties and obligations owed to society. Claims that citizens regard as founded on duties and obligations based on their conception of the good and the moral doctrine they affirm in their own life are also, for our purposes here, to be counted as self-authenticating. Doing this is reasonable in a political conception of justice for a constitutional democracy, for provided the conceptions of the good and the moral doctrine citizens affirm are compatible with the public conception of justice, these duties and obligations are self-authenticating from a political point of view.

When we describe the way in which citizens regard themselves as free, we are relying on how citizens tend to think of themselves in a democratic society when questions of political justice arise. That this aspect belongs to a particular political conception is clear from the contrast with a different political conception in which the members of society are not viewed as self-authenticating sources of valid claims. In this case their claims have no weight except insofar as they can be derived from the duties and obligations owed to society, or from their ascribed roles in a social hierarchy justified by religious or aristocratic values.

To take an extreme case, slaves are human beings who are not counted as sources of claims, not even claims based on social duties or obligations, for slaves are not counted as capable of having duties or obligations. Laws that prohibit the abuse and maltreatment of slaves are not founded on claims made by slaves in their own behalf, but on claims originating either from slaveholders or from the general interests of society (which do not include the interests of slaves). Slaves are, so to speak, socially dead: they are not recognized as persons at all.[20] This contrast with a political conception of justice that allows slavery makes clear why conceiving of citizens as free persons in virtue of their moral powers and their having a conception of the good goes with a particular political conception of the justice.

7.6. I emphasize that the conception of the person as free and equal is a normative conception: it is given by our moral and political thought and practice, and it is studied by moral and political philosophy and by the philosophy of law. Since ancient Greece, both in philosophy and in law, the concept of the person has been that of someone who can take part in, or play a role in, social life, and hence who can exercise and respect its various rights and duties. In specifying the central organizing idea of society as a fair system of cooperation, we use the companion idea of free and equal persons as those who can play the role of fully cooperating members. As suits a political conception of justice that views society as a fair system of cooperation, a citizen is someone who can be a free and equal participant over a complete life.

This conception of the person is not to be mistaken for the conception of a human being (a member of the species homo sapiens) as the latter might be specified in biology or psychology without the use of normative concepts of various kinds, including, for example, the concepts of the moral powers and of the moral and political virtues. Moreover, to characterize the person, we must add to these concepts those used to formulate the powers of reason, inference, and judgment. These are essential companion powers to the two moral powers and are required for their exercise and for the practice of the virtues.

## §8. Relation between the Fundamental Ideas

8.1. The five fundamental ideas we have discussed so far are closely related when laid out in the sequence by which they were introduced: from society as a fair system of cooperation to the idea of a well-ordered society,

---

20. For the idea of social death, see Orlando Patterson, *Slavery and Social Death* (Cambridge, Mass.: Harvard University Press, 1982), esp. pp. 5–9, 38–45, 337.

to the idea of the basic structure of such a society, to the idea of the original position, and finally to the idea of citizens, those engaged in cooperation, as free and equal.

In this sequence we start with the organizing idea of society as a fair system of cooperation and then make it more determinate by spelling out what results when this idea is fully realized (a well-ordered society), and what this idea applies to (the basic structure). We then say how the fair terms of cooperation are specified (by the parties in the original position) and explain how the persons engaged in cooperation are to be regarded (as free and equal citizens).

8.2. This spelling out of the central organizing idea of social cooperation is not a deductive argument. The steps starting with that idea and proceeding to the next are not said to follow from, or to be derived from, it. We specify the organizing idea and make it more determinate as we connect it with the other ideas.

To illustrate: there are various ways of specifying the central idea of social cooperation. As we noted, we might say that the fair terms of cooperation are fixed by natural law viewed either as God's law or as given by a prior and independent moral order publicly known by rational intuition. Such ways of fixing those terms have not been excluded by deductive argument: for instance, by showing them to be incompatible with the idea of social cooperation. Instead, they are ruled out by the historical conditions and the public culture of democracy that set the requirements for a political conception of justice in a modern constitutional regime. Among those historical conditions is the fact of reasonable pluralism, which rules out comprehensive doctrines as a basis for a workable political agreement on a conception of justice. Since justice as fairness looks for such a basis, it follows a different course.

8.3. We cannot tell in advance whether the idea of social cooperation, and its two companion ideas, will provide the organizing ideas we need for a workable political conception of justice. The public political culture is not unambiguous: it contains a variety of possible organizing ideas that might be used instead, various ideas of liberty and equality, and other ideas of society. All we need claim is that the idea of society as a fair system of cooperation is deeply embedded in that culture, and so it is not unreasonable to examine its merits as a central organizing idea. The point is that whatever idea we select as the central organizing idea cannot be fully justified by its own intrinsic reasonableness,[21] as its intrinsic reasonableness cannot suffice for that. Such an idea can be fully justified (if at all) only by the conception of political justice to which it eventually leads when worked out, and by how well that conception coheres with our considered convictions of political justice at all levels of generality in what we may call wide (and general) reflective equilibrium (§10). The idea of reflective equilibrium connects with that of public justification, to which we now turn.

## §9. The Idea of Public Justification

9.1. So far we have discussed five fundamental ideas beginning with the central organizing idea of society as a fair system of social cooperation. Now we turn to a sixth and last fundamental idea, the idea of public justification, and three other ideas related to it: those of reflective equilibrium (§10),[22] of an overlapping consensus (§11), and of free public reason (§26). The aim of the idea of public justification is to specify the idea of justification in a way appropriate to a political conception of justice for a society characterized, as a democracy is, by reasonable pluralism.

The idea of public justification goes with the idea of a well-ordered society, for such a society is effectively regulated by a publicly recognized conception of justice (§3). From the preceding discussion, we see that to fill this role a conception of justice should have three features. These make it a political conception of justice:

(a) While it is, of course, a moral conception, it is worked out for a specific subject, namely, the basic structure of a democratic society. It does not apply directly to associations and groups within society, and only later do we try to extend it to connect it with the principles of local justice and to cover the relations between peoples.

(b) Accepting this conception does not presuppose accepting any particular comprehensive doctrine. A political conception presents itself as a rea-

---

21. Intrinsic reasonableness, or acceptability, is a difficult idea. It means that a judgment or conviction strikes us as reasonable, or acceptable, without our deriving it from, or basing it on, other judgments. Of course, that a conviction strikes us as reasonable may indeed turn out to depend on our other beliefs and convictions, but that is not how it strikes us. On due reflection we may affirm the conviction as having a certain reasonableness, or acceptability, on its own.

22. See also *Theory*, §§4, 9.

sonable conception for the basic structure alone and its principles express a family of political values that characteristically apply to that structure.

(c) A political conception of justice is formulated so far as possible solely in terms of fundamental ideas familiar from, or implicit in, the public political culture of a democratic society: for example, the idea of society as a fair system of cooperation and the idea of citizens as free and equal. That there are such ideas in their public culture is taken as a fact about democratic societies.

9.2. We saw that in a well-ordered society effectively regulated by a publicly recognized political conception of justice, everyone accepts the same principles of justice. These principles provide, then, a mutually acceptable point of view from which citizens' claims on the main institutions of the basic structure can be adjudicated. An essential feature of a well-ordered society is that its public conception of political justice establishes a shared basis for citizens to justify to one another their political judgments: each cooperates, politically and socially, with the rest on terms all can endorse as just. This is the meaning of public justification.

So understood, justification is addressed to others who disagree with us (*Theory*, §87). If there is no conflict in judgment about questions of political justice—judgments about the justice of certain principles and standards, particular institutions and policies, and the like—there is nothing so far to justify. To justify our political judgments to others is to convince them by public reason, that is, by ways of reasoning and inference appropriate to fundamental political questions, and by appealing to beliefs, grounds, and political values it is reasonable for others also to acknowledge. Public justification proceeds from some consensus: from premises all parties in disagreement, assumed to be free and equal and fully capable of reason, may reasonably be expected to share and freely endorse.

Public justification is not, then, simply valid argument from given premises (though of course it is that). Valid argument is instructive in setting out the relations between statements: it joins basic ideas and general statements with one another and with more particular judgments; it exhibits the overall structure of conceptions of any kind. By connecting the elements of a conception into an intelligible and perspicuous whole, it serves as a mode of exposition. But when the premises and conclusions are not acceptable on due reflection to all parties in disagreement, valid argument falls short of public justification. For justice as fairness to succeed, it must be acceptable, not only to our own considered convictions, but also to those of others, and this at all levels of generality in more or less wide and general reflective equilibrium (as explained below in §10).

9.3. Of course, it is too much to expect complete agreement on all political questions. The practicable aim is to narrow disagreement at least regarding the more divisive controversies, and in particular those that involve the constitutional essentials (§13.5); for what is of greatest urgency is consensus on those essentials, for example:

(1) the fundamental principles that specify the general structure of government and the political process; the powers of the legislature, executive, and the judiciary; the limits of majority rule; and

(2) the equal basic rights and liberties of citizenship that legislative majorities must respect, such as the right to vote and to participate in politics, freedom of thought and of association, liberty of conscience, as well as the protections of the rule of law.

These and other matters are a complex story; I merely hint at what is meant. The point is that if a political conception of justice covers the constitutional essentials, it is already of enormous importance even if it has little to say about many economic and social issues that legislative bodies must consider. To resolve these it is often necessary to go outside that conception and the political values its principles express, and to invoke values and considerations it does not include. But so long as there is firm agreement on the constitutional essentials, the hope is that political and social cooperation between free and equal citizens can be maintained.

9.4. Clearly one leading aim of public justification is to preserve the conditions of effective and democratic social cooperation on a footing of mutual respect between citizens regarded as free and equal. Such justification depends on an agreement in judgment at least on constitutional essentials; and so, when that agreement is in jeopardy, one task of political philosophy is to try to work out a conception of justice that narrows disagreement on at least the most disputed questions.

Contrast two ideas of public justification on matters political: the first appeals to a political conception of justice, the second appeals to a comprehensive doctrine, religious, philosophical, or moral. Thus a comprehensive moral doctrine tries to show which political judgments are true as specified, say, by rational intuitionism, or by a variant of utilitarianism. Now, so far as possible, political liberalism neither accepts nor rejects any particular comprehensive doctrine, moral or religious. It does allow that it belongs to these doctrines to search for religious, philosophical, and moral truth. Justice as fairness hopes to put aside long-standing religious and philosophical controversies and to avoid relying on any particular comprehensive view. It uses a different idea, that of public justification, and seeks to moderate divisive political conflicts and to specify the conditions of fair social cooperation between citizens. To realize this aim we try to work up, from the fundamental ideas implicit in the political culture, a public basis of justification that all citizens as reasonable and rational can endorse from within their own comprehensive doctrines. If this is achieved, we have an overlapping consensus of reasonable doctrines (§11), and with it, the political conception affirmed in reflective equilibrium. It is this last condition of reasoned reflection that, among other things, distinguishes public justification from mere agreement.

## §10. The Idea of Reflective Equilibrium

10.1. To explain the idea of reflective equilibrium we start from the thought (included in the idea of free and equal persons) that citizens have a capacity for reason (both theoretical and practical) as well as a sense of justice. Under the normal circumstances of human life, these powers gradually develop, and after the age of reason are exercised in many kinds of judgments of justice ranging over all kinds of subjects, from the basic structure of society to the particular actions and character of people in everyday life. The sense of justice (as a form of moral sensibility) involves an intellectual power, since its exercise in making judgments calls upon the powers of reason, imagination and judgment.

We select from our judgments of political justice those we refer to as considered judgments or considered convictions. These are judgments given under conditions in which our capacity for judgment is most likely to have been fully exercised and not affected by distorting influences (*Theory*, §9). Considered judgments are those given when conditions are favorable to the exercise of our powers of reason and sense of justice: that is, under conditions where we seem to have the ability, the opportunity, and the desire to make a sound judgment; or at least we have no apparent interest in not doing so, the more familiar temptations being absent. Some judgments we view as fixed points: ones we never expect to withdraw, as when Lincoln says: "If slavery is not wrong, nothing is wrong."[23] The positions of judges,

---

23. Abraham Lincoln, letter to A. G. Hodges, April 4, 1864, *The Collected Works of Abraham Lincoln*, ed. Roy P. Basler (New Brunswick, N.J.: Rutgers University Press, 1953), 7:281–283.

umpires, and referees are designed to include conditions that encourage the exercise of the judicial virtues, among them impartiality and judiciousness, so that their verdicts can be seen as approximating considered judgments, so far as the case allows.

10.2. Not only do our considered judgments often differ from those of other persons, but our own judgments are sometimes in conflict with one another. The implications of the judgments we render on one question may be inconsistent or incongruent with those we render on other questions. This point deserves emphasis. Many of our most serious conflicts are conflicts within ourselves. Those who suppose their judgments are always consistent are unreflective or dogmatic; not uncommonly they are ideologues and zealots. The question arises: how can we make our own considered judgments of political justice more consistent both within themselves and with the considered judgments of others without imposing on ourselves an external political authority?

We approach this problem as follows: we note that we make considered political judgments at all levels of generality, ranging from particular judgments on the particular actions of individuals to judgments about the justice and injustice of particular institutions and social policies, and ending finally at highly general convictions. Among these convictions are those about the restrictions to impose on reasons for favoring principles of justice for the basic structure, and these convictions we model by the idea of the veil of ignorance in the original position (§6).

Justice as fairness regards all our judgments, whatever their level of generality—whether a particular judgment or a high-level general conviction—as capable of having for us, as reasonable and rational, a certain intrinsic reasonableness. Yet since we are of divided mind and our judgments conflict with those of other people, some of these judgments must eventually be revised, suspended, or withdrawn, if the practical aim of reaching reasonable agreement on matters of political justice is to be achieved.

10.3. Focusing now on any one person, suppose we (as observers) find the conception of political justice that makes the fewest revisions in that person's initial judgments and proves to be acceptable when the conception is presented and explained. When the person in question adopts this conception and brings other judgments in line with it we say this person is in narrow reflective equilibrium. The equilibrium is narrow because, while general convictions, first principles, and particular judgments are in line, we looked for the conception of justice that called for the fewest revisions to achieve consistency, and neither alternative conceptions of justice nor the force of the various arguments for those conceptions have been taken into account by the person in question.

This suggests that we regard as wide reflective equilibrium (still in the case of one person) that reflective equilibrium reached when someone has carefully considered alternative conceptions of justice and the force of various arguments for them. More exactly, this person has considered the leading conceptions of political justice found in our philosophical tradition (including views critical of the concept of justice itself (some think Marx's view is an example)), and has weighed the force of the different philosophical and other reasons for them. In this case, we suppose this person's general convictions, first principles, and particular judgments are in line; but now the reflective equilibrium is wide, given the wide-ranging reflection and possibly many changes of view that have preceded it. Wide and not narrow reflective equilibrium is plainly the important concept (*Theory*, §9, though the terms "narrow" and "wide" are unfortunately not used there).

10.4. Recall that a well-ordered society is a society effectively regulated by a public conception of justice. Think of each citizen in such a society as having achieved wide (versus narrow) reflective equilibrium. But since citizens recognize that they affirm the same public conception of political justice, reflective equilibrium is also general: the same conception is affirmed in everyone's considered judgments. Thus citizens have achieved general and wide, or what we may refer to as full, reflective equilibrium. (The adjective "full" we reserve for features as realized in a well-ordered society.) In such a society not only is there a public point of view from which all citizens can adjudicate their claims, but also this point of view is mutually recognized as affirmed by them all in full reflective equilibrium.

From what we said above (in §10.2), the idea of justification paired with full reflective equilibrium is nonfoundationalist in this way: no specified kind of considered judgment of political justice or particular level of generality is thought to carry the whole weight of public justification. Considered judgments of all kinds and levels may have an intrinsic reasonableness, or acceptability, to reasonable persons that persists after due reflection. The most reasonable political conception for us is the one that best fits all our considered convictions on reflection and organizes them into a coherent view. At any given time, we cannot do better than that.

In justice as fairness, full reflective equilibrium is characterized by its practical aim, reasoned reflection, and its nonfoundationalist aspect, as described above. In this way it meets the need for a basis of public justification on questions of political justice; for coherence among considered convictions at all levels of generality and in wide and general reflective equilibrium is all that is required for the practical aim of reaching reasonable agreement on matters of political justice. With other ideas of justification specified by certain comprehensive doctrines, coherence of this kind presumably does not suffice. But endorsing other ideas of justification alone will not prevent such doctrines from belonging to an overlapping consensus.

## §11. The Idea of an Overlapping Consensus

11.1. The idea of an overlapping consensus is introduced to make the idea of a well-ordered society more realistic and to adjust it to the historical and social conditions of democratic societies, which include the fact of reasonable pluralism. While in a well-ordered society all citizens affirm the same political conception of justice, we do not assume they do so for all the same reasons, all the way down.[24] Citizens have conflicting religious, philosophical, and moral views and so they affirm the political conception from within different and opposing comprehensive doctrines, and so, in part at least, for different reasons. But this does not prevent the political conception from being a shared point of view from which they can resolve questions concerning the constitutional essentials.

Thus to formulate a realistic idea of a well-ordered society, given the historical conditions of the modern world, we do not say that its public political conception of justice is affirmed by citizens from within the same comprehensive doctrine. The fact of reasonable pluralism implies that there is no such doctrine, whether fully or partially comprehensive, on which all citizens do or can agree to settle the fundamental questions of political justice. Rather, we say that in a well-ordered society the political conception is affirmed by what we refer to as a reasonable overlapping consensus. By this we mean that the political conception is supported by the reasonable though opposing religious, philosophical, and moral doctrines that gain a significant body of adherents and endure over time from one generation to the next. This is, I believe, the most reasonable basis of political and social unity available to citizens of a democratic society.

24. The phrase is from Nozick's *Anarchy, State, and Utopia*, p. 225, where it is italicized.

11.2. The thought is that citizens in a well-ordered society affirm two distinct although closely related views. One of these is the political conception of justice they all affirm. The other is one of the opposing comprehensive (or partially comprehensive) doctrines, religious, philosophical, and moral, found in society. For those who hold well-articulated, highly systematic, comprehensive doctrines, it is from within such a doctrine (that is, starting from its basic assumptions) that these citizens affirm the political conception of justice. The fundamental concepts, principles, and virtues of the political conception are theorems, as it were, of their comprehensive views.

Justice as fairness has the three features of a political conception that should help it to gain the support of a reasonable overlapping consensus. Its requirements are limited to society's basic structure, its acceptance presupposes no particular comprehensive view, and its fundamental ideas are familiar and drawn from the public political culture. The three features allow different comprehensive views to endorse it. These include religious doctrines that affirm liberty of conscience and support the basic constitutional freedoms, as well as various liberal philosophical doctrines, such as those of Kant and Mill, that likewise do so.

We need not enumerate further possibilities (of which there are many) except to add that many citizens may not hold any well-articulated comprehensive doctrine at all. Perhaps most do not. Rather, they affirm various religious and philosophical, associational and personal values together with the political values expressed by the political conception. These political values are not derived within any overall, systematic view. People may think that the political values realized by a just basic structure are normally of sufficient weight to override whatever other values are likely come in conflict with them. So while their whole view is comprehensive in that it includes nonpolitical values, it is only partially comprehensive in being neither systematic nor complete. In §58 we shall find that this lack of system and completeness is indeed fortunate, and helps to permit a modus vivendi to change over time into an overlapping consensus.

11.3. In giving an important place to the idea of an overlapping consensus, we assume the fact of reasonable pluralism to be a permanent condition of a democratic society. Any political conception has a view of the political and social world and relies on certain general facts of political sociology and human psychology. The fact of reasonable pluralism is the first of five such facts that are especially important in justice as fairness.

To elaborate: the diversity of religious, philosophical, and moral doctrines found in modern democratic societies is not a mere historical condition that may soon pass away; it is a permanent feature of the public culture of democracy. Under the political and social conditions secured by the basic rights and liberties of free institutions, a diversity of conflicting and irreconcilable yet reasonable comprehensive doctrines will come about and persist, should it not already exist. This fact about free societies is what I call the fact of reasonable pluralism.

A second and related general fact is that a continuing shared adherence to one comprehensive doctrine can be maintained only by the oppressive use of state power, with all its official crimes and the inevitable brutality and cruelties, followed by the corruption of religion, philosophy, and science. If we say a political society is a community when it is united in affirming one and the same comprehensive doctrine (recall §7.3), then the oppressive use of state power with these attendant evils is necessary to maintain political community. Let us call this the fact of oppression. In the society of the Middle Ages, more or less united in affirming the Catholic faith, the Inquisition was not an accident; its suppression of heresy was needed to preserve the shared religious belief. The same holds, we suppose, for any comprehensive philosophical and moral doctrine, even secular ones. A society united on a form of utilitarianism, or on the moral views of Kant or Mill, would likewise require the oppressive sanctions of state power to remain so.[25]

A third general fact is that an enduring and secure democratic regime, one not divided by bitter doctrinal disputes and hostile social classes, must be willingly and freely supported by at least a substantial majority of its politically active citizens. Together with the first general fact, this means that to serve as a public basis of justification for a constitutional regime a conception of justice must be one that can be endorsed by widely different and even irreconcilable comprehensive doctrines. Otherwise the regime will not be enduring and secure. This leads us to introduce the idea of a political conception of justice, as specified in §9.

We add, then, a fourth general fact: that the political culture of a demo-

25. The content and tone of one's conception of justice, political or other, is undoubtedly influenced by dwelling upon certain facts of historical experience. For justice as fairness, important among these facts are the endless oppressions and cruelties of state power and inquisition used to sustain Christian unity beginning as early as St. Augustine and extending into the eighteenth century. Political liberalism begins with the division of Christendom after the Reformation, though that was hardly the Reformers' intent. As Hegel believed, that it occurred was not a misfortune but a good thing for both church and state. See G. F. W. Hegel, *Elements of the Philosophy of Right,* trans. H. B. Nisbet and ed. Allen Wood (Cambridge: Cambridge University Press, 1991), §270 (end of the long comment), pp. 301f.

cratic society that has worked reasonably well over a considerable period of time normally contains, at least implicitly, certain fundamental ideas from which it is possible to work up a political conception of justice suitable for a constitutional regime.

11.4. What lies behind these first four general facts? Surely all, and especially the first two (the fact of reasonable pluralism and the fact of oppression), call for explanation. For why should free institutions with their basic rights and liberties lead to diversity; and why should state power be required to overcome it? Why doesn't our sincere and conscientious attempt to reason with one another lead us to agreement? It seems to do so in science, or in natural science anyway, at least in the long run.

There are several possible explanations. We might suppose that most people hold views that advance their own more narrow interests; and since their interests are different, so are their views. Or perhaps people are often irrational and not very bright, and this mixed with logical errors leads to conflicting opinions. But these explanations are too easy, and not the kind we want. We want to know how reasonable disagreement is possible, for we always begin work within ideal theory. Thus we ask: how might reasonable disagreement come about?

An explanation of the right kind is that the sources of reasonable disagreement—what I call the burdens of judgment—among reasonable persons are the many obstacles to the correct (and conscientious) exercise of our powers of reason and judgment in the ordinary course of political life. These obstacles include the following:

(a) The evidence—empirical and scientific—bearing on a case may be conflicting and complex, and thus hard to assess and evaluate.

(b) Even where we agree fully about the kinds of considerations that are relevant, we may disagree about their weight, and so arrive at different judgments.

(c) To some degree all our concepts, and not only our moral and political concepts, are vague and subject to hard cases. This indeterminacy means that we must rely on judgment and interpretation (and on judgments about interpretations) within some range (not sharply specifiable) where reasonable persons may differ.

(d) The way we assess evidence and weigh moral and political values is shaped (how much so we cannot tell) by our total experience, our whole course of life up to now; and our total experiences surely differ. So in a modern society with its numerous offices and positions, its many divisions of labor, its many social groups and often their ethnic variety, citizens' total experiences differ enough for their judgments to diverge to some degree on many if not most cases of any significant complexity.

(e) Often there are different kinds of normative considerations of different force on both sides of a question and it is difficult to make an overall assessment.[26]

A fifth and last general fact may be stated as follows: that many of our most important political judgments involving the basic political values are made subject to conditions such that it is highly unlikely that conscientious and fully reasonable persons, even after free and open discussion, can exercise their powers of reason so that all arrive at the same conclusion.

11.5. This fact must not be understood to imply a philosophical doctrine of skepticism.[27] It does not mean that reasonable persons do not agree in political judgment because objective values do not exist, or are subjective; or that what we take as judgments about values are simply historically conditioned opinions giving voice to interests rooted in time and place. It refers instead to the many difficulties in reaching agreement arising with all kinds of judgment. These difficulties are particularly acute in the case of political judgments in view of the very great complexity of the questions raised, the often impressionistic nature of the evidence, and the severity of the conflicts they commonly address.

The burdens of judgment alone can account for the fact of reasonable pluralism (there are of course other reasons); and since we cannot eliminate these burdens, pluralism is a permanent feature of a free democratic culture. We do not deny that vanity and greed, the will to dominate and the desire for glory are prominent in politics and affect the rise and fall of nations. Yet since we cannot as a democracy use state power, with its attendant cruelties and corruptions of civic and cultural life, to eradicate diver-

---

26. A related point has often been stressed by Isaiah Berlin; namely, that any system of social institutions is limited in the range of values it can accommodate, so that some selection must be made from the full range of moral and political values that might be realized. This is because any system of institutions has, as it were, but a limited social space. In being forced to select among cherished values, we face great difficulties in setting priorities, and face other hard decisions that may seem to have no clear answer. See his statement in "On the Pursuit of the Ideal," in *The Crooked Timber of Humanity*, ed. Henry Hardy (New York: Knopf, 1991).

27. This follows *Theory*, §34: 188, in holding it essential to avoid resting liberty of conscience and toleration on philosophical skepticism and indifference to religion.

sity, we look for a political conception of justice that can gain the support of a reasonable overlapping consensus to serve as a public basis of justification.

11.6. In conclusion, two remarks to prevent misunderstandings of the idea of an overlapping consensus:

First, given the actual comprehensive views existing in society, no matter what their content, there is plainly no guarantee that justice as fairness, or any reasonable conception for a democratic regime, can gain the support of an overlapping consensus and in that way underwrite the stability of its political institutions. Many doctrines are plainly incompatible with the values of democracy. Moreover, political liberalism does not say that the values articulated by a political conception of justice, though of basic significance, outweigh the transcendent values (as people may interpret them)—religious, philosophical, or moral—with which the political conception may possibly conflict. To say that would go beyond the political.

A second remark is that we start from the conviction that a constitutional democratic regime is reasonably just and workable, and worth defending. But given the fact of reasonable pluralism, we try to design our defense of it so as to gain the allegiance of reasonable people and to win wide support. We do not look to the comprehensive doctrines that in fact exist and then frame a political conception that strikes a balance between them expressly designed to gain their allegiance. To do that would make the political conception political in the wrong way (§56).

Instead, we ask how to frame a conception of justice for a constitutional regime that both seems defensible in its own right and is such that those who support, or who might be brought to support, that kind of regime can also endorse that conception. We assume that we know nothing in advance about people's comprehensive views, and we try to put no unnecessary obstacles in the way of their affirming the political conception. This leads to the idea of a political conception of justice that presupposes no particular comprehensive view, and hence may be supported by an enduring overlapping consensus of reasonable doctrines, given good fortune and enough time to gain allegiance to itself.

In Part V we consider whether a well-ordered democratic society is possible, and if so, how its possibility is consistent with human nature and the requirements of workable political institutions. We try to show that the well-ordered society of justice as fairness is indeed possible according to our nature and those requirements. This endeavor belongs to political philosophy as reconciliation; for seeing that the conditions of a social world at least allow for that possibility affects our view of the world itself and our attitude toward it. No longer need it seem hopelessly hostile, a world in which the will to dominate and oppressive cruelties, abetted by prejudice and folly, must inevitably prevail. None of this may ease our loss, situated as we may be in a corrupt society. But we may reflect that the world is not in itself inhospitable to political justice and its good. Our social world might have been different and there is hope for those at another time and place.

# PART II

# Principles of Justice

## §12. Three Basic Points

12.1. In Part II we discuss the content of the two principles of justice that apply to the basic structure, as well as various grounds in favor of them and replies to a number of objections. A more formal and organized argument for these principles is presented in Part III, where we discuss the reasoning that moves the parties in the original position. In that argument the original position serves to keep track of all our assumptions and to bring out their combined force by uniting them into one framework so that we can more easily see their implications.

I begin with three basic points which review some matters discussed in Part I and introduce others we are about to examine. Recall first that justice as fairness is framed for a democratic society. Its principles are meant to answer the question: once we view a democratic society as a fair system of social cooperation between citizens regarded as free and equal, what principles are most appropriate to it? Alternatively: which principles are most appropriate for a democratic society that not only professes but wants to take seriously the idea that citizens are free and equal, and tries to realize that idea in its main institutions? The question of whether a constitutional regime is to be preferred to majoritarian democracy, we postpone until later (Part IV, §44).

12.2. The second point is that justice as fairness takes the primary subject of political justice to be the basic structure of society, that is, its main political and social institutions and how they fit together into one unified system of cooperation (§4). We suppose that citizens are born into society and will normally spend their whole lives within its basic institutions. The nature and role of the basic structure importantly influence social and economic inequalities and enter into determining the appropriate principles of justice.

In particular, let us suppose that the fundamental social and economic inequalities are the differences in citizens' life-prospects (their prospects over a complete life) as these are affected by such things as their social class of origin, their native endowments, their opportunities for education, and their good or ill fortune over the course of life (§16). We ask: by what principles are differences of that kind—differences in life-prospects—made legitimate and consistent with the idea of free and equal citizenship in society seen as a fair system of cooperation?

12.3. The third point is that justice as fairness is a form of political liberalism: it tries to articulate a family of highly significant (moral) values that characteristically apply to the political and social institutions of the basic structure. It gives an account of these values in the light of certain special features of the political relationship as distinct from other relationships, associational, familial, and personal.

(a) It is a relationship of persons within the basic structure of society, a structure we enter only by birth and exit only by death (or so we may assume for the moment). Political society is closed, as it were; and we do not, and indeed cannot, enter or leave it voluntarily.

(b) Political power is always coercive power applied by the state and its apparatus of enforcement; but in a constitutional regime political power is at the same time the power of free and equal citizens as a collective body. Thus political power is citizens' power, which they impose on themselves and one another as free and equal.

The idea of political liberalism arises as follows. We start from two facts: first, from the fact of reasonable pluralism, the fact that a diversity of reasonable comprehensive doctrines is a permanent feature of a democratic society; and second, from the fact that in a democratic regime political power is regarded as the power of free and equal citizens as a collective body. These two points give rise to a problem of political legitimacy. For if the fact of reasonable pluralism always characterizes democratic societies and if political power is indeed the power of free and equal citizens, in the light of what reasons and values—of what kind of a conception of justice—can citizens legitimately exercise that coercive power over one another?

Political liberalism answers that the conception of justice must be a political conception, as defined in §9.1. Such a conception when satisfied allows us to say: political power is legitimate only when it is exercised in accordance with a constitution (written or unwritten) the essentials of which all citizens, as reasonable and rational, can endorse in the light of their common human reason. This is the liberal principle of legitimacy. It is a further desideratum that all legislative questions that concern or border on these essentials, or are highly divisive, should also be settled, so far as possible, by guidelines and values that can be similarly endorsed.

In matters of constitutional essentials, as well as on questions of basic justice, we try to appeal only to principles and values each citizen can endorse. A political conception of justice hopes to formulate these values: its shared principles and values make reason public, while freedom of speech and thought in a constitutional regime make it free. In providing a public basis of justification, a political conception of justice provides the framework for the liberal idea of political legitimacy. As noted in §9.4, however, and discussed further in §26, we do not say that a political conception formulates political values that can settle all legislative questions. This is neither possible nor desirable. There are many questions legislatures must consider that can only be settled by voting that is properly influenced by nonpolitical values. Yet at least on constitutional essentials and matters of basic justice we do try for an agreed basis; so long as there is at least rough agreement here, fair social cooperation among citizens can, we hope, be maintained.[1]

12.4. Given these three points, our question is: viewing society as a fair system of cooperation between citizens regarded as free and equal, what principles of justice are most appropriate to specify basic rights and liberties, and to regulate social and economic inequalities in citizens' prospects over a complete life? These inequalities are our primary concern.

To find a principle to regulate these inequalities, we look to our firmest considered convictions about equal basic rights and liberties, the fair value

1. It is not always clear whether a question involves a constitutional essential, as will be mentioned in due course. If there is doubt about this and the question is highly divisive, then citizens have a duty of civility to try to articulate their claims on one another by reference to political values, if that is possible.

of the political liberties as well as fair equality of opportunity. We look outside the sphere of distributive justice more narrowly construed to see
whether an appropriate distributive principle is singled out by those firmest
convictions once their essential elements are represented in the original position as a device of representation (§6). This device is to assist us in working out which principle, or principles, the representatives of free and equal
citizens would select to regulate social and economic inequalities in these
prospects over a complete life when they assume that the equal basic liberties and fair opportunities are already secured.

The idea here is to use our firmest considered convictions about the nature of a democratic society as a fair system of cooperation between free
and equal citizens—as modeled in the original position—to see whether the
combined assertion of those convictions so expressed will help us to identify an appropriate distributive principle for the basic structure with its economic and social inequalities in citizens' life-prospects. Our convictions
about principles regulating those inequalities are much less firm and assured; so we look to our firmest convictions for guidance where assurance
is lacking and guidance is needed (*Theory*, §§4, 20).

## §13. Two Principles of Justice

13.1. To try to answer our question, let us turn to a revised statement of
the two principles of justice discussed in *Theory*, §§11–14. They should
now read:[2]

(a) Each person has the same indefeasible claim to a fully adequate
scheme of equal basic liberties, which scheme is compatible with
the same scheme of liberties for all; and

(b) Social and economic inequalities are to satisfy two conditions: first,
they are to be attached to offices and positions open to all under
conditions of fair equality of opportunity; and second, they are to

2. This section summarizes some points from "The Basic Liberties and Their Priority,"
*Tanner Lectures on Human Values*, vol. 3, ed. Sterling McMurrin (Salt Lake City: University
of Utah Press, 1982), §I, reprinted in *Political Liberalism*. In that essay I try to reply to what
I believe are two of the more serious objections to my account of liberty in *Theory* raised by
H. L. A. Hart in his splendid critical review essay, "Rawls on Liberty and Its Priority," *University of Chicago Law Review* 40 (Spring 1973): 551–555, reprinted in his *Essays in Jurisprudence and Philosophy* (Oxford: Oxford University Press, 1983). No changes made in justice as fairness in this restatement are more significant than those forced by Hart's review.

be to the greatest benefit of the least-advantaged members of society (the difference principle).[3]

As I explain below, the first principle is prior to the second; also, in the second principle fair equality of opportunity is prior to the difference principle. This priority means that in applying a principle (or checking it against test cases) we assume that the prior principles are fully satisfied. We seek a principle of distribution (in the narrower sense) that holds within the setting of background institutions that secure the basic equal liberties (including the fair value of the political liberties)[4] as well as fair equality of opportunity. How far that principle holds outside that setting is a separate question we shall not consider.[5]

13.2. The revisions in the second principle are merely stylistic. But before noting the revisions in the first principle, which are significant, we should attend to the meaning of fair equality of opportunity. This is a difficult and not altogether clear idea; its role is perhaps best gathered from why it is introduced: namely, to correct the defects of formal equality of opportunity—careers open to talents—in the system of natural liberty, so-called (*Theory*, §12: 62ff.; §14). To this end, fair equality of opportunity is said to require not merely that public offices and social positions be open in the formal sense, but that all should have a fair chance to attain them. To

3. Instead of "the difference principle," many writers prefer the term "the maximin principle," or simply "maximin justice," or some such locution. See, for example, Joshua Cohen's very full and accurate account of the difference principle in "Democratic Equality," *Ethics* 99 (July 1989): 727–751. But I still use the term "difference principle" to emphasize first, that this principle and the maximin rule for decision under uncertainty (§28.1) are two very distinct things; and second, that in arguing for the difference principle over other distributive principles (say a restricted principle of (average) utility, which includes a social minimum), there is no appeal at all to the maximin rule for decision under uncertainty. The widespread idea that the argument for the difference principle depends on extreme aversion to uncertainty is a mistake, although a mistake unhappily encouraged by the faults of exposition in *Theory*, faults to be corrected in Part III of this restatement.

4. See *Theory*, §36: 197–199.

5. Some have found this kind of restriction objectionable; they think a political conception should be framed to cover all logically possible cases, or all conceivable cases, and not restricted to cases that can arise only within a specified institutional context. See for example Brian Barry, *The Liberal Theory of Justice* (Oxford: Oxford University Press, 1973), p. 112. In contrast, we seek a principle to govern social and economic inequalities in democratic regimes as we know them, and so we are concerned with inequalities in citizens' life-prospects that may actually arise, given our understanding of how certain institutions work.

specify the idea of a fair chance we say: supposing that there is a distribution of native endowments, those who have the same level of talent and ability and the same willingness to use these gifts should have the same prospects of success regardless of their social class of origin, the class into which they are born and develop until the age of reason. In all parts of society there are to be roughly the same prospects of culture and achievement for those similarly motivated and endowed.

Fair equality of opportunity here means liberal equality. To accomplish its aims, certain requirements must be imposed on the basic structure beyond those of the system of natural liberty. A free market system must be set within a framework of political and legal institutions that adjust the long-run trend of economic forces so as to prevent excessive concentrations of property and wealth, especially those likely to lead to political domination. Society must also establish, among other things, equal opportunities of education for all regardless of family income (§15).[6]

13.3. Consider now the reasons for revising the first principle.[7] One is that the equal basic liberties in this principle are specified by a list as follows: freedom of thought and liberty of conscience; political liberties (for example, the right to vote and to participate in politics) and freedom of association, as well as the rights and liberties specified by the liberty and integrity (physical and psychological) of the person; and finally, the rights and liberties covered by the rule of law. That the basic liberties are specified by a list is quite clear from *Theory*, §11: 61 (1st ed.); but the use of the singular term "basic liberty" in the statement of the principle on *Theory*, §11: 60 (1st ed.), obscures this important feature of these liberties.

This revision brings out that no priority is assigned to liberty as such, as if the exercise of something called "liberty" had a preeminent value and were the main, if not the sole, end of political and social justice. While there is a general presumption against imposing legal and other restrictions on conduct without a sufficient reason, this presumption creates no special priority for any particular liberty. Throughout the history of democratic

6. These remarks are the merest sketch of a difficult idea. We come back to it from time to time.

7. This principle may be preceded by a lexically prior principle requiring that basic needs be met, as least insofar as their being met is a necessary condition for citizens to understand and to be able fruitfully to exercise the basic rights and liberties. For a statement of such a principle with further discussion, see R. G. Peffer, *Marxism, Morality, and Social Justice* (Princeton: Princeton University Press, 1990), p. 14.

thought the focus has been on achieving certain specific rights and liberties as well as specific constitutional guarantees, as found, for example, in various bills of rights and declarations of the rights of man. Justice as fairness follows this traditional view.

13.4. A list of basic liberties can be drawn up in two ways. One is historical: we survey various democratic regimes and assemble a list of rights and liberties that seem basic and are securely protected in what seem to be historically the more successful regimes. Of course, the veil of ignorance means that this kind of particular information is not available to the parties in the original position, but it is available to you and me in setting up justice as fairness.[8] We are perfectly free to use it to specify the principles of justice we make available to the parties.

A second way of drawing up a list of basic rights and liberties is analytical: we consider what liberties provide the political and social conditions essential for the adequate development and full exercise of the two moral powers of free and equal persons (§7.1). Following this we say: first, that the equal political liberties and freedom of thought enable citizens to develop and to exercise these powers in judging the justice of the basic structure of society and its social policies; and second, that liberty of conscience and freedom of association enable citizens to develop and exercise their moral powers in forming and revising and in rationally pursuing (individually or, more often, in association with others) their conceptions of the good.

Those basic rights and liberties protect and secure the scope required for the exercise of the two moral powers in the two fundamental cases just mentioned: that is to say, the first fundamental case is the exercise of those powers in judging the justice of basic institutions and social policies; while the second fundamental case is the exercise of those powers in pursuing our conception of the good. To exercise our powers in these ways is essential to us as free and equal citizens.

8. Here I should mention that there are three points of view in justice as fairness that it is essential to distinguish: the point of view of the parties in the original position, the point of view of citizens in a well-ordered society, and the point of view of you and me who are setting up justice as fairness as a political conception and trying to use it to organize into one coherent view our considered judgments at all levels of generality. Keep in mind that the parties are, as it were, artificial persons who are part of a procedure of construction that we frame for our philosophical purposes. We may know many things that we keep from them. For these three points of view, see *Political Liberalism*, p. 28.

13.5. Observe that the first principle of justice applies not only to the basic structure (both principles do this) but more specifically to what we think of as the constitution, whether written or unwritten. Observe also that some of these liberties, especially the equal political liberties and freedom of thought and association, are to be guaranteed by a constitution (*Theory*, chap. IV). What we may call "constituent power," as opposed to "ordinary power,"[9] is to be suitably institutionalized in the form of a regime: in the right to vote and to hold office, and in so-called bills of rights, as well as in the procedures for amending the constitution, for example.

These matters belong to the so-called constitutional essentials, these essentials being those crucial matters about which, given the fact of pluralism, working political agreement is most urgent (§9.4). In view of the fundamental nature of the basic rights and liberties, explained in part by the fundamental interests they protect, and given that the power of the people to constitute the form of government is a superior power (distinct from the ordinary power exercised routinely by officers of a regime), the first principle is assigned priority.

This priority means (as we have said) that the second principle (which includes the difference principle as one part) is always to be applied within a setting of background institutions that satisfy the requirements of the first principle (including the requirement of securing the fair value of the political liberties), as by definition they will in a well-ordered society.[10] The fair value of the political liberties ensures that citizens similarly gifted and motivated have roughly an equal chance of influencing the government's policy and of attaining positions of authority irrespective of their economic and social class.[11] To explain the priority of the first principle over the second:

9. This distinction is derived from Locke, who speaks of the people's power to constitute the legislative as the first and fundamental law of all commonwealths. John Locke, *Second Treatise of Government*, §§134, 141, 149.

10. It is sometimes objected to the difference principle as a principle of distributive justice that it contains no restrictions on the overall nature of permissible distributions. It is concerned, the objection runs, solely with the least advantaged. But this objection is incorrect: it overlooks the fact that the parts of the two principles of justice are designed to work in tandem and apply as a unit. The requirements of the prior principles have important distributive effects. Consider the effects of fair equality of opportunity as applied to education, say, or the distributive effects of the fair value of the political liberties. We cannot possibly take the difference principle seriously so long as we think of it by itself, apart from its setting within prior principles.

11. [See *Political Liberalism*, p. 358.]

this priority rules out exchanges ("trade-offs," as economists say) between the basic rights and liberties covered by the first principle and the social and economic advantages regulated by the difference principle. For example, the equal political liberties cannot be denied to certain groups on the grounds that their having these liberties may enable them to block policies needed for economic growth and efficiency.

Nor can we justify a selective service act that grants educational deferments or exemptions to some on the grounds that doing this is a socially efficient way both to maintain the armed forces and to provide incentives to those otherwise subject to conscription to acquire valuable skills by continuing their education. Since conscription is a drastic interference with the basic liberties of equal citizenship, it cannot be justified by any needs less compelling than those of the defense of these equal liberties themselves (*Theory,* §58: 333f.).

A further point about priority: in asserting the priority of the basic rights and liberties, we suppose reasonably favorable conditions to obtain. That is, we suppose historical, economic and social conditions to be such that, provided the political will exists, effective political institutions can be established to give adequate scope for the exercise of those freedoms. These conditions mean that the barriers to constitutional government (if such there are) spring largely from the political culture and existing effective interests, and not from, for instance, a lack of economic means, or education, or the many skills needed to run a democratic regime.[12]

13.6. It is important to note a distinction between the first and second principles of justice. The first principle, as explained by its interpretation, covers the constitutional essentials. The second principle requires fair equality of opportunity and that social and economic inequalities be governed by the difference principle, which we discuss in §§17–19. While some principle of opportunity is a constitutional essential—for example, a principle requiring an open society, one with careers open to talents (to use the eighteenth-century phrase)—fair equality of opportunity requires more than that, and is not counted a constitutional essential. Similarly, although a

12. The priority (or the primacy) of the basic equal liberties does not, contrary to much opinion, presuppose a high level of wealth and income. See Amartya Sen and Jean Dreze, *Hunger and Public Action* (Oxford: Oxford University Press, 1989), chap. 13; and Partha Dasgupta, *An Inquiry into Well-Being and Destitution* (Oxford: Oxford University Press, 1993), chaps. 1–2, 5 and passim.

social minimum providing for the basic needs of all citizens is also a constitutional essential (§38.3–4; §49.5), the difference principle is more demand-
ing and is not so regarded.

The basis for the distinction between the two principles is not that the
first expresses political values while the second does not. Both principles
express political values. Rather, we see the basic structure of society as having two coordinate roles, the first principle applying to one, the second
principle to the other (*Theory*, §11: 53). In one role the basic structure
specifies and secures citizens' equal basic liberties (including the fair value
of the political liberties (§45)) and establishes a just constitutional regime.
In the other role it provides the background institutions of social and economic justice in the form most appropriate to citizens seen as free and
equal. The questions involved in the first role concern the acquisition and
the exercise of political power. To fulfill the liberal principle of legitimacy
(§12.3), we hope to settle at least these questions by appeal to the political
values that constitute the basis of free public reason (§26).

The principles of justice are adopted and applied in a four-stage sequence.[13] In the first stage, the parties adopt the principles of justice behind a veil of ignorance. Limitations on knowledge available to the parties
are progressively relaxed in the next three stages: the stage of the constitutional convention, the legislative stage in which laws are enacted as the constitution allows and as the principles of justice require and permit, and the
final stage in which the rules are applied by administrators and followed by
citizens generally and the constitution and laws are interpreted by members
of the judiciary. At this last stage, everyone has complete access to all the
facts. The first principle applies at the stage of the constitutional convention, and whether the constitutional essentials are assured is more or less
visible on the face of the constitution and in its political arrangements and
the way these work in practice. By contrast the second principle applies at
the legislative stage and it bears on all kinds of social and economic legislation, and on the many kinds of issues arising at this point (*Theory*, §31: 172–
176). Whether the aims of the second principle are realized is far more difficult to ascertain. To some degree these matters are always open to reasonable differences of opinion; they depend on inference and judgment in assessing complex social and economic information. Also, we can expect
more agreement on constitutional essentials than on issues of distributive
justice in the narrower sense.

13. [See *Theory*, §31: 172–176, and *Political Liberalism*, pp. 397–398.]

Thus the grounds for distinguishing the constitutional essentials covered by the first principle and the institutions of distributive justice covered by the second are not that the first principle expresses political values and the second does not. Rather, the grounds of the distinction are four:

(a) The two principles apply to different stages in the application of principles and identify two distinct roles of the basic structure;

(b) It is more urgent to settle the constitutional essentials;

(c) It is far easier to tell whether those essentials are realized; and

(d) It seems possible to gain agreement on what those essentials should be, not in every detail, of course, but in the main outlines.

13.7. One way to see the point of the idea of constitutional essentials is to connect it with the idea of loyal opposition, itself an essential idea of a constitutional regime. The government and its loyal opposition agree on these constitutional essentials. Their so agreeing makes the government legitimate in intention and the opposition loyal in its opposition. Where the loyalty of both is firm and their agreement mutually recognized, a constitutional regime is secure. Differences about the most appropriate principles of distributive justice in the narrower sense, and the ideals that underlie them, can be adjudicated, though not always properly, within the existing political framework.

While the difference principle does not fall under the constitutional essentials, it is nevertheless important to try to identify the idea of equality most appropriate to citizens viewed as free and equal, and as normally and fully cooperating members of society over a complete life. I believe this idea involves reciprocity[14] at the deepest level and thus democratic equality properly understood requires something like the difference principle. (I say "something like," for there may be various nearby possibilities.) The re-

14. [As understood in justice as fairness, reciprocity is a relation between citizens expressed by principles of justice that regulate a social world in which all who are engaged in cooperation and do their part as the rules and procedures require are to benefit in an appropriate way as assessed by a suitable benchmark of comparison. The two principles of justice, including the difference principle with its implicit reference to equal division as a benchmark, formulate an idea of reciprocity between citizens. For a fuller discussion of the idea of reciprocity, see *Political Liberalism,* pp. 16–17, and the introduction to the paperback edition, pp. xliv, xlvi, li. The idea of reciprocity also plays an important part in "The Idea of Public Reason Revisited," *University of Chicago Law Review,* 64 (Summer 1997): 765–807, reprinted in *The Law of Peoples* (Cambridge, Mass.: Harvard University Press, 1999) and *Collected Papers.*]

maining sections of this part (§§14-22) try to clarify the content of this principle and to clear up a number of difficulties.

## §14. The Problem of Distributive Justice

14.1. The problem of distributive justice in justice as fairness is always this: how are the institutions of the basic structure to be regulated as one unified scheme of institutions so that a fair, efficient, and productive system of social cooperation can be maintained over time, from one generation to the next? Contrast this with the very different problem of how a given bundle of commodities is to be distributed, or allocated, among various individuals whose particular needs, desires, and preferences are known to us, and who have not cooperated in any way to produce those commodities. This second problem is that of allocative justice (*Theory*, §11: 56; §14: 77).

To illustrate: accepting the assumptions implied by interpersonal cardinal comparisons of well-being, we might, for example, allocate the bundle of commodities so as to achieve the greatest satisfaction summed over these individuals from the present into the future. As a political conception of justice, the classical principle of utility (as found in Bentham and Sidgwick) can be seen as adapting the idea of allocative justice so as to be a single principle for the basic structure over time.

14.2. We reject the idea of allocative justice as incompatible with the fundamental idea by which justice as fairness is organized: the idea of society as a fair system of social cooperation over time. Citizens are seen as cooperating to produce the social resources on which their claims are made. In a well-ordered society, in which both the equal basic liberties (with their fair value) and fair equality of opportunity are secured, the distribution of income and wealth illustrates what we may call pure background procedural justice. The basic structure is arranged so that when everyone follows the publicly recognized rules of cooperation, and honors the claims the rules specify, the particular distributions of goods that result are acceptable as just (or at least as not unjust) whatever these distributions turn out to be.

To elaborate: within the framework of background justice set up by the basic structure, individuals and associations may do as they wish insofar as the rules of institutions permit. Observe that particular distributions cannot be judged at all apart from the claims (entitlements) of individuals earned by their efforts within the fair system of cooperation from which those distributions result. In contrast to utilitarianism, the concept of allocative justice has no application. There is no criterion for a just distribution apart from background institutions and the entitlements that arise from actually working through the procedure.[15] It is background institutions that provide the setting for fair cooperation within which entitlements arise.

14.3. These points can be made clearer as follows. The word "background" in the phrase "background procedural justice" above is intended to indicate that certain rules must be included in the basic structure as a system of social cooperation so that this system remains fair over time, from one generation to the next.[16]

Consider an example. The draft rule in a professional sport such as basketball ranks teams in the opposite order from their standing in the league at the end of the season: championship teams go last in the draft of new players. This rule provides for regular and periodic changes in the roster of teams and is designed to ensure that teams in the league are more or less evenly matched from year to year, so that in any given season each team can give any other a decent game. These changes of players are necessary to achieve the aims and attractions of the sport and are not foreign to its purpose.

The required background rules are specified by what is necessary to fulfill the two principles of justice. Later on we survey some of these as found in a property-owning democracy (Part IV).[17] For example, background institutions must work to keep property and wealth evenly enough shared over time to preserve the fair value of the political liberties and fair equality of opportunity over generations. They do this by laws regulating bequest and inheritance of property, and other devices such as taxes, to prevent excessive concentrations of private power (*Theory*, §43: 245ff.).

14.4. Since the difference principle applies to institutions as public systems of rules, their requirements are foreseeable. They do not involve any more continuous or regular interference with individuals' plans and actions than do, say, familiar forms of taxation. Since the effects of those rules are foreseen, they are taken into account when citizens draw up their plans in

15. See *Theory*, §14: 74–77, and note the distinction made there between the three kinds of procedural justice.

16. The term "background" is introduced here and is not used in *Theory*.

17. Property-owning democracy is discussed in *Theory*, chap. V, but unfortunately the contrast between it and welfare-state capitalism is not made clear enough. This defect I aim to correct in Part IV.

the first place. Citizens understand that when they take part in social cooperation, their property and wealth, and their share of what they help to produce, are subject to the taxes, say, which background institutions are known
to impose. Moreover, the difference principle (as well as the first principle
and the first part of the second principle) respects legitimate expectations
based on the publicly recognized rules and the entitlements earned by individuals (*Theory,* §§47–48).[18]

The rules of background institutions required by the two principles of
justice (including the difference principle) are designed to achieve the aims
and purposes of fair social cooperation over time. They are essential to preserve background justice, such as the fair value of the political liberties and
fair equality of opportunity, as well as to make it likely that economic and
social inequalities contribute in an effective way to the general good or,
more exactly, to the benefit of the least-advantaged members of society. Like
the draft rule in professional sports, the arrangements required by the difference principle are part of, and not foreign to, the conception of fair social
cooperation in justice as fairness. Even with these rules of background justice, distributive justice may still be understood as a case of pure procedural
justice.

## §15. The Basic Structure as Subject: First Kind of Reason

15.1. A characteristic feature of justice as fairness as a political conception
is that it takes the basic structure as its primary subject. I note two broad
kinds of reasons for this: the first notes how social institutions work and the
nature of the principles required to regulate them over time to maintain
background justice.

Consider an important criticism of Locke. Suppose we begin, as it seems
he does, with the attractive idea that persons' social circumstances and their
relations with one another should develop over time in accordance with fair
agreements fairly arrived at. Much as with Locke's conception of ideal history, we might use certain principles to specify various rights and duties of
persons, as well as their rights to acquire and transfer property. Now suppose we start with a just initial state in which everyone's possessions are
justly held. We then say that when everyone respects persons' rights and

18. The remarks in this paragraph reply to the kind of objection Nozick raises to the difference principle in *Anarchy, State, and Utopia.* His description of the Wilt Chamberlin example, chap. 7, pp. 160–164, suggests that to apply that principle to government must involve continual interference with particular individual transactions.

duties, as well as the principles for acquiring and transferring property, the succeeding states are also just, no matter how distant in time. Call this an ideal historical process view.[19]

To work out this idea we need an account not only of the just initial state and of fair agreements, but also of just social conditions under which fair agreements are to be reached. Even though the initial state may have been just, and subsequent social conditions may also have been just for some time, the accumulated results of many separate and seemingly fair agreements entered into by individuals and associations are likely over an extended period to undermine the background conditions required for free and fair agreements. Very considerable wealth and property may accumulate in a few hands, and these concentrations are likely to undermine fair equality of opportunity, the fair value of the political liberties, and so on. The kind of limits and provisos that in Locke's view apply directly to the separate transactions of individuals and associations in the state of nature are not stringent enough to ensure that fair background conditions are maintained.[20]

15.2. To preserve these conditions is the task of the rules of pure procedural background justice. Unless the basic structure is regulated over time, earlier just distributions of assets of all kinds do not ensure the justice of later distributions, however free and fair particular transactions between individuals and associations may look when viewed locally and apart from background institutions. For the outcome of these transactions taken together is affected by all kinds of contingencies and unforeseeable consequences. It is necessary to regulate, by laws governing inheritance and bequest, how people acquire property so as to make its distribution more equal, to provide fair equality of opportunity in education, and much else. That such rules of background justice are in force over time does not detract from but rather makes possible the important values expressed by free and fair agreements reached by individuals and associations within the basic structure. This is because principles applying to these agreements directly (for example, the law of contract) do not alone suffice to preserve background justice.

What is needed, then, is a division of labor between two kinds of princi-

19. Nozick's *Anarchy, State, and Utopia* is an example of this kind of view.

20. For example, in Locke's case they fail to guarantee the equal political liberties, as we can tell from *Second Treatise*, §158. See Joshua Cohen, "Structure, Choice, and Legitimacy: Locke's Theory of the State," *Philosophy and Public Affairs* 15 (Fall 1986): 301–324.

ples, each kind suitably specified: first, those that regulate the basic structure over time and are designed to preserve background justice from one generation to the next; and second, those that apply directly to the separate and free transactions between individuals and associations. Defects in either kind of principle can result in a serious failure of the conception of justice as a whole.

15.3. Once the many transactions and agreements of individuals and associations are framed within a just basic structure, we have an ideal social process view, of which justice as fairness is an example. The contrast with Locke's ideal historical process view is in part this: while both views use the concept of pure procedural justice, they specify this concept in different ways. The historical process view focuses on the transactions of individuals and associations as these are constrained by the principles and provisos applying directly to the parties in particular transactions.

By contrast, as a social process view, justice as fairness focuses first on the basic structure and on the regulations required to maintain background justice over time for all persons equally, whatever their generation or social position. Since a public conception of justice needs clear, simple, and intelligible rules, we rely on an institutional division of labor between principles required to preserve background justice and principles that apply directly to particular transactions between individuals and associations. Once this division of labor is set up, individuals and associations are then left free to advance their (permissible) ends within the framework of the basic structure, secure in the knowledge that elsewhere in the social system the regulations necessary to preserve background justice are in force.

Taking the basic structure as the primary subject enables us to regard distributive justice as a case of pure background procedural justice: when everyone follows the publicly recognized rules of cooperation, the particular distribution that results is acceptable as just whatever that distribution turns out to be (§14.2). This allows us to abstract from the enormous complexities of the innumerable transactions of daily life and frees us from having to keep track of the changing relative positions of particular individuals (*Theory*, §14: 76f.). Society is an ongoing scheme of fair cooperation over time without any specified beginning or end relevant for political justice. The principles of justice specify the form of background justice apart from all particular historical conditions. What counts is the workings of social institutions now, and a benchmark of the state of nature—the level of well-being (however specified) of individuals in that state—plays no role. It is a historical surd, unknowable, but even if it could be known, of no significance.[21]

## §16. The Basic Structure as Subject: Second Kind of Reason

16.1. The second kind of reason for taking the basic structure as the primary subject derives from its profound and pervasive influence on the persons who live under its institutions. Recall that in explaining the emphasis put on the basic structure as subject, we said that we view citizens as born into society: it is there that they will lead a complete life. They enter that social world only by birth, leave it only by death. And since any modern society, even a well-ordered one, must rely on some inequalities to be well designed and effectively organized, we ask what kinds of inequalities a well-ordered society would allow or be particularly concerned to avoid.

Justice as fairness focuses on inequalities in citizens' life-prospects—their prospects over a complete life (as specified by an appropriate index of primary goods)—as these prospects are affected by three kinds of contingencies:

(a) their social class of origin: the class into which they are born and develop before the age of reason;

(b) their native endowments (as opposed to their realized endowments); and their opportunities to develop these endowments as affected by their social class of origin;

(c) their good or ill fortune, or good or bad luck, over the course of life (how they are affected by illness and accident; and, say, by periods of involuntary unemployment and regional economic decline).

Even in a well-ordered society, then, our prospects over life are deeply affected by social, natural, and fortuitous contingencies, and by the way the basic structure, by setting up inequalities, uses those contingencies to meet certain social purposes.

Pointing out these three kinds of contingencies is not enough, of course, to show conclusively that the basic structure is the appropriate subject of political justice. No such decisive arguments are available, as everything de-

21. See *Theory*, §12: 69, though the point is not stated sufficiently sharply.

pends on how the conception of justice as fairness hangs together as a whole. Yet if we ignore the inequalities in people's prospects in life arising from these contingencies and let those inequalities work themselves out while failing to institute the regulations necessary to preserve background justice, we would not be taking seriously the idea of society as a fair system of cooperation between citizens as free and equal. This reminds us that what we are asking is precisely: what principles of background justice are presupposed in taking seriously that idea of society (§12.1)?

16.2. If citizens of a well-ordered society are to recognize one another as free and equal, basic institutions must educate them to this conception of themselves, as well as publicly exhibit and encourage this ideal of political justice. This task of education belongs to what we may call the wide role of a political conception.[22] In this role such a conception is part of the public political culture: its first principles are embodied in the institutions of the basic structure and appealed to in their interpretation. Acquaintance with and participation in that public culture is one way citizens learn to conceive of themselves as free and equal, a conception which, if left to their own reflections, they would most likely never form, much less accept and desire to realize.

Consider further how the three contingencies (noted above) affect the content of people's final ends and purposes, as well as the vigor and confidence with which they pursue them. We assess our prospects in life according to our place in society and we form our ends and purposes in the light of the means and opportunities we can realistically expect. So whether we are hopeful and optimistic about our future, or resigned and apathetic, depends both on the inequalities associated with our social position and on the public principles of justice that society not merely professes but more or less effectively uses to regulate the institutions of background justice. Hence the basic structure as a social and economic regime is not only an arrangement that satisfies given desires and aspirations but also an arrangement that arouses further desires and aspirations in the future. This it does by the expectations and ambitions it encourages in the present, and indeed over a complete life.

Moreover, native endowments of various kinds (say, native intelligence

22. By contrast, the narrow role might be something like that of specifying the basic principles and most essential rules that must be followed for political society to be enduring and stable. H. L. A. Hart's idea of the minimum content of natural law, which draws on Hume, is an example. See *The Concept of Law* (Oxford: Oxford University Press, 1961), pp. 189–195.

and natural ability) are not fixed natural assets with a constant capacity. They are merely potential and cannot come to fruition apart from social conditions; and when realized they can take but one or a few of many possible forms. Educated and trained abilities are always a selection, and a small selection at that, from a wide range of possibilities that might have been fulfilled. Among what affects their realization are social attitudes of encouragement and support, and institutions concerned with their early discipline and use. Not only our conception of ourselves, and our aims and ambitions, but also our realized abilities and talents, reflect our personal history, opportunities and social position, and the influence of good and ill fortune.

16.3. To sum up: for the two kinds of reasons noted in this and the preceding section, we take the basic structure as the primary subject. This structure comprises social institutions within which human beings may develop their moral powers and become fully cooperating members of a society of free and equal citizens. And as a framework that preserves background justice over time from one generation to the next it realizes the idea (central to justice as fairness) of pure background procedural justice as an ideal social process (as explained under the first kind of reason). It also answers to the public role of educating citizens to a conception of themselves as free and equal; and, when properly regulated, it encourages in them attitudes of optimism and confidence in their future, and a sense of being treated fairly in view of the public principles which are seen as effectively regulating economic and social inequalities (as explained under the second kind of reason).

So far, then, starting with the basic structure seems to accord with the other ideas of justice as fairness, something we could not have foreseen at the outset. A sharp definition of that structure might have gotten in the way of fitting it into these other ideas, just as a sharp definition of them would have gotten in the way of fitting them to it. (Recall the remarks in §4.3.)

## §17. Who Are the Least Advantaged?

17.1. We have referred to the least advantaged, but who are they and how are they singled out? To answer these questions we introduce the idea of primary goods. These are various social conditions and all-purpose means that are generally necessary to enable citizens adequately to develop and fully exercise their two moral powers, and to pursue their determinate conceptions of the good. Here we look to the social requirements and the normal circumstances of human life in a democratic society. Primary goods are things needed and required by persons seen in the light of the political conception of persons, as citizens who are fully cooperating members of society, and not merely as human beings apart from any normative conception. These goods are things citizens need as free and equal persons living a complete life; they are not things it is simply rational to want or desire, or to prefer or even to crave. We use the political conception, and not a comprehensive moral doctrine, in specifying those needs and requirements.

What count as primary goods depends, of course, on various general facts about human needs and abilities, their normal phases and requirements of nurture, relations of social interdependence, and much else. We need at least a rough idea of rational plans of life showing why these plans usually have a certain structure and depend on certain primary goods for their formation, revision, and successful execution.[23] But, as stressed above, the account of primary goods does not rest solely on psychological, social, or historical facts. While the list of primary goods rests in part on the general facts and requirements of social life, it does so only together with a political conception of the person as free and equal, endowed with the moral powers, and capable of being a fully cooperating member of society. This normative conception is necessary to identify the appropriate list of primary goods.[24]

17.2. We distinguish five kinds of such goods:

(i) The basic rights and liberties: freedom of thought and liberty of conscience, and the rest (§13). These rights and liberties are essential institutional conditions required for the adequate development and full and informed exercise of the two moral powers (in the two fundamental cases (§13.4)).

(ii) Freedom of movement and free choice of occupation against a background of diverse opportunities, which opportunities allow the pursuit of a variety of ends and give effect to decisions to revise and alter them.

(iii) Powers and prerogatives of offices and positions of authority and responsibility.

(iv) Income and wealth, understood as all-purpose means (having an ex-

23. A sketch of the features of rational plans is given in *Theory,* chap. VII.

24. Unhappily *Theory* is at best ambiguous on this matter. I am indebted to a number of people, especially to Joshua Cohen and Joshua Rabinowitz; and to Allen Buchanan, T. M. Scanlon, and Samuel Scheffler for valuable discussion; and to Michael Teitelman, who first raised the difficulty.

change value)[25] generally needed to achieve a wide range of ends whatever they may be.

(v) The social bases of self-respect, understood as those aspects of basic institutions normally essential if citizens are to have a lively sense of their worth as persons and to be able to advance their ends with self-confidence.

17.3. The two principles of justice assess the basic structure according to how it regulates citizens' shares of primary goods, these shares being specified in terms of an appropriate index. Note that primary goods are given by reference to objective features of citizens' social circumstances, features open to public view: their secured institutional rights and liberties, their available fair opportunities, their (reasonable) expectations of income and wealth seen from their social position, and so on. As we have said, the inequalities to which the difference principle applies are differences in citizens' (reasonable) expectations of primary goods over a complete life. These expectations are their life-prospects. In a well-ordered society where all citizens' equal basic rights and liberties and fair opportunities are secure, the least advantaged are those belonging to the income class with the lowest expectations.[26] To say that inequalities in income and wealth are to be arranged for the greatest benefit of the least advantaged simply means that we are to compare schemes of cooperation by seeing how well off the least advantaged are under each scheme, and then to select the scheme under

25. For this idea of exchange value, see Rawls, "Fairness to Goodness," *Philosophical Review* 84 (October 1975): §III. Also in *Collected Papers*.

26. Note here that in the simplest form of the difference principle the individuals who belong to the least advantaged group are not identifiable apart from, or independently of, their income and wealth. The least advantaged are never identifiable as men or women, say, or as whites or blacks, or Indians or British. They are not individuals identified by natural or other features (race, gender, nationality, and the like) that enable us to compare their situation under all the various schemes of social cooperation it is feasible to consider. Taking these cooperative schemes as possible social worlds (let's say) over which the names of individuals refer to (rigidly designate) the same individuals in each possible (social) world, the term "the least advantaged" is not a rigid designator (to use Saul Kripke's term, see *Naming and Necessity* (Cambridge, Mass.: Harvard University Press, 1972)). Rather, the worst off under any scheme of cooperation are simply the individuals who are worst off under that particular scheme. They may not be those worst off in another. Even supposing, for example, that it turns out, as commonsense political sociology might suggest, that the least advantaged, identified by income and wealth, include many individuals born into the least-favored social class of origin, and many of the least (naturally) endowed and many who experience more bad luck and misfortune (§16), nevertheless those attributes do not define the least advantaged. Rather, it happens that there may be a tendency for such features to characterize many who belong to that group.

which the least advantaged are better off than they are under any other scheme.

To highlight the objective character of primary goods, note that it is not self-respect as an attitude toward oneself but the social bases of self-respect that count as a primary good.[27] These social bases are things like the institutional fact that citizens have equal basic rights, and the public recognition of that fact and that everyone endorses the difference principle, itself a form of reciprocity. The objective character of primary goods also is shown in the fact that in applying the principles of justice we do not consider estimates of citizens' overall happiness as given, say, by the fulfillment of their (rational) preferences, or their desires (as in a utilitarian view). Nor do we consider their good in the light of some moral or associational or personal ideal. We also do not need a measure of citizens' moral powers and other abilities, or of how far citizens have actually realized them, so long as their powers and abilities suffice for them to be normal cooperating members of society.[28]

Citizens' appropriate shares of primary goods are not regarded as approximating to their good as specified by any particular comprehensive religious, philosophical, or moral doctrine; or even as specified by what several such doctrines may hold in common concerning our (comprehensive) good. The account of primary goods belongs, then, wholly within justice as fairness as a political conception of justice. The reason for remaining within the political conception is by now familiar: it is in order to hold open the possibility of finding a public basis of justification supported by an overlapping consensus.

Primary goods, then, are what free and equal persons (as specified by the political conception) need as citizens. These goods belong to a partial conception of the good that citizens, who affirm a plurality of conflicting comprehensive doctrines, can agree upon for the purpose of making the interpersonal comparisons required for workable political principles. While pluralism means that there can be no agreement on a complete conception of the good grounded in a comprehensive doctrine, some conceptions of the good are indispensable for any account of justice, political or other; and they can be freely used in justice as fairness so long as they fit within it as political conceptions (§43). The partial conception of the good set out by the account of primary goods is one of them.

27. *Theory* is ambiguous on this point. It fails to distinguish between self-respect as an attitude, the preserving of which is a fundamental interest, and the social bases that help to support that attitude.

28. On this point, see the discussion of the provision of health care in Part IV, §51.

17.4. A final comment: there are at least two ways to proceed in specifying a list of primary goods. One is to look at the various comprehensive doctrines actually found in society and specify an index of such goods as a kind of average of what those who affirm the opposing doctrines would need by way of institutional protections and all-purpose means. Doing this might seem the best way to achieve an overlapping consensus.

But this is not how justice as fairness proceeds. Instead, it works up a political conception from the fundamental idea of society as a fair system of social cooperation. The hope is that this conception with its account of primary goods can win the support of an overlapping consensus. We leave aside the comprehensive doctrines that now exist, or have existed, or might exist. Our thought is not that primary goods are fair to conceptions of the good associated with comprehensive doctrines by striking a fair balance between them. Rather, primary goods are fair to free and equal citizens: these goods enable them to advance their permissible conceptions of the good (those the pursuit of which are compatible with justice).

## §18. The Difference Principle: Its Meaning

18.1. We now turn to the difference principle as a principle of distributive justice in the narrow sense. Recall that it is subordinate to both the first principle of justice (guaranteeing the equal basic liberties) and the principle of fair equality of opportunity (§13.1). It works in tandem with these two prior principles and it is always to be applied within background institutions in which those principles are satisfied.[29]

Social cooperation, we assume, is always productive, and without cooperation there would be nothing produced and so nothing to distribute. This assumption is not emphasized sufficiently in *Theory*, §§12–13. Figure 1 implies that there is production: MAG and LAG ($x_1$ and $x_2$ in the figure in *Theory*) are now representative individuals of the more and the less advantaged groups respectively, the two groups engaged in productive cooperation.[30] The OP curve (P for production) runs northeast from the origin until it bends downward to the southeast.[31]

29. The explanation of the principle of (Pareto) efficiency for institutions is found in *Theory*, §12: 58–62.

30. This figure is similar to figure 6 in *Theory*, §13: 66.

31. For example, the figures in *Theory*, §12: 59f. assume that there is an already given bundle of goods to be shared between the two persons $x_1$ and $x_2$. This is shown in the fact that the efficiency frontier runs northwest and southeast. And no mention is made of these persons as being engaged in cooperation to produce those goods.

**Figure 1**

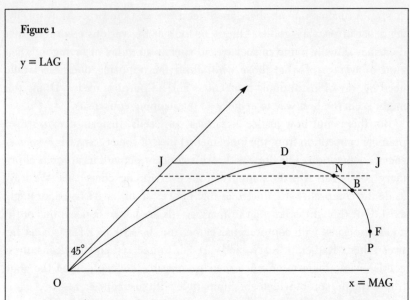

In this figure the distances along the two axes are measured in terms of an index of primary goods, with the x-axis the more advantaged group (MAG), the y-axis the less advantaged (LAG). The line JJ parallel to the x-axis is the highest equal-justice line touched by the OP curve at its maximum at D. Note that D is the efficient point nearest to equality, represented by the 45-degree line. N is the Nash point, where the product of utilities is maximized (if we assume utilities to be linear in indexes of primary goods), and B is the Bentham point, where the sum of individual utilities is maximized (again with the same assumption). The set of efficient points goes from D to the feudal point F, at which the OP curve becomes vertical.

We imagine the whole space southeast of the 45-degree line to be filled with parallel equal-justice lines. Thus from each point on the 45-degree line running northeast from the origin, there is an equal-justice line. The line JJ is simply the highest such line that can be reached when we are constrained to move along the OP curve. Society aims, other things equal, to reach the highest equal-justice line measured by the distance from O along the 45-degree line. To do this it moves as far northeast as possible along the OP curve and stops when this curve bends to the southeast.

Observe that the parallel lines are equal-justice lines and not indifference lines of the familiar kind that represent evaluations of individual or social welfare. Equal-justice lines represent how claims to goods cooperatively produced are to be shared among those who produced them, and they reflect an idea of reciprocity. They are equal-justice lines in the sense that any point on a line is equally acceptable provided it is reached by an OP curve of a scheme of cooperation satisfying the principles of justice prior to the difference principle. The fact that they are parallel means that a greater index of primary goods (here understood as a person's prospects of income and wealth over a complete life) for one group (the MAG) is justified only insofar as it adds to the index of the other group (the LAG). When this is no longer true, even though the index increases for the more advantaged group, as it does beyond D, then the reciprocity implicit in the difference principle no longer obtains. This is shown by the fact that N and B are on lower equal-justice lines than D. A utilitarian equal-justice line through B would be a smooth curve convex to the origin running from northwest to southeast, showing the MAG may gain more even though the LAG receive less. Contrary to reciprocity, trade-offs are permitted.

Finally, note that as indicated in §17, the MAG and the LAG are specified by reference to their shares in the output and not as particular individuals identifiable independently of the scheme of cooperation. When we represent the index of the MAG on the x-axis, the OP curve lies everywhere southeast of the 45-degree line.

18.2. A scheme of cooperation is given in large part by how its public rules organize productive activity, specify the division of labor, assign various roles to those engaged in it, and so on. These schemes include schedules of wages and salaries to be paid out of output. By varying wages and salaries, more may be produced. This is because over time the greater returns to the more advantaged serve, among other things, to cover the costs of training and education, to mark positions of responsibility and encourage persons to fill them, and to act as incentives. A given OP curve is paired with a particular scheme of cooperation: it indicates the returns to the two groups when only wages and salaries are changed. The origin of the OP curve represents the equal division point: both groups receive the same remuneration.

To explain: take any point on the OP curve: if the wages to the more advantaged is the corresponding point on the x-axis, then the wages to the less advantaged is the corresponding point on the y-axis. Thus there are, in general, different OP curves for different schemes of cooperation; and some schemes are more effectively designed than others. One scheme is more effective than another if its OP curve always gives a greater return to the less advantaged for any given return to the more advantaged.[32] Other things being equal, the difference principle directs society to aim at the highest point on the OP curve of the most effectively designed scheme of cooperation.

18.3. A further feature of the difference principle is that it does not require continual economic growth over generations to maximize upward indefinitely the expectations of the least advantaged (assessed in terms of

---

32. When these curves criss-cross, the one tangent to the highest JJ line is best; if they touch the same JJ line, the one whose tangent is to the left of the other is best.

income and wealth). That would not be a reasonable conception of justice. We should not rule out Mill's idea of a society in a just stationary state where (real) capital accumulation may cease.[33] A well-ordered society is specified so as to allow for this possibility. What the difference principle does require is that during an appropriate interval of time the differences in income and wealth earned in producing the social product be such that if the legitimate expectations of the more advantaged were less, those of the less advantaged would also be less. Society would always be on the upward-rising part or at the top of the OP curve.[34] Permissible inequalities (thus defined) satisfy that condition and are compatible with a social product of a steady-state equilibrium in which a just basic structure is supported and reproduced over time.

Another aspect of the same point is this: the difference principle requires that however great the inequalities in wealth and income may be, and however willing people are to work to earn their greater shares of output, existing inequalities must contribute effectively to the benefit of the least advantaged. Otherwise the inequalities are not permissible. The general level of wealth in society, including the well-being of the least advantaged, depends on people's decisions as to how to lead their lives. The priority of liberty means that we cannot be forced to engage in work that is highly productive in terms of material goods. What kind of work people do, and how hard they do it, is up to them to decide in light of the various incentives society offers. What the difference principle requires, then, is that however great the general level of wealth—whether high or low—the existing inequalities are to fulfill the condition of benefiting others as well as ourselves. This condition brings out that even if it uses the idea of maximizing the expectations of the least advantaged, the difference principle is essentially a principle of reciprocity.

18.4. We have seen that the two principles of justice apply to citizens as identified by their indexes of primary goods. It is natural to ask: Why are distinctions of race and gender not explicitly included among the three contingencies noted earlier (§16)? How can one ignore such historical facts as slavery (in the antebellum South) and the inequalities between men and women resulting from the absence of provisions to make good women's ex-

33. See his *Principles of Political Economy,* bk. IV, ch. VI.
34. See the distinction at *Theory,* §13: 68 between perfectly just schemes and those just throughout.

tra burden in the bearing, raising, and educating of children so as to secure their fair equality of opportunity?

The answer is that we are mainly concerned with ideal theory: the account of the well-ordered society of justice as fairness. Within that account we need to distinguish two questions: first, what contingencies tend to generate troubling inequalities even in a well-ordered society and thus prompt us, along with other considerations, to take the basic structure as the primary subject of justice; and second, how within ideal theory should the least advantaged be specified?

While there is some tendency for individuals most adversely affected by the three contingencies (§16.1) to be among the least advantaged, this group is defined not by reference to those contingencies but by an index of primary goods (§17, n. 26). Taking the simplest form of the difference principle, the least advantaged are those who share with other citizens the basic equal liberties and fair opportunities but have the least income and wealth. We use income and wealth to specify this group; and the particular individuals who belong to it may change from one arrangement of the basic structure to another.

18.5. In ideal theory, as stated in *Theory*, §16, the two principles of justice are to be applied to the basic structure by assessing it from certain standard points of view: namely, those of the representative equal citizen (whose basic equal liberties and fair opportunities are secure) and of the representatives of various levels of income and wealth. Nevertheless, sometimes other positions must be taken into account. Suppose, for example, that certain fixed natural characteristics are used as grounds for assigning unequal basic rights, or allowing some persons only lesser opportunities; then such inequalities will single out relevant positions. Those characteristics cannot be changed, and so the positions they specify are points of view from which the basic structure must be judged.

Distinctions based on gender and race are of this kind. Thus if men, say, have greater basic rights or greater opportunities than women, these inequalities can be justified only if they are to the advantage of women and acceptable from their point of view. Similarly for unequal basic rights and opportunities founded on race (*Theory*, §16: 85). It appears that historically these inequalities have arisen from inequalities in political power and control of economic resources. They are not now, and it would seem never have been, to the advantage of women or less favored races. To be sure, so sweeping a historical judgment may occasionally be uncertain. However, in a well-ordered society in the present age no such uncertainty obtains, so justice as fairness supposes that the standard relevant positions specified by the primary goods should suffice.

18.6. To conclude: when used in a certain way, distinctions of gender and race give rise to further relevant positions to which a special form of the difference principle applies (*Theory*, §16: 85). We hope that in a well-ordered society under favorable conditions, with the equal basic liberties and fair equality of opportunity secured, gender and race would not specify relevant points of view. *Theory* takes up only two questions of partial compliance (or nonideal) theory, civil disobedience and conscientious refusal to serve in an unjust war. The serious problems arising from existing discrimination and distinctions based on gender and race are not on its agenda, which is to present certain principles of justice and then to check them against only a few of the classical problems of political justice as these would be settled within ideal theory.

This is indeed an omission in *Theory;* but an omission is not as such a fault, either in that work's agenda or in its conception of justice. Whether fault there be depends on how well that conception articulates the political values necessary to deal with these questions. Justice as fairness, and other liberal conceptions like it, would certainly be seriously defective should they lack the resources to articulate the political values essential to justify the legal and social institutions needed to secure the equality of women and minorities. In Part IV, §50, there is a brief discussion of the nature of the family and the equality of women.

## §19. Objections via Counterexamples

19.1. Part of the idea of reflective equilibrium is to test the soundness of first principles by seeing whether we can endorse on reflection the judgments to which they lead in cases sometimes framed for this purpose: counterexamples so-called. To be a proper counterexample a case must satisfy all the relevant assumptions made in applying or in arguing for the principles of justice; otherwise it misses the mark. Let us look at three objections via counterexamples to illustrate this.

Consider first two related objections: (a) suppose the most effective OP curve rises very slowly to its maximum; then the share of the more advantaged is much greater than the share to the less advantaged. (In Figure 1 (§18.1), imagine D moved far to the right along the line JJ.) This may seem unjust to the less advantaged. On the other hand: (b) suppose that the most effective OP curve falls very slowly after its maximum; then the more advantaged do not receive a much greater share even though their receiving this share would only slightly reduce the share of the less advantaged. (In the figure, imagine the arc from D through N and B and beyond stretched far to the right). This may seem unjust to the more advantaged.

In both cases, the troubling feature is the rather flat slope of the OP curve, in one case before, in the other after, the maximum. This means that large potential gains (or losses) to one group are paired with small potential losses (or gains) for the other group. In such cases we are tempted to think some adjustments should be made to achieve a greater overall gain. The reply is that, given the required background institutions securing both the equal basic liberties and fair equality of opportunity, and the many possibilities of social organization, the most effective OP curve is very unlikely to have the flat slopes described above. Thus:

(i) In reply to (a): if citizens have fair and equal opportunities to develop their native endowments and to acquire socially productive skills, and if the scheme of cooperation is effectively designed, then the OP curve should rise quickly enough to its maximum so that the ratio of shares in favor of the more advantaged is not likely to strike us as unjust. The idea is that given the equal basic liberties and fair equality of opportunity, the open competition between the greater numbers of the well-trained and better educated reduces the ratio of shares until it lies within an acceptable range. Notice here how, in meeting the objection, we rely on the way the difference principle works in tandem with the prior principles. With background institutions of fair equality of opportunity and workable competition required by the prior principles of justice, the more advantaged cannot unite as a group and then exploit their market power to force increases in their income.[35] This has been mentioned before; here we see it illustrated.

(ii) In reply to (b): given the same assumptions as in (i), there surely ex-

35. For example, background institutions prevent doctors from forming an association to push up the cost of medical care and thus to raise the income of doctors, say by restricting entry into the medical profession, or by agreeing to charge higher fees. High earnings, however, are not sufficient proof of collusion. The income of opera singers seems largely determined by free demand and supply; the demand is high, the supply is low, and in the short run nearly fixed, but not forever fixed as is the supply of the paintings by old masters. The number of opera singers is small enough so that their earnings are not a serious worry in any case; besides they work hard and spread joy. Whereas doctors are a large group, and should competitive background institutions with fair opportunity not work properly in their case, or in similar cases, we would have to examine the causes for the failure of competitive arrangements and try to fix them if that can be done consistent with the prior principles. We might also have to reconsider the soundness of the difference principle.

ists some institutional device to transfer at least part of the large return of the more advantaged to the less advantaged, by taxation, say, to reduce their return beyond the maximum of the OP curve.

19.2. In each reply the idea is that the shapes of OP curves assumed in objections (a) and (b) do not in fact occur when the basic structure satisfies the prior principles. Our aim is achieved should the difference principle yield satisfactory conclusions in social worlds that fulfill the principles prior to it. The difference principle specifies no definite limits within which the ratio of the shares of the more and less advantaged is to fall. Indeed, we hope to avoid having to specify such limits, since we want to leave this ratio to fall where it may, as the outcome of pure background procedural justice. This is perfectly acceptable unless, on due reflection, the actual ratio strikes us as unjust.[36]

The ratio of shares is, of course, an observable feature of the distribution of goods, and one that can be ascertained apart from the scheme of cooperation itself. We simply tabulate who gets what. Now it seems impossible to specify plausible limits on this ratio that can gain wide assent. One reason is that it is not observable shares alone, or their ratio, that count, but whether those receiving these shares have made an appropriate contribution to the good of others by training and educating their native endowments and putting them to work within a fair system of social cooperation. We cannot tell simply by listing who gets what whether the distribution arises from the most (or an) effectively designed system of cooperation satisfying the difference principle. It is best to leave the limits unspecified and try to ignore the observable features of distributions, or their overall shape. In a society well ordered by the two principles of justice, we hope that the observable features of the distributions that result fall in a range where they do not seem unjust.

The simplest limit, or shape, to impose on distributions is strict equality in all social goods. Plainly the difference principle is not egalitarian in that sense, since it recognizes the need for inequalities in social and economic organization, of which their role as incentives is but one. It is, however, egalitarian in a sense to be discussed later in Part III: it selects the efficient point on the OP curve closest to equality (this is obvious from Figure 1, in

36. Of course, within justice as fairness, we do not have any further criterion to judge whether the ratio is unjust, for all our principles are met. It is simply that the actual ratio may disturb us and make us wonder. It is as if a state of reflective equilibrium is a bit upset. We hope the disparities that do occur fall within a range where we are not thus troubled. I am indebted to Ronald Dworkin for pointing out the need to make this point explicit.

which the 45-degree line represents equality and the segment D to B and beyond is the set of efficient points).

19.3. Finally, I consider a third counterexample meant to show that the difference principle needs revision. Discussing it in some detail will bring out several points to remember in testing that principle.[37]

|     | *Indians* | *British* |
| --- | --- | --- |
| (1) | 100 | 100 |
| (2) | 120 | 110 |
| (3) | 115 | 140 |

In this example there are only three alternative constitutions for India in 1800, with the distributions of primary goods as shown. Looking at the three alternatives, the difference principle selects (3) because it is the scheme in which the least-advantaged group (not always the Indians) does best.

The example is meant to show that it is not correct, as *Theory* is alleged to say, that the representative Briton's advantages under constitution (3) are gained in ways that promote the representative Indian's prospects: it is not correct because the particular individuals least advantaged under (3), the Indians, would have been even better off under (2). Only one place is cited (*Theory*, §17: 103, 1st ed.) as grounds for this interpretation: "B (the least-favored representative man) can accept A's (the more favored representative man) being better off since A's advantages have been gained in ways that improve B's prospects."

The mistake in the alleged counterexample is clear: the cited passage occurs early in *Theory*, §17, right after §16, in which, as we have seen, the relevant groups for applying the difference principle are specified by their prospects in terms of primary goods; or in the simplest form of the principle, by income and wealth. In ideal theory, rigid designators such as Indians and British are excluded.[38] The idea of a representative man ("individual" would have been better) is a familiar and handy way of speaking about

37. This example is from Derek Parfit, *Reasons and Persons* (Oxford: Oxford University Press, 1984), pp. 490–493. I am grateful to Brian Barry for sending me his comments on the example which he presented at the annual meeting of the American Political Science Association in 1985. I have drawn heavily on Barry's comments and any merits of my remarks are due to him. I should add that the example is of no importance in Parfit's book, occurring among several appendixes, this one written with John Broome. What I say is not in any way a criticism of that remarkable work.

38. See §17, n. 26.

a group already specified in some way. The passage cited (and others similar to it) should be read as referring to groups specified by income and wealth. What the numerical example does bring out is that the difference principle must not say (we already know it does not say (§18)) that the particular individuals, who are worst off under the basic structure it selects, would not be better off under any other practicable structure.

19.4. We might be tempted simply to dismiss the example as violating the restrictions on relevant groups. This would be too hasty, since the passage cited from *Theory* mentions (and so do many other passages) a kind of reciprocity between groups appropriately named. What lies behind this way of talking? Ignoring the matter of names for the moment, consider what can be said to the Indians in favor of (3). Accepting the conditions of the example, we cannot say the Indians would do no better under any alternative arrangement. Rather, we say that, in the neighborhood of (3), there is no alternative arrangement that by making the British worse off could make the Indians better off. The inequality in (3) is justified because in that neighborhood the advantages to the British do contribute to the advantages of the Indians. The condition of the Indians' being as well off as they are (in that neighborhood) is that the British are better off.

This reply depends, as does the difference principle itself, on there being a rough continuum of basic structures, each very close (practically speaking) to some others in the aspects along which these structures are varied as available systems of social cooperation. (Those close to one another are said to be in the same neighborhood.) The main question is not (3) against (2) but (3) against (1). If the Indians ask why there are inequalities at all, the reply focuses on (3) in relation to reasonably close and available alternatives in the neighborhood. It is in this neighborhood that reciprocity is thought to hold. If the Indians ask why we select the neighborhood of (3) rather than that of (2), the answer is that in the latter the worst off would be even worse off.

19.5. Note further that the example has the odd feature that there is a crossing over of the positions of the two groups: the Indians are best off in (2), the British in (3). Plainly if we use income and wealth classes, as the difference principle requires, the supposed difficulty cannot arise. As before, we don't have a counterexample. Moreover, the example is artificial, not only because it overlooks the assumption of a rough continuum of basic structures but because it is hard to see how, consistent with the principles of justice prior to the difference principle, together with the facts of commonsense political sociology, the crossover cases could be actual alternatives. In one the Indians predominate in the more advantaged group, in the other the British. Thus both groups can take part effectively in political and economic life.

If this is so, why wouldn't there be an intermediate constitution in which the difference principle is satisfied and there is at least an approximate equality between Indians and British? That is, the inequality within both groups is the same, and each has the same average income and wealth. Since members of both groups can be effective participants in society, as crossing-over shows, there is no justification for any inequality between them as groups. Of course, what would in fact happen is that when the prior principles of the equal liberties and of fair equality of opportunity are both satisfied, some of the Indians would be among the better off and some among the worse off, and similarly for the British. The example is unrealistic and so the difference principle need not cover it.

Of course, the Indians might still say that they want to be as well off as they can be; it doesn't matter to them that the British are even worse off in (2) than they (the Indians) are in (3). To this the reply is that the difference principle does not appeal to the self-interest of those particular persons or groups identifiable by their proper names who are in fact the least advantaged under existing arrangements, rather, it is a principle of justice.[39] In ideal theory, the only defense of inequalities in the basic structure is that they make the worst off (whoever they may be, Indians, British, or any other group, however ethnically composed, mixed or otherwise) better off than the worst off (whoever they may be) under any alternative (practicable) scheme consistent with all the requirements of the two principles of justice. In this way, the difference principle expresses, as any principle of political justice must, a concern for all members of society. The question is: how to express the concern that is most appropriate to the freedom and equality of democratic citizenship?

I have discussed this example to illustrate the care that must be taken in framing counterexamples to the difference principle. The example reminds us: (a) that the principle is meant to hold only when the prior principles of justice are satisfied; (b) that it presupposes a rough continuum of practicable basic structures; (c) that arbitrary numerical examples can easily be misleading unless we attend carefully to the commonsense institutional back-

---

39. This point is emphasized by Barry in his remarks referred to in note 37.

ground; (d) that the difference principle is a principle of justice and not an appeal to the self-interest of any particular group; and of course, finally, (e) that relevant social positions must be specified correctly (and not, for example, by rigid designators). If we apply the principle as a single principle by itself, ignoring these points, we get nonsense.

## §20. Legitimate Expectations, Entitlement, and Desert

20.1. Recall from §14 that in justice as fairness distribution takes place in accordance with legitimate claims and earned entitlements. These expectations and entitlements are specified by the public rules of the scheme of social cooperation. Suppose, for example, that these rules include provisions for agreements about wages and salaries, or for workers' compensation based on an index of the firm's market performance, as in a share economy.[40] Then those who make and honor these agreements have, by definition, a legitimate expectation of receiving the agreed amounts at the agreed times. They are entitled to these amounts. What individuals do depends on what the rules and agreements say they would be entitled to; what individuals are entitled to depends on what they do (*Theory*, §14: 74, 76).

Once more I stress that there is no criterion of a legitimate expectation, or of an entitlement, apart from the public rules that specify the scheme of cooperation. Legitimate expectations and entitlements are always (in justice as fairness) based on these rules. Here we assume, of course, that these rules are compatible with the two principles of justice. Given that these principles are satisfied by the basic structure, and given that all legitimate expectations and entitlements are honored, the resulting distribution is just, whatever it is. Apart from existing institutions, there is no prior and independent idea of what we may legitimately expect, or of what we are entitled to, that the basic structure is designed to fulfill. All these claims arise within the background system of fair social cooperation; they are based on its public rules and on what individuals and associations do in the light of those rules.

20.2. Now this statement is easily misunderstood. Within our comprehensive view we have a concept of moral desert specified independently of the rules of existing institutions. To say justice as fairness rejects such a

40. See Martin Weitzman, *The Share Economy* (Cambridge, Mass.: Harvard University Press, 1984).

concept is incorrect. It recognizes at least three ideas that in ordinary life are viewed as ideas of moral desert.

First, the idea of moral desert in the strict sense, that is, the moral worth of a person's character as a whole (and of a person's several virtues) as given by a comprehensive moral doctrine; as well as the moral worth of particular actions;

Second, the idea of legitimate expectations (and its companion idea of entitlements), which is the other side of the principle of fairness (*Theory*, §48); and

Third, the idea of deservingness as specified by a scheme of public rules designed to achieve certain purposes.

The concept of moral desert is not questioned. Rather, the thought is that a conception of moral desert as moral worth of character and actions cannot be incorporated into a political conception of justice in view of the fact of reasonable pluralism. Having conflicting conceptions of the good, citizens cannot agree on a comprehensive doctrine to specify an idea of moral desert for political purposes. In any case, moral worth would be utterly impracticable as a criterion when applied to questions of distributive justice. We might say: Only God could make those judgments. In public life we need to avoid the idea of moral desert and to find a replacement that belongs to a reasonable political conception.

20.3. The idea of a legitimate expectation is suggested as precisely such a replacement: it belongs to a political conception of justice and is framed to apply to that domain. While the political conception as a whole does apply to the family as an institution belonging to the basic structure (§50), its several principles are not intended to apply directly to the relations between members of the family, or to personal relationships between individuals, nor again to relations between members of small groups, or associations.[41] For example, the political conception of justice does not require parents to treat their children according to the difference principle, any more than friends are required so to treat one another. Each of these cases presumably requires its own distinctive criteria. How far the idea of legitimate expectations holds must be considered separately in each case.

Finally, the idea of deservingness as specified by a scheme of public rules is illustrated at *Theory*, §48: 276, by games, as when we say that the losing

---

41. This is not to deny that in general the principles of justice restrict the form these arrangements can take (cf. §4.2 and §50).

team deserved to win. Here it is not denied that to the winners go the victory and the honors; what is meant is that the losers exhibited to a higher degree the qualities and skills the game is designed to encourage, the display of which makes the game enjoyable both to play and to watch. Yet chance and luck, or other mishaps, denied the losers what they deserved. This usage also fits the case where, after a particularly well played game, we say that both teams deserved to win; and while better a victory than a tie, it is too bad either had to lose.

20.4. Justice as fairness uses only the second and third ideas of desert. The second we have already covered in discussing legitimate expectations and entitlements. The third is mentioned only at *Theory*, §48: 276, but it is generally implied, as it holds for public rules effectively designed to achieve social purposes. Schemes of cooperation satisfying the difference principle are such rules; they serve to encourage individuals to educate their endowments and to use them for the general good.

Thus when individuals, moved by the public rules of social arrangements, try conscientiously to act accordingly, they may become deserving. But, as in games, there are competitors, and even when the competition is fair, one's success is not assured. Although well-designed arrangements may help to avoid large discrepancies between deservingness and success, this is not always possible. The relevant point here is that there are many ways to specify deservingness depending on the public rules in question together with the ends and purposes they are meant to serve. Yet none of those ways specifies an idea of moral desert, properly understood.

## §21. On Viewing Native Endowments as a Common Asset

21.1. In *Theory*, §17, it is said that we do not deserve (in the sense of moral desert) our place in the distribution of native endowments. This statement is meant as a moral truism.[42] Who would deny it? Do people really think that they (morally) deserved to be born more gifted than others?

42. This remark is not made from within justice as fairness, since this conception contains no idea of moral desert in the sense meant. On the other hand, the remark is not made from within any particular comprehensive philosophical or moral doctrine. Rather, I assume that all reasonable such doctrines would endorse this remark and hold that moral desert always involves some conscientious effort of will, or something intentionally or willingly done, none of which can apply to our place in the distribution of native endowments, or to our social class of origin.

Do they think that they (morally) deserved to be born a man rather than a woman, or vice versa? Do they think that they deserved to be born into a wealthier rather than into a poorer family? No.

The second and third ideas of desert do not depend on whether we morally deserve our place in the distribution of native endowments. A basic structure satisfying the difference principle rewards people, not for their place in that distribution, but for training and educating their endowments, and for putting them to work so as to contribute to others' good as well as their own. When people act in this way they are deserving, as the idea of legitimate expectations requires. The idea of entitlement presupposes, as do ideas of (moral) desert, a deliberate effort of will, or acts intentionally done. As such they provide the basis of legitimate expectations.

21.2. In *Theory* it is said (§17: 101, 1st ed.) that the difference principle represents an agreement to regard the distribution of native endowments as a common asset and to share in the benefits of this distribution whatever it turns out to be. It is not said that this distribution is a common asset: to say that would presuppose a (normative) principle of ownership that is not available in the fundamental ideas from which we begin the exposition. Certainly the difference principle is not to be derived from such a principle as an independent premise.

The text of *Theory* mentioned above is commenting on what is involved in the parties' agreeing to the difference principle: namely, by agreeing to that principle, it is as if they agree to regard the distribution of endowments as a common asset. What this regarding consists in is expressed by the difference principle itself. The remark about the distribution of endowments as a common asset elucidates its meaning.

21.3. Note that what is regarded as a common asset is the distribution of native endowments and not our native endowments per se. It is not as if society owned individuals' endowments taken separately, looking at individuals one by one. To the contrary, the question of the ownership of our endowments does not arise; and should it arise, it is persons themselves who own their endowments: the psychological and physical integrity of persons is already guaranteed by the basic rights and liberties that fall under the first principle of justice (§13.1).

What is to be regarded as a common asset, then, is the distribution of native endowments, that is, the differences among persons. These differences consist not only in the variation of talents of the same kind (variation in strength and imagination, and so on) but in the variety of talents of different kinds. This variety can be regarded as a common asset because it makes possible numerous complementarities between talents when organized in appropriate ways to take advantage of these differences. Consider how these talents are organized and coordinated in games and in performances of musical compositions. For example, consider a group of musicians every one of whom could have trained himself to play equally well as the others any instrument in the orchestra, but who each have by a kind of tacit agreement set out to perfect their skills on the one they have chosen so as to real-ize the powers of all in their joint performances (*Theory*, §79: 459n4). Vari-ations of talent of the same kind (as in degrees of strength and endurance) also allow for mutually beneficial complementarities, as economists have long known and formulated in the principle of comparative advantage.

21.4. We use the phrase "common asset" to express a certain attitude, or point of view, toward the natural fact of the distribution of endowments. Consider the question: Is it possible for persons as free and equal not to view it a misfortune (though not an injustice) that some are by nature better endowed than others? Is there any political principle mutually acceptable to citizens as free and equal to guide society in its use of the distribution of native endowments? Is it possible for the more and the less advantaged to be reconciled to a common principle? Should there be no such principle, the structure of social worlds and the general facts of nature would be to this extent hostile to the very idea of democratic equality.

To resolve the question, we try to show in Part III that the original posi-tion is a point of view from which the representatives of citizens as free and equal would agree to the difference principle, and so to the use of the distri-bution of endowments as, so to speak, a common asset. If we can show this, then that principle offers a way of seeing nature and the social world as no longer hostile to democratic equality; and in formulating such a principle justice as fairness does the work of political philosophy as reconciliation.

Here it is crucial that the difference principle includes an idea of reci-procity: the better endowed (who have a more fortunate place in the distri-bution of native endowments they do not morally deserve) are encouraged to acquire still further benefits—they are already benefited by their fortu-nate place in that distribution—on condition that they train their native en-dowments and use them in ways that contribute to the good of the less en-dowed (whose less fortunate place in the distribution they also do not morally deserve). Reciprocity is a moral idea situated between impartiality, which is altruistic, on the one side and mutual advantage on the other.[43]

## §22. Summary Comments on Distributive Justice and Desert

22.1. Looking back on our discussion, I add a few summary comments. Justice as fairness does not reject the concept of moral desert as given by a fully or partially comprehensive religious, philosophical, or moral doctrine. Rather, in view of the fact of reasonable pluralism, it holds that no such doctrine can serve as a political conception of distributive justice. Moreover, it would not be workable, or practicable, for the purposes of political life.

The problem, then, is to find a replacement—a conception that does the kind of work needed for a political view that we might naturally, though incorrectly, suppose could only be done by a concept of moral desert belonging to a comprehensive view. To this end justice as fairness introduces a conception of legitimate expectations and its companion conception of entitlements.

22.2. For this replacement to be satisfactory, it must not only be workable, and answer the needs of a political conception of justice, but also:

(a) It should authorize the social and economic inequalities necessary, or else highly effective, in running an industrial economy in a modern state. Such inequalities (as already noted) cover the costs of training and education, act as incentives, and the like.

(b) It should express a principle of reciprocity, since society is viewed as a fair system of cooperation from one generation to the next between free and equal citizens, and since the political conception is to apply to the basic structure which regulates background justice.

(c) It should appropriately handle the most serious inequalities from the point of view of political justice: inequalities in citizens' prospects as given by their reasonable expectations over a complete life. These inequalities are those likely to arise between different income levels in society as these are affected by the social position into which individuals are born and spend the early years of life up to the age of reason, as well as by their place in the distribution of native endowments. We are concerned with the long-lasting

43. See *Political Liberalism*, pp. 16–17.

effects of these contingencies, together with the consequences of accident and luck throughout life.

In addition to these desiderata, there are two others that deserve notice:

(d) Principles specifying fair distribution must, so far as possible, be stated in terms that allow us publicly to verify whether they are satisfied.[44]

(e) We should look for principles that are reasonably simple and whose basis can be explained in ways citizens may be assumed to understand in the light of ideas available in the public political culture.

22.3. The question, then, is whether the difference principle (working in tandem with the prior principles of the basic liberties and fair opportunity, and understood in the light of the ideas of entitlement and legitimate expectation) meets these desiderata as well as if not better than other available political principles. Justice as fairness holds that it may do so, and that it is worth considering, once we recognize that the role of commonsense precepts of justice, and of inequalities in distributive shares in modern societies, is not to reward moral desert as distinguished from deservingness. Their role is rather to attract people to positions where they are most needed from a social point of view, to cover the costs of acquiring skills and educating abilities, to encourage them to accept the burdens of particular responsibilities, and to do all this in ways consistent with free choice of occupation and fair equality of opportunity (*Theory*, §47). Of course, we are only beginning to explore this question (we will say more later) and can never provide a conclusive answer.

In considering the merits of the difference principle, keep in mind what we have already said: when justice as fairness says we do not morally deserve either our initial place in society or our place in the distribution of native endowments, it views this as a truism. It does not say that we never deserve in an appropriate way the social position or the offices we may hold in later life, or the realized skills and educated abilities we may have after we have reached the age of reason. In a well-ordered society we usually do deserve these things, when desert is understood as entitlement earned under fair conditions. Justice as fairness holds that the idea of desert as entitlement is fully adequate for a political conception of justice; and this is a moral idea (though not the idea of moral desert defined by a comprehensive doctrine) because the political conception to which it belongs is itself a moral conception.

---

44. This feature has been emphasized in connection with primary goods in §17.

The substantive question, then, is whether we need, or should want, more than this in a political conception. Doesn't it suffice to cooperate on fair terms that all of us as free and equal can publicly endorse before one another? Wouldn't this be reasonably close to the practicable, political best? Certainly some will insist that they do morally deserve certain things in ways a political conception does not account for. This people may do from within their comprehensive doctrines, and indeed, if the doctrine is sound, they may be correct in doing so. Justice as fairness does not deny this. Why should it? It only says that since these conflicting doctrines say that we morally deserve different things in different ways for different reasons, they cannot all be correct; and in any case, none of them is politically feasible. To find a public basis of justification, we must look for a workable political conception of justice.

22.4. Recall that we started in §12.1 by asking: what are the principles most appropriate to specify the fair terms of social cooperation between citizens regarded as free and equal? We are concerned with principles that take seriously the idea of citizens as free and equal, and so with principles suited to shape political and social institutions so that they may effectively realize this idea. But, of course, this raises the question of whether there may not be a number of principles that take the idea seriously. What could these alternatives be? How can we select among them? The answer that justice as fairness proposes is that the most appropriate principles taking this idea seriously are those that would be selected by citizens themselves when fairly represented as free and equal. To carry out this suggestion leads to the original position as a device of representation (§6). The argument from that position is presented in Part III.

The background worry present in asking these questions is that we may not know of any principles that take seriously the idea of citizens as free and equal; or that if we do, we know of several conflicting ones. They impose very different requirements and there is endless dispute about them influenced by which favors us most. Or it may be that we know of at least one family of principles that takes the idea seriously but we are not willing to act from it, for whatever variety of reasons. Should any of these things be the case, the question arises whether our speaking of citizens as free and equal is seriously meant. Is it simply talk? Does it serve other than an ideological purpose, understanding this term in Marx's sense? Plainly the integrity of constitutional democratic thought depends on the answers to these questions.

## PART III

# *The Argument from the Original Position*

### §23. The Original Position: The Setup

23.1. Part III considers two main topics in this order: the setup of the original position (§§23–26), and the argument from the original position for the two principles of justice. This argument is divided into two fundamental comparisons: the first fundamental comparison (§§27–33); and the second fundamental comparison (§§34–40). Since we have already discussed the original position as a device of representation, I focus here on a few details about how it is set up.[1]

Keep in mind throughout that, as a device of representation, the original position models two things (§6.4).

First, it models what we regard—here and now—as fair conditions under which the representatives of citizens, viewed solely as free and equal persons, are to agree to the fair terms of social cooperation (as expressed by principles of justice) whereby the basic structure is to be regulated.

Second, it models what we regard—here and now—as acceptable restrictions on the reasons on the basis of which the parties (as citizens' representatives), situated in those fair conditions, may properly put forward certain principles of justice and reject others.

1. See *Theory*, §§20–25.

Keep in mind also that the original position serves other purposes as well. As we have said (§12.1), it provides a way to keep track of our assumptions. We can see what we have assumed by looking at the way the parties and their situation have been described. The original position also brings out the combined force of our assumptions by uniting them into one surveyable idea that enables us to see their implications more easily.

23.2. I now turn to matters of detail. Note first the similarity between the argument from the original position and arguments in economics and social theory. The elementary theory of the consumer (the household) contains many examples of the latter. In each case we have rational persons (or agents) making decisions, or arriving at agreements, subject to certain conditions. From these persons' knowledge and beliefs, their desires and interests, and the alternatives they face, as well as the likely consequences they expect from adopting each alternative, we can figure out what they will decide, or agree to, unless they make a mistake in reasoning or otherwise fail to act sensibly. If the main elements at work can be modeled by mathematical assumptions, it may be possible to prove what they will do, ceteris paribus.

Despite the similarity between familiar arguments in economics and social theory and the argument from the original position, there are fundamental differences. One difference is that our aim is not to describe and explain how people actually behave in certain situations, or how institutions actually work. Our aim is to uncover a public basis for a political conception of justice, and doing this belongs to political philosophy and not social theory. In describing the parties we are not describing persons as we find them. Rather, the parties are described according to how we want to model rational representatives of free and equal citizens. In addition, we impose on the parties certain reasonable conditions as seen in the symmetry of their situation with respect to one another and the limits of their knowledge (the veil of ignorance).

23.3. Here again we distinguish (as we did in §2.2) between the rational and the reasonable, a distinction that parallels Kant's distinction between the hypothetical imperative and the categorical imperative. Kant's categorical imperative procedure subjects an agent's rational and sincere maxim (drawn up in the light of the agent's empirical practical reason) to the reasonable constraints contained in that procedure, and thus constrains the agent's conduct by the requirements of pure practical reason. Similarly, the reasonable conditions imposed on the parties in the original position constrain them in reaching a rational agreement on principles of justice as they try to advance the good of those they represent. In each case the reasonable has priority over the rational and subordinates it absolutely. This priority expresses the priority of right; and justice as fairness resembles Kant's view in having this feature.[2]

The terms "reasonable" and "rational" will not be explicitly defined. We gather their meaning by how they are used and by attending to the contrast between them. Yet a remark may help: the reasonable is viewed as a basic intuitive moral idea; it may be applied to persons, their decisions and actions, as well as to principles and standards, to comprehensive doctrines and to much else. We are concerned at first with reasonable principles of justice for the basic structure. These are principles it would be reasonable for free and equal citizens to accept as specifying the fair terms of their social cooperation. Justice as fairness conjectures that the principles that will seem reasonable for this purpose, all things considered, are the same principles that rational representatives of citizens, when subject to reasonable constraints, would adopt to regulate their basic institutions. What constraints, though, are reasonable? We say: those that arise from situating citizens' representatives symmetrically when they are represented solely as free and equal, and not as belonging to this or that social class, or as possessing these or those native endowments, or this or that (comprehensive) conception of the good. While this conjecture may have an initial plausibility, only its detailed elaboration can show how far it is sound.

23.4. We should like the argument from the original position to be, so far as is possible, a deductive one, even if the reasoning we actually give falls short of this standard.[3] The point in aiming for this is that we do not want the parties' accepting the two principles to depend on psychological hypotheses or social conditions not already included in the description of the original position. Consider the proposition in economics that the agent for

2. Here I correct a remark in *Theory*, §3: 15 and §9: 47 (1st ed.), where it is said that the theory of justice is a part of the theory of rational choice. From what we have just said, this is simply a mistake, and would imply that justice as fairness is at bottom Hobbesian (as Hobbes is often interpreted) rather than Kantian. What should have been said is that the account of the parties, and of their reasoning, uses the theory of rational choice (decision), but that this theory is itself part of a political conception of justice, one that tries to give an account of reasonable principles of justice. There is no thought of deriving those principles from the concept of rationality as the sole normative concept.

3. See *Theory*, §20: 104f.

the household buys the commodity-bundle indicated by the (unique) point in commodity-space at which the budget line is tangent to the (highest) in-difference curve touching that line. This proposition follows deductively from the premises of demand theory. The necessary psychology is already included in those premises. Ideally we want the same to be true of the argu-ment from the original position: we include the necessary psychology in the description of the parties as rational representatives who are moved to se-cure the good of those they represent, as this good is specified by the ac-count of primary goods (§25.4). As such, the parties are artificial persons, merely inhabitants of our device of representation: they are characters who have a part in the play of our thought-experiment.

With respect to the alternatives available to the parties, we do not try to say what principles they would think of as possible alternatives. To do so would be a complicated business and a distraction from our practical aim. Rather, we simply hand the parties a list of principles, a menu, as it were. Included on the list are the more important conceptions of political justice found in our tradition of political philosophy, together with several other al-ternatives we want to examine. The parties must agree on one alternative on this menu.

The principles of justice agreed to are not, then, deduced from the con-ditions of the original position: they are selected from a given list. The orig-inal position is a selection device: it operates on a familiar family of con-ceptions of justice found in, or shaped from, our tradition of political philosophy. If it is objected that certain principles are not on the list, say libertarian principles of justice,[4] those principles must be added to it. Jus-tice as fairness then argues that the two principles of justice would still be agreed to. Should this argument succeed, libertarians must object to the setup of the original position itself as a device of representation. For exam-ple, they must say that it fails to represent considerations they regard as es-sential, or that it represents them in the wrong way. The argument contin-ues from there.

To argue from a given list cannot, of course, establish what is the most appropriate conception of justice among all possible alternatives, the best conception, as it were. It may, however, suffice for our first and minimum objective: namely, to find a conception of political justice that can specify an appropriate moral basis of democratic institutions and can hold its own against the known existing alternatives.

4. See Nozick's formulation of them in *Anarchy, State, and Utopia*, p. 151.

## §24. The Circumstances of Justice

24.1. We are to think of the circumstances of justice as reflecting the historical conditions under which modern democratic societies exist. These include what we may call the objective circumstances of moderate scarcity and the necessity of social cooperation for all to have a decent standard of life. Also especially important are the circumstances that reflect the fact that in a modern democratic society citizens affirm different, and indeed incommensurable and irreconcilable, though reasonable, comprehensive doctrines in the light of which they understand their conceptions of the good. This is the fact of reasonable pluralism (§11). There is no politically practicable way to eliminate this diversity except by the oppressive use of state power to establish a particular comprehensive doctrine and to silence dissent, the fact of oppression (§11). This seems evident not only from the history of democratic states but also from the development of thought and culture in the context of free institutions. We take this pluralism to be a permanent feature of a democratic society, and view it as characterizing what we may call the subjective circumstances of justice.

One role of political philosophy is to help us reach agreement on a political conception of justice, but it cannot show, clearly enough to gain general and free political agreement, that any single reasonable comprehensive doctrine, with its conception of the good, is superior. It does not follow (and justice as fairness as a political conception of justice does not say, and must not say) that there is no true comprehensive doctrine, or no best conception of the good. It only says that we cannot expect to reach a workable political agreement as to what it is. Since reasonable pluralism is viewed as a permanent condition of a democratic culture, we look for a conception of political justice that takes that plurality as given. Only in this way can we fulfill the liberal principle of legitimacy (§12.3): when constitutional essentials are involved, political power, as the power of free and equal citizens, is to be exercised in ways that all citizens as reasonable and rational might endorse in the light of their common human reason. Social unity is based on citizens' accepting a political conception of justice and uses ideas of the good fitting within it. It is not based on a complete conception of the good rooted in a comprehensive doctrine.

24.2. The parties, as representatives of free and equal citizens, act as trustees or guardians. Thus, in agreeing to principles of justice, they must secure the fundamental interests of those they represent. This does not mean that the parties are self-interested, much less selfish, as these words are normally used. Nor does it mean this when applied to citizens in society for whom the parties are responsible. True, the parties take no direct interest in the interests of persons represented by other parties. But whether people are self-interested, or even selfish, depends on the content of their final ends; on whether these are interests in themselves, in their own wealth and position, in their own power and prestige. In acting responsibly as trustees to secure persons' fundamental interests in their freedom and equality—in the conditions adequate for the development and exercise of their moral powers and the effective pursuit of their conception of the good on fair terms with others—the parties are not viewing those they represent as selfish, or self-interested. Certainly we expect and indeed want people to care about their liberties and opportunities so that they can achieve their good. We think they would show a lack of self-respect and weakness of character in not doing so.

That the parties take no direct interest in the interests of those represented by the other parties reflects an essential aspect of how citizens are quite properly moved when questions of political justice arise about the basic structure. Deep religious and moral conflicts characterize the subjective circumstances of justice. Those engaged in these conflicts are surely not in general self-interested, but rather, see themselves as defending their basic rights and liberties which secure their legitimate and fundamental interests. Moreover, these conflicts can be the most intractable and deeply divisive, often more so than social and economic ones.

Similarly, without an appreciation of the depth of the conflict between comprehensive doctrines as they enter the political domain, the case for formulating a reasonable political conception of justice with its idea of public reason (§26) is less likely to seem convincing. But this is getting ahead.

## §25. Formal Constraints and the Veil of Ignorance

25.1. Once again recall (§6) that the original position is a device of representation: it models, first, what we regard (here and now) as fair conditions for the terms of social cooperation to be agreed to (reflected in the symmetry of the parties' situation); and second, it models what we regard (here and now) as reasonable restrictions on reasons that may be used in arguing for principles of justice to regulate the basic structure. Various formal constraints of the concept of right are modeled in the original position by requiring the parties to evaluate principles of justice from a suitably general

point of view. However rational it might be for the parties to favor principles framed to promote the determinate and known interests of those they
represent, should they have the opportunity, the constraints of right, joined
with the limits on information (modeled by the veil of ignorance), make that
impossible.[5]

It is a commonplace of moral philosophy to require first principles to be
general and universal. Principles are general when it is possible to state
them without the use of proper names or rigged definite descriptions. They
are universal when they can be applied without inconsistency or self-defeat-
ing incoherence to all moral agents, in our case, to all citizens in the society
in question. Justice as fairness also requires, and this is much less common,
that first principles of political justice be public. This condition is applied
to political conceptions, not to moral conceptions generally; whether it applies to the latter is a separate question. In the case of political conceptions
for the basic structure the publicity condition seems appropriate. It means
that in evaluating principles the parties in the original position are to take
into account the consequences, social and psychological, of public recognition by citizens that these principles are mutually acknowledged and that
they effectively regulate the basic structure. These consequences are important in the argument from the original position, as we see in due course.

25.2. Although the argument from the original position could be presented formally, I use the idea of the original position as a natural and vivid
way to convey the kind of the reasoning the parties may engage in. Many
questions about the original position answer themselves if we remember
this and see it is a device of representation modeling reasonable constraints
that limit the reasons that the parties as rational representatives may appeal
to. Is that position a general assembly which includes at one moment everyone who lives at some time? No. Is it a gathering of all actual or possible
persons? Plainly not. Can we enter it, so to speak, and if so when? We can
enter it at any time. How? Simply by reasoning in accordance with the
modeled constraints, citing only reasons those constraints allow.

It is essential that the parties as rational representatives be led to the
same judgment as to which principles to adopt. This allows that a unanimous agreement can be reached. The veil of ignorance achieves this result

5. *Theory* doesn't use the phrase "a device of representation," but at various places it
makes the points in this paragraph. See *Theory,* §4: 16f., 18f.; §20: 104f.; §24: 119f.; §78: 453;
§87: 514.

by limiting the parties to the same body of general facts (the presently accepted facts of social theory (§26)) and to the same information about the general circumstances of society: that it exists under the circumstances of justice, both objective and subjective, and that reasonably favorable conditions making a constitutional democracy possible obtain (§13.5).

Along with other conditions on the original position, the veil of ignorance removes differences in bargaining advantages, so that in this and other respects the parties are symmetrically situated. Citizens are represented solely as free and equal persons: as those who have to the minimum sufficient degree the two moral powers and other capacities enabling them to be normal cooperating members of society over a complete life. By situating the parties symmetrically, the original position respects the basic precept of formal equality, or Sidgwick's principle of equity: those similar in all relevant respects are to be treated similarly. With this precept satisfied, the original position is fair.

25.3. We suppose that the parties are rational, where rationality (as distinguished from reasonableness) is understood in the way familiar from economics. Thus the parties are rational in that they can rank their final ends consistently; they deliberate guided by such principles as: to adopt the most effective means to one's ends; to select the alternative most likely to advance those ends; to schedule activities so that, ceteris paribus, more rather than less of those ends can be fulfilled.

There is, be it noted, one important modification in this idea of rationality in regard to certain special psychologies.[6] These include a liability to envy and spite, a peculiarly high aversion to risk and uncertainty, and a strong will to dominate and exercise power over others. The parties (in contrast to persons in society) are not moved by such desires and inclinations. Remember it is up to us, you and me, who are setting up justice as fairness, to describe the parties (as artificial persons in our device of representation) as best suits our aims in developing a political conception of justice. Since envy, for instance, is generally regarded as something to be avoided and feared, at least when it becomes intense, it seems desirable that, if possible, the choice of principles should not be influenced by this trait.[7] So we stipulate that the parties are not influenced by these psychologies as they try to secure the good of those they represent.

6. See *Theory*, §25: 123ff.
7. [See *Theory*, §80: 465.]

25.4. Since the veil of ignorance prevents the parties from knowing the (comprehensive) doctrines and conceptions of the good of the persons they represent, they must have some other grounds for deciding which principles to select in the original position. Here we face a serious problem: unless we can set up the original position so that the parties can agree on principles of justice moved by appropriate grounds, justice as fairness cannot be carried through.

To solve this problem is one reason we introduced the idea of primary goods and enumerated a list of items falling under this heading (§17.2). As we saw, these goods are identified by asking which things are generally necessary as social conditions and all-purpose means to enable citizens, regarded as free and equal, adequately to develop and fully exercise their two moral powers, and to pursue their determinate conceptions of the good. Primary goods, we said, are things persons need as citizens, rather than as human beings apart from any normative conception. Here the political conception, and not a comprehensive moral doctrine, helps to specify these needs and requirements.

25.5. Finally, a basic point about the argument from the original position. We split this argument into two parts.[8] Above we said the parties themselves are not swayed by the special psychologies: in the first part we say they think the same of the persons they represent. Their reasoning aims at selecting the principles of justice that best secure those persons' good, their fundamental interests, ignoring any inclinations that might arise from envy, or a special aversion to uncertainty, and the like. (Aversion to uncertainty is discussed in §31.)

In the second part of the argument, which we take up in Part V, the parties consider the psychology of citizens in the well-ordered society of justice as fairness: that is, the psychology of people who grow up and live in a society in which the two principles of justice (the principles the parties have selected) effectively regulate the basic structure and in which this fact is publicly recognized. In that part the question will be whether a basic structure so regulated actually generates in citizens a high degree of excusable envy and spite,[9] or a will to dominate and the like. If so, citizens' sense of justice is likely to be weak, or too frequently overridden by attitudes rooted in the special psychologies. Just institutions are too often violated

8. *Theory*, §25: 124; §76: 441; §80: 465.
9. See *Theory*, §81.

and the favored principles of justice fail to generate their own support. The associated well-ordered society is unstable. Thus the parties must reconsider the principles agreed to and examine whether, on balance, other principles should be adopted. If the principles already selected turn out to be (sufficiently) stable, the argument is complete.[10]

## §26. The Idea of Public Reason

26.1. In presenting the argument for the two principles we have to refer to the parties' general knowledge of social theory and human psychology. But how is this knowledge specified? It must be settled by you and me as we set up justice as fairness. It is up to us to say what the parties are to know in view of our aims in working out a political conception of justice that can be, we hope, the focus of a reasonable overlapping consensus and hence a public basis of justification.

For an agreement on the principles of justice to be effective, and to support a public basis of justification, there must be a companion agreement on the guidelines for public inquiry and on the criteria as to what kind of information and knowledge is relevant in discussing political questions, at least when these involve the constitutional essentials and questions of basic justice (§13.6). The original agreement, then, has two parts:

(1) First, an agreement on the principles of political justice for the basic structure (for example, those of justice as fairness); and

(2) Second, an agreement on the principles of reasoning and the rules of evidence in the light of which citizens are to decide whether the principles of justice apply, when and how far they are satisfied, and which laws and policies best fulfill them in existing social conditions.

26.2. Faced with the fact of reasonable pluralism, and granted that, on matters of constitutional essentials, basic institutions and public policies should be justifiable to all citizens (as the liberal principle of legitimacy requires), we allow the parties the general beliefs and forms of reasoning

10. Note here that (sufficient) stability is imposed as a condition on a reasonable conception of political justice: such a conception must be able to generate its own sufficiently strong supporting sense of justice. This idea of stability is taken up in Part V. Meanwhile do not mistake this sense of stability with the stability of a modus vivendi, or with stability as a balance of political forces.

found in common sense, and the methods and conclusions of science, when not controversial. The principle of legitimacy makes this the most appropriate and perhaps the only way to specify the companion agreement. So we say the parties have that kind of general knowledge and they use those ways of reasoning. This excludes comprehensive religious and philosophical doctrines (the whole truth, as it were) from being specified as public reasons. The same holds for elaborate economic theories of general equilibrium and the like, if these are in dispute. If we are to speak of public reason, the knowledge and ways of reasoning—the plain truths now common and available to citizens generally—that ground the parties' selection of the principles of justice must be accessible to citizens' common reason.[11] Otherwise, the political conception does not provide a basis of political legitimacy.

This does not mean, however, that reasonable comprehensive doctrines cannot be introduced and discussed in public reason.[12] People are in general free to do this. It has the advantage of citizens informing one another where they come from, so to speak, and on what basis they support the public political conception of justice. All this may have desirable consequences and may strengthen the forces working for stability. It is also less restrictive and gives citizens a deeper understanding of their several points of view. Nevertheless, though we can introduce our comprehensive doctrine, the duty of civility requires us in due course to make our case for the legislation and public policies we support in terms of public reasons, or the political values covered by the political conception of justice (or one of a suitable family of such).

One ground for introducing the idea of public reason is this: while political power is always coercive—backed by the government's monopoly of legal force—in a democratic regime it is also the power of the public, that is, the power of free and equal citizens as a corporate body. But if each citizen has an equal share in political power, then, so far as possible, political power should be exercised, at least when constitutional essentials and ques-

11. Thus we suppose the parties accept the four general facts of political sociology in §11.3.

12. We may call this the "wide view" of public reason, as distinct from the narrower view of it called the "inclusive view" found in *Political Liberalism,* lect. VI, §8. The difference is that the inclusive view allowed comprehensive doctrines to be introduced only in nonideal circumstances, as illustrated by slavery in the antebellum South and the civil rights movement in the 1960s and later. The idea of public reason is further developed in "The Idea of Public Reason Revisited."

tions of basic justice are at stake, in ways that all citizens can publicly endorse in the light of their own reason. This is the principle of political legitimacy that justice as fairness is to satisfy.

Citizens must be able, then, to present to one another publicly acceptable reasons for their political views in cases raising fundamental political questions. This means that our reasons should fall under the political values expressed by a political conception of justice. If free and equal persons are to cooperate politically on a basis of mutual respect, we must justify our use of our corporate and coercive political power, where those essential matters are at stake, in the light of public reason.

Here we are concerned solely with the way the idea of public reason holds for questions about the constitutional essentials and questions of basic justice. Most legislative questions do not concern these matters, although they often touch upon them, for example, tax legislation and laws regulating property; legislation protecting the environment and controlling pollution; laws establishing national parks and voting funds for museums and the arts. A satisfactory account of public reason would show how these questions differ from fundamental questions, and why the restrictions imposed by public reason do not apply to them, or if they do, at least not in the same way or so stringently.[13]

26.3. The political values expressed by justice as fairness as a political conception are of two kinds, each paired with one of the two parts of the original agreement as stated above (§26.1).

(a) The first kind—the values of political justice—fall under the principles of justice for the basic structure. They include the values of equal political and civil liberty; fair equality of opportunity; social equality and reciprocity (expressed by the difference principle), and so on.

(b) The second kind of political values—the values of public reason—fall under the guidelines for public inquiry and for the steps to be taken to ensure that inquiry is free and public as well as informed and reasonable. They include not only the appropriate use of the fundamental concepts of

13. If we define a justification as publicly based when it is based solely on political values covered by the political conception of justice, then we strive for publicly based justifications for questions regarding the constitutional essentials and basic questions of distributive justice but not in general for all the questions to be settled by the legislature within a constitutional framework. We should distinguish, then, between these two cases, the first attainable (we hope) and desirable, the second neither attainable nor desirable. For the importance of this distinction I am indebted to T. M. Scanlon and Peter de Marneffe.

judgment, inference, and evidence, but also the virtues of reasonableness and fair-mindedness as shown in the adherence to the criteria and procedures of commonsense knowledge and to the methods and conclusions of science when not controversial. These values reflect an ideal of citizenship: our willingness to settle the fundamental political matters in ways that others as free and equal can acknowledge are reasonable and rational. This ideal gives rise to a duty of public civility (§33), one aspect of which directs us, when constitutional essentials and questions of basic justice are involved, to reason within the limits set by the principle of legitimacy.

In sum, public reason is the form of reasoning appropriate to equal citizens who as a corporate body impose rules on one another backed by sanctions of state power. As we have said, shared guidelines for inquiry and methods of reasoning make that reason public, while freedom of speech and thought in a constitutional regime make that reason free. By contrast, nonpublic reason is the reason appropriate to individuals and associations within society: it guides how they quite properly deliberate in making their personal and associational decisions. The nonpublic reasons of churches and universities, of scientific associations and private clubs differ. These associations have diverse aims and purposes, and within the limits of political justice, they quite rightly view themselves in their own way.

26.4. Let us elaborate this last point and consider the distinction between public reason and nonpublic reason. To act reasonably and responsibly, corporate bodies as well as individuals need some recognized way of reasoning about what is to be done. This holds for government and its citizens as a corporate body and also for associations such as firms and labor unions, universities and churches. We say the recognized ways of reasoning of associations are public with respect to their members, but nonpublic with respect to political society, and so nonpublic with respect to citizens generally.

All ways of reasoning—whether individual, associational, or political—must accept certain common elements: principles of inference and rules of evidence; they must incorporate the fundamental concepts of judgment, inference, and evidence, and include standards of correctness and criteria of truth. Otherwise they would not be ways of reasoning but something else: mere rhetoric or artifices of persuasion. The capacity to learn and to apply those concepts and principles is part of our common human reason. We are concerned with reason, not simply with discourse.

Nevertheless, different procedures and methods are appropriate in view of the different conceptions of themselves held by individuals and corporate bodies, and given the different conditions under which their reasoning is carried out as well as the different constraints to which their reasoning is properly subject. To illustrate: the rules for weighing evidence in a court of law—the rules relating to hearsay evidence and requiring that the defendant be guilty beyond a reasonable doubt—are suited to the special role of courts. These rules are different from the rules of evidence used by a scientific society; moreover, different authorities are recognized as relevant or binding by different corporate bodies. Consider the differences between a church council discussing a point of theological doctrine, a university faculty debating educational policy, and a meeting of a scientific association trying to assess the harm to the public from a nuclear accident. The criteria and methods of the public reason of these associations depend in part on how the nature (the aim and point) of each association is understood and the conditions under which it pursues its ends.

In a democratic society, nonpublic authority as seen, for example, in the authority of churches over their members, is freely accepted. In the case of ecclesiastical authority, since apostasy and heresy are not legal offenses, those who are no longer able to recognize a church's authority may cease being members without running afoul of state power. Whatever comprehensive religious, philosophical, or moral views we hold are also freely accepted; for given liberty of conscience and freedom of thought, we impose any such doctrine on ourselves, politically speaking. By this I do not claim that we do this by an act of free choice, as it were, apart from all prior loyalties and commitments, attachments and affections. I mean that, as free and equal citizens, whether we affirm these views is regarded as within our political competence as specified by the basic constitutional rights and liberties (§7:4–5).

26.5. By contrast with associations within society, the power of the government cannot be evaded except by leaving the state's territory. That power's being guided by public reason in the form appropriate to the all-inclusive citizen body of a democratic society does not change this. Yet normally, leaving is a grave step: it involves leaving the society and culture in which we have been raised, the society and culture whose language we use in speech and thought to express and understand ourselves, our aims, goals, and values; the society and culture whose history, customs, and conventions we depend on to find our place in our social world. In large part we affirm this society and culture, having an intimate and inexpressible knowledge of it, even though much of it we may question and even reject.

The state's authority cannot, then, be freely accepted in the sense that the bonds of society and culture, of history and social place of origin, begin so early to shape our life and are normally so strong that the right of emigration (suitably qualified)[14] does not suffice to make accepting its authority free, politically speaking, in the way that liberty of conscience suffices to make accepting ecclesiastical authority free, politically speaking.[15] Nevertheless we may over the course of life come freely to accept, as the outcome of reflective thought and reasoned judgment, the ideals, principles, and standards that specify our basic rights and liberties and effectively guide and moderate the political power to which we are subject. This is the outer limit of our freedom.

These contrasts between public and nonpublic reason (the reason of associations) are significant. They show that political liberalism does not view political society as an association. Quite the contrary, it insists on the distinction between a political society and an association. Associations within society can be communities united on shared final ends; indeed this is essential: were it not the case social life would lose its point.

## §27. First Fundamental Comparison

27.1. The preceding survey (§§23–26) completes a brief account of the setup of the original position. We now start on the second topic of this part, the reasoning of the parties for the two principles of justice. This reasoning is organized as two fundamental comparisons.[16] Doing this enables us to separate the reasons that lead the parties to select the difference principle from the reasons that lead them to select the principle of the basic equal liberties. Despite the formal resemblance between the difference principle as a

14. I shall not discuss these qualifications. I have in mind, for example, that those properly convicted of certain sufficiently serious crimes may not be allowed to emigrate pending serving their sentence.

15. I mean simply that it is no defense of the principles of political justice to say to those protesting them: You can always leave the country. The analogue of this may hold for associations but not for political society itself. Here is another place where the difference between political society and the associations within it is clear.

16. This way of organizing the reasoning for the two principles was first sketched in "Reply to Alexander and Musgrave," *Quarterly Journal of Economics* 88 (November 1974), §§III–VI, pp. 639–653, reprinted in *Collected Papers*.

principle of distributive justice and the maximin rule as a rule of thumb for decisions under uncertainty (stated below in §28.1), the reasoning for the difference principle does not rely on this rule. The formal resemblance is misleading.[17]

To proceed: we assume that the parties reason by comparing alternatives two at a time. They begin with the two principles of justice and compare those principles with the other available alternatives on the list. If the two principles are supported by a stronger balance of reasons in each such comparison, the argument is complete and those principles are adopted. In any comparison there may be reasons, possibly strong ones, for and against each of the two alternatives. Still, it may be clear that the balance of reasons favors one alternative over the other. Plainly an argument for the two principles depends on judgment—on judging the balance of reasons—and is also relative to a given list. We do not claim that the two principles would be agreed to from a complete, or any possible, list.[18] To claim that would be excessive and I attempt no general argument.

The two comparisons we will discuss are, then, but a small part of the argument that would be required to provide a reasonably conclusive argument for the two principles of justice. This is because the two principles are compared, each time in a different way, with the principle of average utility, and the comparison shows at best their superiority over that principle. The first comparison, which gives the reasoning for the first principle, is, I think, quite conclusive; the second comparison, which gives the reasoning for the difference principle, is less conclusive. It turns on a more delicate balance of less decisive considerations. Nevertheless, despite the limited scope of this two-part argument, it is instructive in suggesting how we can proceed in other comparisons to bring out the merits of the two principles.

27.2. The two comparisons arise as follows. In the history of democratic thought two contrasting ideas of society have a prominent place: one is the idea of society as a fair system of social cooperation between citizens regarded as free and equal; the other is the idea of society as a social system organized so as to produce the most good summed over all its members, where this good is a complete good specified by a comprehensive doctrine.

17. The failure to explain this was a serious fault in *Theory*.
18. See *Theory*, §87: 509.

The tradition of the social contract elaborates the first idea, the utilitarian tradition is a special case of the second.

Between these two traditions there is a basic contrast: the idea of society as a fair system of social cooperation is quite naturally specified so as to include the ideas of equality (the equality of basic rights, liberties, and fair opportunities) and of reciprocity (of which the difference principle is an example). By contrast, the idea of society organized to produce the most good expresses a maximizing and aggregative principle of political justice. In utilitarianism, the ideas of equality and of reciprocity are accounted for only indirectly, as what is thought to be normally necessary to maximize the sum of social welfare. The two comparisons turn on this contrast: the first brings out the advantage of the two principles with respect to equality, the second their advantage with respect to reciprocity, or mutuality.

As I said above, presenting the case for the two principles by way of these two comparisons separates the reasons that particularly favor the equal basic liberties from the reasons that particularly favor the difference principle. Given this separation, the situation is not as one might have thought. The first comparison, which uses the guidelines of the maximin rule for decisions under uncertainty, is quite decisive in supporting the equal basic rights and liberties; but those guidelines lend little support to the difference principle. In fact, when we formulate the second comparison they are not used at all.

27.3. In the first comparison the two principles of justice, taken as a unit, are compared with the principle of average utility as the sole principle of justice. The principle of average utility says that the institutions of the basic structure are to be arranged so as to maximize the average welfare of the members of society, beginning now and extending into the foreseeable future.

The second fundamental comparison is that in which the two principles, again taken as a unit, are compared with an alternative formed by substituting for the difference principle the principle of average utility (combined with a stipulated social minimum). In all other respects the two principles of justice are unchanged. In the second comparison, then, the principles prior to the difference principle are already accepted and the parties are selecting a principle for regulating economic and social inequalities (differences in citizens' prospects over a complete life) for a society in which those prior principles are assumed to be effective in regulating the basic structure. This means that people already view themselves as free and equal citizens of a democratic society, and the parties must take that into account.

27.4. The first comparison is the more fundamental because the aim of justice as fairness is to work out an alternative conception of political justice to those found in utilitarianism, perfectionism, and intuitionism (the first has been particularly dominant in our political tradition), while at the same time finding a more appropriate moral basis for the institutions of a modern democratic society. Should the two principles win in the first comparison, this aim is already in good part achieved; but should they lose, all is lost. The first comparison is also essential in replying to recent libertarian views, as we may call them, of Buchanan, Gauthier, and Nozick (see §6: n. 16), the first two being explicitly contractarian.

The first comparison with the principle of average utility is important for another reason: it illustrates how arguments from the original position proceed, and it provides a fairly simple case which displays the nature of those arguments. Surveying them prepares us for the second comparison, which turns on a less decisive balance of reasons.

## §28. The Structure of the Argument and the Maximin Rule

28.1. First, a statement of the maximin rule: it tells us to identify the worst outcome of each available alternative and then to adopt the alternative whose worst outcome is better than the worst outcomes of all the other alternatives. To follow this rule in selecting principles of justice for the basic structure we focus on the worst social positions that would be allowed when that structure is effectively regulated by those principles under various circumstances. What this means will become clearer by looking at the argument from the original position in the first comparison.[19]

The argument can be described as follows:

(i) If there are certain conditions in which it is rational to be guided by the maximin rule when agreeing to principles of justice for the basic structure, then under those conditions the two principles of justice would be agreed to rather than the principle of average utility.

19. *Theory*, §26: 132–135. As the account of this and later sections shows, the maximin rule was never proposed as the general principle of rational decision in all cases of risk and uncertainty, as some seem to have thought. For example, see J. C. Harsanyi, in his review essay, "Can the Maximin Principle Serve as a Basis for Morality?" *American Political Science Review* 69 (1975): 594–606, and reprinted in his *Essays on Ethics, Social Behavior, and Scientific Explanation* (Dordrecht: D. Reidel Pub. Co., 1976). Such a proposal would be simply irrational, as Harsanyi argues, pp. 39f. On this point there was, and is, no disagreement. The only question is whether, given the highly special, indeed unique, conditions of the original position, the maximin rule is a useful heuristic rule of thumb for the parties to use to organize their deliberations.

(ii) There are certain conditions, three in particular, such that, when they obtain, it is rational to be guided by the maximin rule when agreeing to principles of justice for the basic structure.

(iii) These three conditions obtain in the original position.

(iv) Therefore, the two principles would be agreed to by the parties rather than the principle of average utility.

While each of the premises (i)–(iii) might be disputed, for the time being let's assume that (i) is acceptable. It is (iii) that calls for the most explanation; but (ii) also requires comment, so let's start with (ii).

28.2. Let us review the three conditions referred to in (ii) above.[20]

(a) Since the maximin rule takes no account of probabilities, that is, of how likely it is that the circumstances obtain for their respective worst outcomes to be realized, the first condition is that the parties have no reliable basis for estimating the probabilities of the possible social circumstances that affect the fundamental interests of the persons they represent. This condition fully obtains when the concept of probability does not even apply.

(b) Since the maximin rule directs the parties to evaluate the alternatives only by their worst possible outcomes, it must be rational for the parties as trustees not to be much concerned for what might be gained above what can be guaranteed (for those they represent) by adopting the alternative whose worst outcome is better than the worst outcomes of all the other alternatives. Let's call this best worst outcome the "guaranteeable level." The second condition obtains, then, when the guaranteeable level is itself quite satisfactory. It fully obtains when this level is completely satisfactory.

(c) Since the maximin rule directs the parties to avoid alternatives whose worst outcomes are below the guaranteeable level, the third condition is that the worst outcomes of all the other alternatives are significantly below the guaranteeable level. When those outcomes are far below that level and altogether intolerable, and must, if possible, be avoided, the third condition fully obtains.

28.3. Three comments about these conditions: First, being guided by the maximin rule in these conditions is compatible with the familiar principle

20. Here we follow William Fellner, *Probability and Profit* (Homewood, Ill.: R. D. Irwin, 1965), pp. 140–142.

of maximizing the fulfillment of one's interests, or (rational) good. The parties' use of the rule to organize their deliberations in no way violates this familiar principle of rationality. Rather, they use the rule to guide them in deciding in accordance with that principle in the highly unusual, if not unique, circumstances of the original position when the matter at hand is of such fundamental significance.

Note, however, this caveat: the argument guided by the rule fits with the idea that rational agents maximize their expected utility, but only if that expected utility is understood to have no substantive content. That is, it does not mean expected pleasure, or agreeable consciousness (Sidgwick), or satisfaction. Expected utility is a purely formal idea specified by a rule or a mathematical function. As such, the rule or function simply represents the order, or ranking, in which the alternatives are judged better and worse in meeting the agent's fundamental interests, which are in this case the interests of citizens as free and equal (§31).

A second point is that it is not necessary that all, or any, of the three conditions fully obtain for the maximin rule to be a sensible way to organize deliberation. For should the third condition fully obtain, this suffices to bring the maximin rule into play, provided that the guaranteeable level is reasonably satisfactory, so long as the first condition at least partially obtains. However, in the first comparison the first condition has a relatively minor role. As we shall see, what is crucial is that the second and third conditions should obtain to a high degree.

Finally, it is not essential for the parties to use the maximin rule in the original position. It is simply a useful heuristic device. Focusing on the worst outcomes has the advantage of forcing us to consider what our fundamental interests really are when it comes to the design of the basic structure. This is not a question that we would often, if ever, ask ourselves in ordinary life. Part of the point of the original position is that it forces us to ask that question and moreover to do so in a highly special situation which gives it a definite sense.

28.4. Let us now review why the second and third conditions obtain to a high degree for the parties given their situation in the original position.

The second condition obtains because the guaranteeable level is quite satisfactory. What is this level? It is the situation of the least-advantaged members of the well-ordered society that results from the full realization of the two principles of justice (given reasonably favorable conditions). Justice as fairness claims that a well-ordered society paired with the two principles of justice is a highly satisfactory political and social world, and we try to support this claim in Part IV. This basic point about the guaranteeable level is crucial for the argument.[21]

The third condition obtains given the assumption we make that there are realistic social circumstances, even with reasonably favorable conditions, under which the principle of utility would require, or allow, that the basic rights and liberties of some be in various ways restricted, or even denied altogether, for the sake of greater benefits for others or for society as a whole. These circumstances are among the possibilities that the parties must guard against on behalf of those they represent.

Utilitarians may question this assumption. But to support it we need not invoke such drastic infringements of liberty as slavery and serfdom, or oppressive religious persecution. Consider instead a possible balance of social advantages to a sizable majority from limiting the political liberties and religious freedoms of small and weak minorities.[22] The principle of average utility seems to allow possible outcomes that the parties, as trustees, must regard as altogether unacceptable and intolerable. So the third condition obtains to a high degree.

21. This important point about the guaranteeable level, while perhaps obvious, is never expressly stated in *Theory*. The failure to do so led some to think of the guaranteeable level as a natural, nonsocial, level below which individual utility drops precipitously to minus infinity, as it were. Thus they hoped to explain why *Theory* used the maximin rule even though they rejected the idea of such a natural, nonsocial level. But, as the text shows, this was not the intention. See the discussion by Joshua Cohen in "Democratic Equality," pp. 733f.

22. To block this kind of argument some utilitarians have imposed restrictions on the kind of advantages to individuals relevant to their utility function. For example, Harsanyi in his essay "Morality and the Theory of Rational Behavior," in *Utilitarianism and Beyond*, ed. Sen and Williams, p. 56, excludes what he calls antisocial preferences, for example, malice, envy, resentment, and the pleasures of cruelty. Now this is a fundamental departure from the classical (and traditional) utilitarian view in which all pleasures, or the satisfaction of actual preferences, regardless of their source, are intrinsically good. When Harsanyi abandons that view (a view he held in 1955 in his "Cardinal Welfare, Individualistic Ethics, and Interpersonal Comparisons," *Journal of Political Economy* 63 (1955): 309–321, reprinted in *Essays on Ethics, Social Behavior, and Scientific Explanation*, pp. 18ff.), he owes us an explanation of the grounds for counting certain pleasures, or satisfactions, for naught. Calling them antisocial is not enough. We need to know where his restrictions on entries in utility functions come from and how they are justified. Until these questions are answered within a suitably specified framework that is recognizably utilitarian, we cannot decide whether Harsanyi is entitled to impose them. One might ask whether a theory of basic rights and liberties, or a nonutilitarian ideal, lies in the background, tacit and unexpressed.

## §29. The Argument Stressing the Third Condition

29.1. Note that although we have not discussed the first condition (directing the parties to discount and not to rely on estimates of probability), we have a strong argument for the two principles based on the fact that the second and third conditions both hold to a high degree. This fact provides the most straightforward argument for the two principles in the first comparison.

In this comparison, then, we do not stress the first condition: we assume it to hold, not fully, but only to some significant degree. This we do because the first condition raises difficult points in the theory of probability that so far as possible we want to avoid. Hence we stipulate that knowledge and well-founded beliefs about probabilities must be based on at least some established facts or well-supported beliefs about the world. This fits any interpretation of probability except a general subjectivist (or Bayesian) one. We then say the parties lack the requisite information, and so cannot have well-founded probabilities in selecting among alternatives.

The point is this: the parties know the general commonsense facts of human psychology and political sociology. They also know that the society in question exists in the circumstances of justice under reasonably favorable conditions. These are conditions that, provided the political will exists, make a constitutional regime possible. Yet whether the political will exists depends on a society's political culture and traditions, its religious and ethnic composition, and much else. Favorable conditions may exist when the political will does not.[23] Thus the knowledge that reasonably favorable conditions exist is far too little for the parties to specify a well-grounded probability distribution over the forms of political culture and tradition that might exist. History tells of more aristocracies and theocracies, dictatorships and class-states, than democracies. Of course, the parties don't have this particular knowledge. In any case, does that make those outcomes more likely than democracy? Surely such speculation is far beyond the reach of common sense, or uncommon sense, for that matter. About the first condition of the maximin rule, we claim, then, only that it holds suf-

23. Germany between 1870 and 1945 is an example of a country where reasonably favorable conditions existed—economic, technological and no lack of resources, an educated citizenry and more—but where the political will for a democratic regime was altogether lacking. One might say the same of the United States today, if one decides our constitutional regime is largely democratic in form only.

ficiently so that the argument of the first comparison emphasizing the second and third conditions is not put in doubt.

29.2. The argument emphasizing the second and third conditions is essentially as follows: if it is indeed the case that a well-ordered society regulated by the two principles of justice is a highly satisfactory form of political society that secures the basic rights and liberties equally for all (and thus represents a highly satisfactory guaranteeable level), and if the principle of utility may sometimes permit or else require the restriction or suppression of the rights and liberties of some for the sake of a greater aggregate of social well-being, then the parties must agree to the two principles of justice. Only in this way (in the first comparison) can they act responsibly as trustees: that is, effectively protect the fundamental interests of the person each represents, and at the same time make sure to avoid possibilities the realization of which would be altogether intolerable.

This argument rests on the parties' assuming that, given the capacity of those they represent to be free and equal persons and fully cooperating members of society over a complete life, those persons would never put their basic rights and liberties in jeopardy so long as there was a readily available and satisfactory alternative. What aim could the parties suppose those persons might have for doing that? Do they wish to take a chance on having ever more adequate material means to fulfill their ends? But the parties as representatives of citizens regarded as free and equal cannot for that purpose jeopardize citizens' basic rights and liberties. Their responsibility as trustees for citizens so regarded does not allow them to gamble with the basic rights and liberties of those citizens.

29.3. There is a further consideration in the argument that proceeds from the third condition. To explain: the parties are seen as making an agreement; it is not simply that they each separately make the same choice. An agreement must be made in good faith, that is, not only with the full intention to honor it but also with a reasonable conviction that one will be able to do so.[24] The class of things we can agree to is included within but smaller than the class of things that we can rationally choose. We can decide to take a chance and at the same time fully intend, should things turn out badly, to do what we can to retrieve our situation.

24. Should none of the alternatives meet this condition, the original position would not be well posed: no undertaking could be given in good faith.

But if we make an agreement, we have to accept the outcome and live with it in accordance with our pledge as given. Since in this case the content of the agreement is the principles of justice to be mutually recognized and acknowledged in perpetuity (there is no second chance), to honor our agreement (the one our representative makes on our instructions) means to apply those principles willingly as the public conception of justice for the basic structure, and to affirm their implications in our thought and conduct over a complete life.

Plainly, then, the parties must weigh what we may call the strains of commitment.[25] They must ask themselves whether those they represent can reasonably be expected to honor the principles agreed to in the manner required by the idea of an agreement.[26] Consider, then, any two conceptions of justice: if in some possible social conditions, the first would permit, or require, a basic structure with positions we could not accept, while the second under all conditions assures basic institutions we can honor whatever our position, the second must be agreed to. Any other agreement would not be made in good faith and the constraint of the strains of commitment would be violated. For the reasons surveyed above, it follows that the two principles of justice must be selected over the principle of utility, for they are the only alternative that guarantees the fundamental interests of citizens as free and equal.[27] Note that if our representative were to choose the principle of utility and things turn out badly for us, we have no grounds for reneging: we cannot plead that the original position situated our representative unfairly, nor can we plead ignorance, or surprise, since the possibility of social conditions leading to institutions we can not accept is an outcome the parties know about and must consider. The original position is framed to rule out all excuses.

25. *Theory*, §29: 153ff. See also "Reply to Alexander and Musgrave," §VI.

26. Whether this is so raises the question of the stability of a political conception of justice, that is, the question whether, when the conception is realized in basic institutions, those who grow up and live under them acquire a sufficiently strong sense of justice. This question falls under the second part of the argument, as defined in §25.5, and it is taken up later in Part V.

27. This fact about the two principles is much clearer in the first comparison than in the second, but it holds in the latter as well. I come back to this in §31. The crucial point is that, as remarked in the previous section, the original position with the maximin rule forces the parties to focus on and to try to specify the fundamental interests of free and equal citizens. A conception of justice ensuring conditions under which citizens can fulfill these interests answers to a basic requirement of stability in ways the principle of utility does not.

29.4. To conclude: given the conception of the person in justice as fairness, we say that the parties assume that, as persons with the two moral powers and a determinate complete conception of the good, citizens have, among other interests, certain religious, philosophical, and moral interests, and that the fulfillment of these interests must, if possible, be guaranteed. There are some things we cannot give up; they are not negotiable. If the advocate of average utility rejects this, then for the moment we have reached an impasse.

It is essential that the two principles are an available and satisfactory alternative which does not impose excessive strains of commitment. They not only protect the basic rights and liberties but provide an adequate complement of the primary goods required for exercising and enjoying those freedoms. There are indeed situations in which there is no way to avoid putting our basic freedoms in jeopardy; but with the two principles available, the original position is not one of them. To agree to the principle of average utility would be to aim for still greater well-being while jeopardizing those rights and liberties without sufficient reason.

## §30. The Priority of the Basic Liberties

30.1. No basic liberty is absolute, since these liberties may conflict in particular cases and their claims must be adjusted to fit into one coherent scheme of liberties. The aim is to make these adjustments in such a way that at least the more significant liberties involved in the adequate development and full exercise of the moral powers in the two fundamental cases are normally compatible. It is the whole scheme of basic liberties which has priority, but it would not have priority unless each of the basic liberties were of fundamental importance and could not be compromised unless doing so were unavoidable. To illustrate, consider liberty of conscience and keep in mind the grounds the parties have for giving it priority.

We said that the force of the first argument emphasizing the second and the third conditions of the maximin rule depends on the idea that given our capacity as citizens to be free and equal, we would not put our basic rights and liberties at risk so long as there is a readily available and satisfactory alternative. The parties are said to reason accordingly. Thus, if but one of the conceptions of justice available to the parties guarantees equal liberty of conscience, that conception must be adopted. The veil of ignorance implies that the parties have no basis for knowing or estimating whether the persons they represent affirm a majority or a minority religious or other doctrine. The point is that the parties cannot take risks by permitting a lesser liberty of conscience for minority religions, say, on the chance that the person each represents belongs to a majority or dominant religion and may, in that event, have an even greater liberty than that secured by equal liberty of conscience.

Were the parties to gamble in that way, they would show that they did not take seriously the religious, philosophical, and moral convictions of the persons they represent. Indeed, they would show that they did not understand the nature of religious belief, or philosophical or moral conviction. This remark is not an argument: it simply calls attention to the special place of such beliefs and convictions, and to the fact that for those who affirm them, they are regarded as nonnegotiable.

30.2. To explain, then, why the first principle of justice has priority over the second, we note that the basic liberties protect fundamental interests that have a special significance. This distinctive feature is connected with the often intractable nature of religious, philosophical, and moral conflicts in the absence of a secure public basis of mutual trust. Later (§32) we maintain that this public basis is best founded on a constitution that guarantees the equal basic liberties once and for all. The same grounds that favor the equality of the basic liberties also favor their priority.

Suppose someone denies that liberty of conscience is a basic liberty and maintains that all human interests are commensurable. This means that, for any two interests, given the extent to which they are satisfied, there is always some rate of exchange at which a rational person is willing to accept a lesser fulfillment of the one in return for a greater fulfillment of the other, and vice versa. One way to make this idea psychologically intelligible is to say that the weights of all interests are ordered according to the degree and duration of the pleasure or agreeable experiences their fulfillment provides. Should this view be maintained, we again reach an apparent impasse, a clash of considered convictions about the reasonableness of some form of hedonism, broadly understood.

Discussion might be carried further[28] but it won't be pursued here, except to say that we can, of course, check the priority of liberty by looking for counterexamples, and consider whether, on due reflection, the resulting priority judgments can be endorsed. Doing this does not provide a decisive

28. See *Theory*, §§83–84.

argument; but if careful search uncovers no counter-cases, the priority of liberty would be so far perfectly reasonable.

## §31. An Objection about Aversion to Uncertainty

31.1. I begin with a familiar distinction often made between uncertainty and risk and then state the objection. The distinction is this: in the case of risk, there is some objective evidential basis for estimating probabilities, for example, relative frequencies, or actuarial tables, or the relative strengths of the various propensities of things (states of affairs) that affect the outcome. In the case of uncertainty there is no such objective basis; such bases as there may be are highly intuitive and sketchy.[29]

One feature of the parties' situation in the original position is that they have no reliable basis for estimating the probabilities of the possible social and historical conditions, or the probability that the persons they represent affirm one comprehensive doctrine (with its conception of the good) and not another. This feature results from how we have set up the original position. Eventually more must be said to justify this stipulation. But in any case we view the parties as faced with uncertainty rather than risk.

31.2. The objection is this: the preceding account of the parties' use of the maximin rule to organize their deliberations describes them as irrationally, even obsessively, averse to uncertainty. Were the parties properly described as rational, as they must be, the two principles would not be adopted. To reply: in both fundamental comparisons we assume that the parties' attitude toward uncertainty rests on what they regard as the fundamental interests of the citizens they represent. Given the conditions of the original position, that attitude is governed by the parties' aim to secure for those citizens the basic rights, liberties and fair opportunities, and at least an adequate share of all-purpose material means (the primary goods of income and wealth) so that the citizens represented will be able to exercise these rights and liberties and to take advantage of those opportunities.

How the parties regard the uncertainty they face depends, then, on the fundamental interests and needs (properly ordered) of citizens viewed as free and equal. If the parties proceed in a cautious manner in organizing their deliberations by the maximin rule, or if it seems as if they are pecu-

29. S. L. Hurley, *Natural Reasons* (Oxford: Oxford University Press, 1989) has an instructive discussion of risk aversion and uncertainty and their relation to the maximin rule. See pp. 376–382.

liarly averse to uncertainty, this is not because they are moved by a special psychology that makes them peculiarly averse to uncertainty. Rather, it is because it is rational for them as trustees, and so as responsible for citizens' (unknown) determinate and complete good, to deliberate in this way, given the overriding importance of establishing a public conception of justice that guarantees the basic rights and liberties. It is the fundamental nature of the interests the parties must protect, and the unusual features of the original position, that support the use of the maximin rule as a rule of thumb, and emphasize the second and third conditions.

31.3. This explanation of the nature of the interests the parties must protect may lead to the further objection that, despite appearances, the argument from the third condition is utilitarian after all. The reasoning behind this thought is given in the caption to Figure 2. Our question now is whether, in view of this reasoning, justice as fairness is utilitarian.[30]

I hold that it is not. This is because the parties use a utility function (I am willing to call it that) so constructed as to reflect the ideal normative conceptions used to organize justice as fairness, that is, the ideas of society as a fair system of cooperation and of citizens as free and equal, and characterized by the two moral powers, and so on. This constructed utility function is based on the needs and requirements of citizens—their fundamental interests—conceived as such persons; it is not based on people's actual preferences and interests.

The reply to the utilitarian, then, is that justice as fairness does not deny that the idea of a utility function can be used to formulate justice as fairness. Indeed, I suppose any conception of justice can be expressed as maximizing a suitably doctored utility function. Surely the debate between utilitarian and nonutilitarian views is not about that trivial formal question! Such a utility function is but a mathematical representation that encodes certain basic features of our normative assumptions. That there is a representation of this kind says nothing about the content of justice as fairness; nor is it the substantive idea of utility in the tradition of utilitarianism.

On the other hand, we should be cheered if utilitarians can find, from within their own point of view, a way to endorse the ideas and principles of

30. I am grateful to Allan Gibbard for raising this question and discussing it with me. A brief account of it should help to clarify the relation between justice as fairness as a political conception and utilitarianism as a comprehensive view.

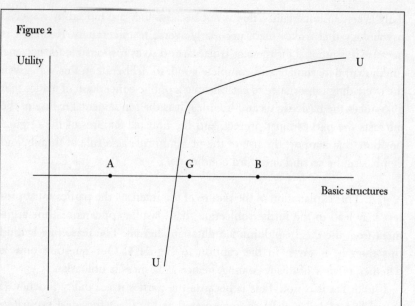

Figure 2

G = the well-ordered society corresponding to the two principles of justice under reasonably favorable conditions.

A = a possible utilitarian society in certain reasonably favorable conditions imposing restrictions on the basic equal liberties as allowed by the principle of average utility.

B = a possible utilitarian society under different reasonably favorable conditions than A and not imposing restrictions on the basic equal liberties.

G, A, B = are situations of the worst-off group, with its corresponding utility given by the UU curve.

UU = the similar utility curve of all citizens derived from the constructed utility function.

Utility is measured on the y-axis. Different basic structures are arranged on the x-axis according to how well they satisfy the two principles of justice. We assume that these structures always exist under reasonably favorable conditions.

The utilitarian is said to reason as follows: the parties' use of the maximin rule rests on their knowing that the total utility curves of the persons they represent are similar and have a rather sharp bend at a point which coincides with the guaranteeable level specified by the well-ordered society of the two principles of justice. Thus to the right of the bend, at point G in the figure, everyone's utility curves become suddenly quite flat. This explains why the parties as citizens' representatives are not much concerned with outcomes superior to the guaranteeable level, and hence the second condition of the maximin rule holds. To the left of the bend everyone's utility curve falls precipitously, and hence the third condition of the maximin rule also holds. This explains why the parties must reject alternatives that fail to guarantee the basic equal liberties. And so in the first comparison the two principles must be agreed to.

From this it is clear that if the aim of the parties is changed from that of securing the fundamental interests of the person each represents to that of maximizing average utility summed over all members of society, they would still agree on the two principle of justice. It is, of course, possible that sometimes the losses imposed by restricting or denying the basic rights and liberties of a few are counterbalanced by a larger sum of advantages accruing to many, and that this could happen in perhaps numerous cases even under the favorable conditions assumed to obtain. But given self- and group-interested tendencies so pervasive in political life, and the great difficulty of making accurate interpersonal comparisons and assessments of total social utility, the parties agree that for the purposes of a political conception of justice there are very strong reasons of simplicity and practicality for adopting the two principles of justice.

justice as fairness. For their doing so means that they can join in an overlapping consensus on that conception. The preceding remarks are not meant, then, as criticism of utilitarianism as a comprehensive doctrine. As a political conception justice as fairness avoids such criticism whenever possible. Nevertheless, we must insist, for the reasons stated, that justice as fairness is not itself utilitarian.

31.4. I append a remark on an instructive point made by Howe and Roemer.[31] It is slightly technical but I believe clear enough. They model the original position as a game with specified withdrawal payoffs and argue that the difference principle is in the core[32] of a game in which no coalition will withdraw after the veil of ignorance is lifted, unless it can guarantee every one of its members a better payoff in a new lottery.[33] The original position,

31. See R. Howe and J. Roemer, "Rawlsian Justice as the Core of a Game," *American Economic Review* 71 (1981): 880–895. I am indebted to Anthony Laden for pointing out to me the relevance of Howe and Roemer's paper for the question of stability. Except for the idea of reasons-stability, implicit in his account, I have merely paraphrased his discussion of their paper in his honors B.A. thesis, Harvard University, 1989.

32. I shall not discuss this idea except to say that the core is the set of imputations of a game such that no coalition, whatever its size, from the grand coalition of all to single individuals, can improve its situation by withdrawing and acting on its own. The core is discussed in any decent text on game theory.

33. Of course this modeling is not accurate to our account of the original position, as the idea of withdrawal payoffs and a new lottery is foreign to it. Howe and Roemer also ignore the basic structure and consider distribution in terms of income and not primary goods. Still, their paper brings out an important point: instead of asking whether there is a coalition that wants to withdraw, we can ask whether there are people in a well-ordered society who are dissatisfied with its regulative principles of justice.

so understood, they view as an extremely risk averse (ERA) game, as distinct from a risk neutral (RN) game, that is, a game in which a coalition will withdraw if it can raise the expectations of its members by having another lottery. The RN game has no core: those below the mean income make up a coalition to withdraw, since in a new lottery they always expect to do better (to receive the mean income). Howe and Roemer conclude that extreme risk aversion is essential to the adoption of the two principles: they think a new lottery is not wanted by any coalition only because no one is willing to take risks.

In reply, we saw in §29 that the setup of the original position forces the parties to focus on the basic needs and requirements, the fundamental interests, of those they represent; and given the strains of commitment, they must adopt principles that secure those interests. As noted above, in doing this they are acting rationally and not in a peculiarly risk-averse manner. Given the setup of the original position, the parties are led to adopt principles that lie in the core, and when realized in the basic structure, these principles achieve a stable society in Howe and Roemer's sense: no coalition wants to withdraw. The reason is that every one's fundamental interests are already cared for; whereas the principle of utility does not ensure this and is unstable.

Thus stability results first, from the availability of principles that guarantee citizens' fundamental interests, and second, from the parties' being moved to secure those interests above all. When everyone's fundamental interests are met, then we have stability. In this way stability is simply a consequence of how the original position is set up. We may call this reasons-stability: it depends in part on what moves the parties. It is distinct from the two kinds of stability discussed later in Part V.

31.5. I should add that many points in this account of the first comparison are highly controversial, among them the assumptions made about probability and the basis of the aversion to uncertainty; the assertion that in the circumstances of justice, even under reasonably favorable conditions, there are situations in which the principle of utility requires at least the restriction if not the suppression of basic rights and liberties; and finally, the idea that some things are not negotiable: from the parties' point of view, at least, our fundamental interests connected with the exercise of citizens' two moral powers take priority over other interests.

## §32. The Equal Basic Liberties Revisited

32.1. To complete the first comparison, we add a second argument for the two principles over the principle of utility. This argument connects with the second condition of the maximin rule, which is that the guaranteeable level is a highly satisfactory social world. Since one reason for this is the central role of the equal basic liberties in a constitutional regime, I survey, by way of preparation, some features of those liberties in addition to those noted in §13.

For one thing, these liberties are bound to conflict with one another; hence the institutional rules specifying them must be adjusted so that each liberty fits into a coherent scheme of liberties. The priority of liberty (the priority of the first principle over the second) means that a basic liberty can be limited or denied only for the sake of one or more other basic liberties, and never for a greater public good understood as a greater net sum of social and economic advantages for society as a whole.

As we have said, none of the basic liberties, such as freedom of thought and liberty of conscience, or political liberty and the guarantees of the rule of law, is absolute, as they may be limited when they conflict with one another. Nor is it required that in the finally adjusted scheme each basic liberty is equally provided for (whatever that would mean). Rather, however these liberties are adjusted, that final scheme is to be secured equally for all citizens.

32.2. In adjusting the basic liberties, we need to distinguish between their restriction and their regulation. The priority of these liberties is not infringed when they are merely regulated, as they must be, in order to be combined into one scheme. So long as what we may call "the central range of application" of each basic liberty is secured, the two principles are fulfilled.

For example, rules of order are essential for regulating free discussion. Not everyone can speak at once, or use the same public facility at the same time for different purposes. Instituting the basic liberties, just like realizing different interests, requires social organization and scheduling as to time and place, and so on. The requisite regulations should not be mistaken for restrictions on the content of speech, for example, prohibitions against publicly arguing for various religious and philosophical, or moral and political doctrines, or against raising questions of general and particular fact about the justice of the basic structure and its social policies.

32.3. Since the basic liberties have a special status in view of their priority, we should count among them only truly essential liberties. We hope that the liberties that are not counted as basic are satisfactorily allowed for by the general presumption against legal restrictions, once we hold that the burden of proof against those restrictions is to be decided by the other requirements of the two principles of justice. If there are many basic liberties, their specification into a coherent scheme securing the central range of application of each may prove too cumbersome. This leads us to ask what are the truly fundamental cases and to introduce a criterion of significance of a particular right or liberty. Otherwise we have no way of identifying a fully adequate scheme of basic liberties of the kind we seek.

A serious defect in *Theory* is that its account of the basic liberties proposes two different and conflicting criteria, both unsatisfactory. One is to specify those liberties so as to achieve the most extensive scheme of the liberties (*Theory*, §32: 203, 1st ed.; §37: 201; §39: 220); the other tells us to take up the point of view of the rational representative equal citizen, and then to specify the scheme of liberties in the light of that citizen's rational interests as known at the relevant stage of the four-stage sequence (*Theory*, §32: 179; §39: 217). But (as Hart maintained)[34] the idea of the extent of a basic liberty is useful only in the least important cases, and citizens' rational interests are not sufficiently explained in *Theory* to do the work asked of them. What is a better criterion?

32.4. The proposed criterion is this: the basic liberties and their priority are to guarantee equally for all citizens the social conditions essential for the adequate development and the full and informed exercise of their two moral powers in what we have referred to as the two fundamental cases (§13.4). These two cases we now specify more fully.[35]

(a) The first fundamental case is connected with the capacity for a sense of justice and concerns the application of the principles of justice to the basic structure and its social policies. The equal political liberties and freedom of thought are to ensure the opportunity for the free and informed ap-

34. See Hart's critical review article "Rawls on Liberty and Its Priority," in his *Essays in Jurisprudence and Philosophy,* especially §III, pp. 232–238.

35. The remarks below summarize (as does §13) points in "The Basic Liberties and Their Priority," §§II, III, IX, also in *Political Liberalism,* lect. VIII, §§2, 3, 9.

plication of the principles of justice to that structure and to its policies by means of the full and effective exercise of citizens' sense of justice. All this is necessary to make possible the free use of public reason (§26).

(b) The second fundamental case is connected with the capacity for a (complete) conception of the good (normally associated with a comprehensive religious, philosophical, or moral doctrine), and concerns the exercise of citizens' powers of practical reason in forming, revising, and rationally pursuing such a conception over a complete life. Liberty of conscience and freedom of association are to ensure the opportunity for the free and informed exercise of this capacity and its companion powers of practical reason and judgment.

(c) The remaining and supporting basic liberties—the liberty and integrity (physical and psychological) of the person and the rights and liberties covered by the rule of law—can be connected with the two fundamental cases by noting that they are necessary if the other basic liberties are to be properly guaranteed. What distinguishes the two fundamental cases is, first, their connection with the realization of the fundamental interests of citizens regarded as free and equal as well as reasonable and rational. In addition, there is the broad scope and basic character of the institutions to which the principles of justice are applied in those two cases.

32.5. Given this division of the basic liberties, the significance of a particular liberty is explained as follows: a liberty is more or less significant depending on whether it is more or less essentially involved in, or is a more or less necessary institutional means to protect, the full and informed exercise of the moral powers in one (or both) of the two fundamental cases. The more significant liberties mark out the central range of application of a particular basic liberty; and in cases of conflict we look for a way to accommodate the more significant liberties within the central range of each.

Consider several illustrative examples. First, the weight of claims to freedom of speech, press, and discussion is to be judged by this criterion. Some kinds of speech are not specially protected, and others may be offenses, for example, libel and defamation of individuals, so-called fighting words (in certain circumstances). Even political speech when it becomes an incitement to the imminent and lawless use of force is no longer protected as a basic liberty.

Why these kinds of speech are offenses may call for careful reflection, and will generally differ from case to case. Libel and defamation of private persons (in contrast with political and other public figures) has no significance at all for the free use of public reason to judge and regulate the basic structure. In addition, those forms of speech are private wrongs. Incitements to imminent and lawless use of force, whatever the significance of the speaker's overall political views, are too disruptive of democratic political procedures to be permitted by the rules of order of public discussion. So long as the advocacy of revolutionary and even seditious doctrines is fully protected, as it should be, there is no restriction on the content of speech, but only regulations as to time and place, and the means used to express it.

32.6. Among the basic rights is the right to hold and to have the exclusive use of personal property. One ground of this right is to allow a sufficient material basis for personal independence and a sense of self-respect, both of which are essential for the adequate development and exercise of the moral powers. Having this right and being able effectively to exercise it is one of the social bases of self-respect.[36] Thus this right is a general right: a right all citizens have in virtue of their fundamental interests. Two wider conceptions of the right to property are not taken as basic: namely,

(i) the right to private property in natural resources and means of production generally, including rights of acquisition and bequest;

(ii) the right to property as including the equal right to participate in the control of the means of production and of natural resources, both of which are to be socially, not privately, owned.

These wider conceptions of property are not used because they are not necessary for the adequate development and full exercise of the moral powers, and so are not an essential social basis of self-respect. They may, however, still be justified. This depends on existing historical and social conditions. The further specification of the rights to property is to be made at the legislative stage, assuming the basic rights and liberties are maintained.[37] As a public political conception, justice as fairness is to provide a shared basis for weighing the case for and against various forms of property, including socialism. To do this, it tries to avoid prejudging, at the fundamental level of basic rights, the question of private property in the means of production. In that way perhaps discussion of this important question can proceed

36. I do not consider here what falls under this personal right, except to say that it would seem to include at least certain forms of real property, such as dwellings and private grounds.

37. See *Theory*, §42: 239–242. The stages of a constitutional convention, the legislature, and the judiciary are discussed in *Theory*, §31.

within a political conception of justice that can gain the support of an overlapping consensus.

## §33. The Argument Stressing the Second Condition

33.1. In §29 we examined the first argument for the two principles of justice guided by the maximin rule. That argument focuses on the possible restrictions or denials of the basic liberties allowed by the principle of (average) utility, and stresses the third condition. I now survey a second argument for the two principles stressing the second condition of the rule, namely, that the guaranteeable level is highly satisfactory. If we ask why this level is highly satisfactory, possibly close to the best that can practicably be achieved, the answer in part is that those principles are more effective than the principle of (average) utility in guaranteeing the equal basic liberties and therefore in meeting three essential requirements for a stable constitutional regime.[38]

The first requirement, given the fact of pluralism, is to fix, once and for all, the basic rights and liberties, and to assign them a special priority. Doing this takes these guarantees off the political agenda of political parties; it puts them beyond the calculus of social interests, thus securing clearly and firmly the terms of social cooperation on a footing of mutual respect. The two principles of justice achieve this.

By contrast, to regard the calculus of social interests as always relevant in specifying basic rights and liberties, as the principle of utility does, leaves the status and content of those freedoms still unsettled. It subjects them to the shifting circumstances of time and place, and by greatly raising the stakes of political controversy, it dangerously increases the insecurity and hostility of public life. Consider the unwillingness to take off the political agenda such questions as which faiths are to have liberty of conscience, or which groups are to have the right to vote. Such an unwillingness perpetuates the deep divisions latent in a society marked by the fact of reasonable pluralism. It may betray a readiness to revive old antagonisms in the hope of gaining a more favorable position should circumstances prove propitious later on. By contrast, securing the basic liberties and affirming their priority more effectively does the work of reconciliation among citizens and promises mutual recognition on a footing of equality.

38. Much of this section is drawn from "The Idea of an Overlapping Consensus," *Oxford Journal of Legal Studies* 7 (1987), pp. 19–21, reprinted in *Collected Papers*, 442ff.

33.2. The second requirement of a stable constitutional regime is that its political conception should specify not only a shared but if possible a clear basis of public reason, and one that can publicly be seen to be sufficiently reliable in its own terms. Now, as we have seen, the publicity condition means that the principles of political right and justice are an essential part of public reason (§§25–26). The idea here, then, is that the two principles of justice specify a clearer and more reliable basis of public reason than the principle of utility. For if the elaborate theoretical calculations involved in applying the principle of utility are publicly viewed as decisive, the highly speculative nature and the great complexity of those estimations are bound to make the application of the principle highly tentative and uncertain. To see this, consider the difficulties of applying it to the basic structure.

Moreover, the principle of utility may prove politically unworkable, for people are likely to be highly suspicious of one another's arguments. The information these complex arguments presuppose is often hard if not impossible to obtain, and frequently there are grave problems in reaching an objective and agreed upon assessment. Moreover, even though we think our arguments sincere and not self-serving when we present them, we must consider what it is reasonable to expect others to think who stand to lose should our reasoning prevail. Arguments supporting political judgments should, if possible, be not only sound, but such that they can be publicly seen to be sound.

The maxim that justice must not only be done, but be seen to be done, holds good not only in law but also in public reason. In these respects, the two principles (with an index of primary goods defined in terms of the objective features of people's social situation) seem superior to the principle of utility. The question is not simply what is true, or what we think is true, but what we can reasonably expect equal citizens, who are often politically at odds, to convince one another is true, or reasonable, even in face of the burdens of judgment and especially the complexities of political judgment.

33.3. The third requirement of a stable constitutional regime is that its basic institutions should encourage the cooperative virtues of political life: the virtues of reasonableness and a sense of fairness, and of a spirit of compromise and a readiness to meet others halfway. These virtues underwrite the willingness if not the desire to cooperate with others on terms that all can publicly accept as fair on a footing of equality and mutual respect. The two principles foster these virtues, first, by removing from the political agenda the most divisive issues, pervasive uncertainty about which must undermine the basis of social cooperation, and second, by specifying a reasonably clear basis of free public reason.

Those principles further encourage the political virtues when, through the publicity condition, they incorporate the ideal of citizens as free and equal persons into public life by way of the shared recognition of the principles of justice and their realization in the basic structure. This incorporation, along with a reasonable moral psychology (to be discussed in Part V), implies that when just institutions are established and working well over time, the cooperative political virtues are encouraged and sustained. Crucial to this process is that the principles of justice express an idea of reciprocity that is lacking in the principle of utility. Observe here that when citizens publicly recognize that the basic structure satisfies the two principles, this public recognition itself not only encourages mutual trust among citizens generally but also nurtures the development of attitudes and habits of mind necessary for willing and fruitful social cooperation. Here is another place where the publicity condition has an important role.

33.4. Among the cooperative virtues of political life is a disposition to honor the duty of public civility (§26.3). It directs us to appeal to political values in cases involving the constitutional essentials, and also in other cases insofar as they border on those essentials and become politically divisive. Abortion is a good example of the latter. Whether it is a constitutional essential may be unclear, but it certainly borders on one and can be the cause of deep conflict. If we accept the idea of public reason we should try to identify political values that may indicate how this question can be settled, or a settlement approached. I have in mind such values as the following: that public law show an appropriate respect for human life, that it properly regulate the institutions through which society reproduces itself over time, that it secure the full equality of women, and finally, that it conform to the requirements of public reason itself, which, for example, bar theological and other comprehensive doctrines from deciding the case. The aim is to formulate these values as political values within the limits of public reason.

The duty of public civility goes with the idea that the political discussion of constitutional essentials should aim at free agreement reached on the basis of shared political values, and that the same holds for other questions bordering on those essentials, especially when they become divisive. In the way that a just war aims at a just peace, and thus restricts the use of those means of warfare that make achieving a just peace more difficult, so, when we aim for free agreement in political discussion, we are to use arguments and appeal to reasons that others are able to accept. But much political debate betrays the marks of warfare. It consists in rallying the troops and intimidating the other side, which must now increase its efforts or back down. In all this one may find the thought that to have character is to have firm convictions and be ready to proclaim them defiantly to others. To be is to confront.

The idea of public reason brings out that what this thought overlooks are the great values achieved by a society that realizes in its public life the cooperative political virtues of reasonableness and a sense of fairness, of a spirit of compromise and the will to honor the duty of public civility. When these virtues are widespread in society and sustain its political conception of justice, they constitute a great public good. They belong to society's political capital. Here the term "capital" is appropriate because these virtues are built up slowly over time and depend not only on existing political and social institutions (themselves slowly built up), but also on citizens' experience as a whole and their public knowledge of the past. Again, like capital, these virtues can depreciate, as it were, and must be constantly renewed by being reaffirmed and acted on in the present.

33.5. To conclude: note that the second argument for the two principles does not, like the first, focus on the individual good of citizens (the need to avoid intolerable denials or restrictions of our basic rights and liberties). Rather, it focuses on the nature of the public political culture realized by the two principles of justice and the desirable effects of that culture on the moral quality of public life and on citizens' political character. The parties in effect try to fashion a certain kind of social world; they regard the social world not as given by history, but, at least in part, as up to them. They view the best agreement as one that guarantees background justice for all, encourages the spirit of cooperation between citizens on a footing of mutual respect, and allows within itself sufficient social space for (permissible) ways of life fully worthy of citizens' allegiance.[39]

39. Consider the following analogy, which I owe to Peter Murrell. A franchiser (say Dunkin' Donuts) is deciding what kind of terms to put in its contract with its many franchisees. Suppose there are two strategies it may follow. The first is to try to make a separate contract with each franchisee, hoping to take a higher percentage of the return in better-situated franchises, as well as increasing the percentage when particular franchises become more profitable. The second strategy is to set once and for all a fixed percentage that seems fair throughout the franchise and to require of franchisees only certain minimum standards of quality and service so as to preserve the franchiser's reputation and the good will of the pub-

Here there is a parallel with J. S. Mill's objection to Bentham's principle of specific consequences.[40] Mill thought that what is fundamental is not the consequences of particular laws taken one by one (although these are not, of course, unimportant), but the main institutions of society as a whole, as one system, as these are shaped by the legal order, and the kind of national character (Mill's term) that the institutions so shaped encourage. He was concerned to specify the idea of utility in line with the permanent interests of man as a progressive being so that the principle of utility would underwrite a social world congenial to human good. Similar reasoning characterizes the second argument for the two principles: the well-ordered society that realizes those principles is a highly satisfactory social world because it encourages a political character that, by taking basic rights and liberties as settled once and for all, sustains the political virtues of social cooperation.

## §34. Second Fundamental Comparison: Introduction

34.1. We have now completed our survey of the first fundamental comparison: the reasoning favoring the two principles of justice (as a unit) over the principle of average utility (as the sole principle of justice). While the outcome of that comparison achieves the most fundamental aim of justice as fairness, it does not give much support to the difference principle. The most it shows is that this principle adequately secures the general all-pur-

---

lic, on which its profits depend. Here I assume that the minimum standards of quality and service are quite clear and can be enforced without seeming arbitrariness.

Note that the second strategy of setting a fixed percentage for all franchises and enforcing minimum standards has the advantage that it fixes once and for all the terms of agreement between the franchiser and its franchisees. The franchiser's interest in its reputation is secured, while at the same time franchisees have an incentive to meet the franchiser's minimum standards and to increase their own return, thus strengthening the franchise as a whole. They know the franchiser will not try to increase its return should they become more prosperous.

Thus, given the very great initial uncertainty the franchiser faces, the great uncertainty in cooperative relations between franchiser and franchisee that the first strategy would perpetuate, and the continuing suspicion and distrust which that uncertainty would cause, the second strategy is superior. From the point of view of the franchiser's own interests it is more rational to try to create a climate of fair cooperation based on clear and fixed terms that strike all parties as reasonable than to try for adjustable fine-tuned contracts that might enable the franchiser to increase profits as particular opportunities arise. There is some evidence that in fact successful franchisers follow the second strategy.

40. See Mill, "Remarks on Bentham's Philosophy," in *Collected Works*, ed. J. M. Robson, vol. 10 (Toronto: University of Toronto Press, 1969), pp. 7ff., 16ff.

pose means we need to take advantage of our basic freedoms. But other principles may be superior to it on that count.

To explore this question let us now discuss a second fundamental comparison in which the two principles of justice taken as a unit are compared to an alternative exactly the same as those principles except in one respect. The principle of average utility, combined with a suitable social minimum, is substituted for the difference principle. A minimum must be included, for the parties will always insist on some insurance of that kind: the question is how much is appropriate. The basic structure is, then, to be arranged so as to maximize average utility consistent, first, with guaranteeing the equal basic liberties (including their fair value) and fair equality of opportunity, and second, with maintaining a suitable social minimum. We refer to this mixed conception as the principle of restricted utility.[41]

34.2. The second comparison is fundamental for this reason: among the conceptions of justice in which the principle of utility has a prominent role, the principle of restricted utility would seem to be the strongest rival to the two principles of justice. Should these principles still be favored in this comparison, then it would appear that other forms of the restricted utility principle would also be rejected. Their role would be that of subordinate norms regulating social policies within the limits allowed by more fundamental principles.

Note that the third condition of the maximin rule no longer obtains since both alternatives ensure against the worst possibilities, not only against the denial or restriction of the basic liberties and of fair equality of opportunity, but also, given the social minimum in the utility principle, against the more serious losses of well-being. Since we do not want to put any weight on the first condition of that rule, we exclude probability arguments entirely. We assume that there are two groups in society, the more and the less advantaged; and then we try to show that both would favor the difference principle over that of restricted utility. In effect, we argue that the second condition of the maximin rule is fully satisfied, or nearly enough so to provide an independent argument for the two principles.

## §35. Grounds Falling under Publicity

35.1. The grounds we consider fall under the ideas of publicity, reciprocity and stability, in that order. I begin, then, with publicity: earlier (§25.1)

41. For mixed conceptions, see *Theory*, §21: 107.

we said that it requires the parties to evaluate principles of justice in the light of the consequences—political, social, and psychological—of the public recognition by citizens generally that these principles are affirmed by them and effectively regulate the basic structure. Before surveying the grounds favoring the difference principle based on this requirement, let us distinguish between three levels of publicity that a well-ordered society may achieve:

(i) The first level is the mutual recognition by citizens of the principles of justice together with the public knowledge (or reasonable belief) that the institutions of the basic structure actually satisfy these principles (§3).

(ii) The second level is the mutual recognition by citizens of the general facts on the basis of which the parties in the original position select those principles. It is by means of these general facts, made available to the parties, that we model in the original position the commonsense knowledge and beliefs of average reasonable citizens about their basic institutions and how they work (§26).

(iii) The third level is the mutual recognition of the complete justification of justice as fairness in its own terms. That is, citizens know its justification as fully as you and I do who are working out that view. Of course, that they will carry reflection so far is unlikely; still, the full justification is available in the public culture for them to consider if they wish.[42] Of course, when there is an overlapping consensus of comprehensive doctrines, citizens will normally have their own further grounds for affirming the political conception, and this fact too is publicly known.

35.2. The hope is that a well-ordered society in which the full publicity condition is satisfied, that is, where all three levels are achieved, is a society without ideology (understood in Marx's sense of false consciousness). But much is required for this to be so. For example, the general facts (at the second level) must be believed by citizens for good reasons; their beliefs must not be illusions or delusions, two forms of ideological consciousness.[43] Since the beliefs we attribute to the parties are those of common sense, as

42. Here I entertain the fantasy that works like this restatement are known in the public culture.

43. In the case of illusions, we are misled, Marx thinks, by the surface appearances of capitalist market arrangements and fail to recognize the exploitation taking place beneath them; whereas delusions are false or unreasonable beliefs we accept, or else irrational and inhuman values we endorse, in both cases because doing so is psychologically necessary for us to assume our role in society and for its basic institutions to work properly.

we called it, and of science when not controversial, there is a decent chance most of those beliefs are accepted for good reasons.

In any case, one way for a society to try to overcome ideological consciousness is to affirm the institutions of freedom of thought and liberty of conscience; for rational inquiry and considered reflection tend over time, if anything does, to expose illusions and delusions. While full publicity cannot guarantee the absence of ideology, much has been gained: people know the principles of political justice their basic institutions satisfy; and, if we affirm justice as fairness, they have reasonable grounds for affirming those principles. And the justice of their institutions will reduce the need they might otherwise have for false beliefs (delusions) about their society in order to assume their role in it, or for its institutions to be effective and stable.

35.3. For our purposes one important consequence of the publicity condition is that it gives the political conception of justice an educational role (§16.2). We suppose, as a general fact of commonsense political sociology, that those who grow up in a well-ordered society will, in good part, form their conception of themselves as citizens from the public culture and from the conceptions of the person and society implicit in it. Since justice as fairness is worked up from fundamental intuitive ideas belonging to that culture, this role is central to it.

The importance of this point in the present context is that in the second comparison the common content of the two alternatives includes the conceptions of citizen and society used in justice as fairness. What is at issue, then, is the most appropriate principle of distributive justice (in the narrower sense); and whether the difference principle or the principle of restricted utility is more appropriate to the conceptions of citizens as free and equal, and of society as a fair system of cooperation between citizens so viewed. Since the idea of society as such a cooperative system contains some idea of mutual advantage, the educational role introduced by the publicity condition means that the common content of the alternatives provides a foothold for grounds of reciprocity.

## §36. Grounds Falling under Reciprocity

36.1. As I have said, the fact that the difference principle includes an idea of reciprocity distinguishes it from the restricted utility principle. The latter is a maximizing aggregative principle with no inherent tendency toward either equality or reciprocity; any such tendency depends on the consequences of applying it in given circumstances, which vary from case to case. The two fundamental comparisons exploit this fact: as we have said, the first brings out the advantage of the two principles with respect to equality (the equal basic liberties), the second with respect to reciprocity.

To simplify matters, let us assume that there are only two groups in society, the more and the less advantaged, and focus on inequalities of income and wealth alone. In its simplest form, the difference principle regulates these inequalities. Since the parties in the original position are symmetrically situated and know (from the common content of the two alternatives) that the principle adopted will apply to citizens viewed as free and equal, they take equal division of income and wealth (equal life-prospects as indexed by those primary goods) as the starting point. They then ask: are there good reasons for departing from equal division, and if so, which inequalities arising in what ways are acceptable?

36.2. A political conception of justice must take into account the requirements of social organization and economic efficiency. The parties would accept inequalities in income and wealth when these work effectively to improve everyone's situation starting from equal division. This suggests the difference principle: taking equal division as the benchmark, those who gain more are to do so on terms acceptable to those who gain less, and in particular to those who gain the least.

We get that principle, then, by taking equal division as the starting point, together with an idea of reciprocity. The principle selects the highest point on the (most efficient) OP curve; and we saw that this point is the efficient point closest to the 45° line, which line represents equality and preserves equal division (see Figure 1, p. 62). The idea of reciprocity implicit in the difference principle selects a natural focal point between the claims of efficiency and equality.[44]

36.3. To see one way the parties might arrive at the difference principle, consider Figure 1. Imagine they have agreed to move from O to D, as everyone gains in the segment OD and D is the first (Pareto) efficient point.

At D the parties ask whether they should proceed from D to B, which is on the southeast-sloping part of the OP curve to the right of D. B is the

---

44. See E. S. Phelps, "Taxation of Wage Income for Economic Justice," *Quarterly Journal of Economics* 87 (1973), §1. The idea of a focal point is due to Thomas Schelling, *Strategy of Conflict* (Cambridge, Mass.: Harvard University Press, 1960), e.g., pp. 57f.

Bentham point at which average utility (so far as it depends on income and wealth) is maximized (subject to the constraints). The points in the segment D to B and on to the point F (the feudal point), where the utility of the most advantaged is maximized, are also efficient points: movements along that segment can raise the index of one group only by lowering the index of the other. The segment DF is the conflict segment in contrast to the segment OD along which everyone benefits by moving northeast.

The difference principle represents an agreement to stop at D and not to enter the conflict segment. D is the only point on the (highest) OP curve that meets the following reciprocity condition: those who are better off at any point are not better off to the detriment of those who are worse off at that point. Since the parties represent citizens as free and equal, and thus take equal division as the appropriate starting point, we say this is an (not the only) appropriate reciprocity condition. We haven't shown there is no other such condition. But it is hard to imagine what it might be.

36.4. To sum up: the difference principle expresses the idea that, starting from equal division, the more advantaged are not to be better off at any point to the detriment of the less well off. But since the difference principle applies to the basic structure, a deeper idea of reciprocity implicit in it is that social institutions are not to take advantage of contingencies of native endowment, or of initial social position, or of good or bad luck over the course of life, except in ways that benefit everyone, including the least favored. This represents a fair undertaking between the citizens seen as free and equal with respect to those inevitable contingencies.

Recall what we said in §21: the better endowed (who have a place in the distribution of native endowments they do not morally deserve) are encouraged to seek still further benefits—they are already favored by their fortunate place in the distribution—provided they train their endowments and use them in ways that contribute to the good of all, and in particular to the good of the least endowed (who have a less fortunate place in the distribution, a place they also do not morally deserve). This idea of reciprocity is implicit in the idea of regarding the distribution of native endowments as a common asset. Parallel but not identical considerations hold for the contingencies of social position and of good and bad luck.

## §37. Grounds Falling under Stability

37.1. The idea of stability can be introduced as follows: in order to be stable, a political conception of justice must generate its own support and the institutions to which it leads must be self-enforcing, at least under reasonably favorable conditions, as we discuss further in Part V. This means that those who grow up in the well-ordered society in which that conception is realized normally develop ways of thought and judgment, as well as dispositions and sentiments, that lead them to support the political conception for its own sake: its ideals and principles are seen to specify good reasons. Citizens accept existing institutions as just and usually have no desire either to violate or to renegotiate the terms of social cooperation, given their present and prospective social position.

Here we suppose that political and social cooperation would quickly break down if everyone, or even many people, always acted self- or group-interestedly in a purely strategic, or game-theoretic fashion. In a democratic regime stable social cooperation rests on the fact that most citizens accept the political order as legitimate, or at any rate as not seriously illegitimate, and hence willingly abide by it.

37.2. In the well-ordered society of justice as fairness it seems that those most likely to be discontent are the more advantaged; and hence they are more likely to violate the terms of cooperation, or to urge renegotiation. For the further they can shift the distribution of income and wealth into the conflict segment (D to F), the more they benefit. Then why aren't they continually urging renegotiations?

Of course, there exists no principle of distribution that can eliminate all tendencies to defect or to renegotiate, if we suppose these tendencies to arise whenever gains to either group (measured in income and wealth) are possible. At any efficient point one group can do better at the expense of the other; such tendencies would fail to exist only if there were no conflict segment and the OP curve, as in some garden of Eden, were to rise indefinitely to the northeast. To ensure stability, the political conception must provide other reasons to counterbalance, or else to silence, the desire to renegotiate or to violate the current terms of cooperation. So while the more advantaged might gain further income and wealth, this consideration is outweighed by other reasons.

37.3. Let us note three such reasons. First, there is the effect of the educational role of a public political conception (§35.3). Thus we suppose all members of society to view themselves as free and equal citizens who, in and through the basic structure of their institutions, are engaged in mutually advantageous social cooperation. Given this conception of themselves, they think that the principle of distribution that applies to that structure should contain an appropriate idea of reciprocity. If the considerations adduced (in §36 above) show that the difference principle contains such an idea, then everyone has this reason to accept it.

We also suppose that in addition to the reason which all have, the more advantaged have a second reason, since they are mindful of the deeper idea of reciprocity implicit in the difference principle when it is applied to the basic structure: namely, that it tends to ensure that the three contingencies (of §16) are taken advantage of only in ways that are to everyone's advantage. The point here is that the more advantaged see themselves as already benefited by their fortunate place in the distribution of native endowments, say, and benefited further by a basic structure (affirmed by the less advantaged) that offers them the opportunity to better their situation, provided that they do so in ways that improve the situation of others.

A third reason connects with the three requirements for a stable constitutional regime. The review of these requirements (in §33) shows how the basic rights and liberties fashion through institutions a public political culture encouraging mutual trust and the cooperative virtues. The difference principle has the same effect; for once it is publicly understood that the three main kinds of contingencies tend to be dealt with only in ways that advance the general good, and that the constant shifts in relative bargaining positions will not be exploited for self- or group-interested ends, mutual trust and the cooperative virtues are further encouraged.

Moreover, since the difference principle expresses an agreement not to enter the conflict segment, and since the more advantaged, who hold positions of authority and responsibility, are better placed to enter it, their publicly affirming that principle conveys to the less advantaged their acceptance of an appropriate idea of reciprocity in the clearest possible way.[45] In this manner the more advantaged also express their recognition of the great importance of the public culture with its political virtues encouraged by the two principles, a culture that inhibits the wastes of endless self- and group-interested bargaining and offers some hope of realizing social concord and civic friendship.

## §38. Grounds against the Principle of Restricted Utility

38.1. The first difficulty with the principle of restricted utility concerns its indeterminacy: that is, where in the conflict segment is the Bentham

---

45. I owe this point to E. F. McClennen, "Justice and the Problem of Stability," *Philosophy and Public Affairs* 18 (Winter 1989): 23f. The whole discussion is instructive.

point; or indeed any other point specified by a utility principle (such as the Nash point)?[46] We require a workable public interpersonal measure to identify it, and moreover one that should be, if possible, recognized by all as reasonably reliable. This is one consideration that led us to introduce the idea of primary goods based on objective features of peoples' circumstances.

The difficulties with the principle of utility on this count are substantial. Uncertainty is likely to increase disputes and mistrust for much the same reason that unclear and ambiguous principles do (§33.2).

38.2. Second, in asking the less advantaged to accept over the whole of their life fewer economic and social advantages (measured in terms of utility) for the sake of greater advantages (similarly measured) for the more advantaged, the principle of utility asks more of the less advantaged than the difference principle asks of the more advantaged. Indeed, asking that of the less advantaged would seem to be an extreme demand. The psychological strains that may lead to instability are bound to be greater. For as a principle of reciprocity, the difference principle rests on our disposition to respond in kind to what others do for (or to) us; while the utility principle puts more weight on what is a considerably weaker disposition, that of sympathy, or better, our capacity for identification with the interests and concerns of others.

Of course, the more advantaged may fail to comply with a just basic structure. But if so, it is not because much is asked of them but because, being more often in positions of authority and political power, they are more strongly tempted to violate any principle of justice. All the more reason, then, not to enter the conflict segment under the guise of maximizing utility. It may be that the inequalities permitted by the difference principle are already too great for stability.

38.3. Finally, the principle of restricted utility contains an idea of a social minimum.[47] But how is this minimum to be determined? We need some

---

46. See Figure 1, §18.

47. In my account of the problem of the social minimum I am much indebted to Jeremy Waldron's discussion, "John Rawls and the Social Minimum," *Journal of Applied Philosophy* 3 (1986), esp. pp. 27–32. At *Theory*, §49: 278–281, I said that in adjusting the minimum in the principle of restricted utility—in striking the most appropriate balance between maximizing average utility and assuring a suitable minimum—it is possible that those who favor that principle are actually guided by the difference principle operating in their reflections implicitly. My thought was that in this case the utility principle does not offer a genuine al-

concept of it that yields guidelines for what it is to provide. There will be different variants of the principle of restricted utility depending on the concept followed. Some concepts of the minimum are incompatible with that principle; for example, the familiar concept of the minimum as a social dividend specified as approximating an equal share of the social product, making allowances as necessary for unavoidable inequalities in running a modern society. The principle of utility rejects this concept, as does justice as fairness.

A concept of the minimum that does fit the restricted utility principle is the following. Earlier (in §29.3) we said the parties must take the strains of commitment into account. This is because, to make an agreement in good faith, they must be reasonably confident that the person each represents will be able to honor it. So let's ask: with the principles of the equal liberties and of fair equality of opportunity already adopted, what is the *lowest* minimum necessary to assure that the strains of commitment are not excessive? These strains are excessive, we said, when, viewing ourselves as free and equal citizens, we can no longer affirm the principles of justice (with their minimum) as the public conception of justice for the basic structure.

The meaning of "affirm" here can be given by noting two ways in which we react when the strains of commitment seem to us excessive. In the first way we become sullen and resentful, and we are ready as the occasion arises to take violent action in protest against our condition. In this case the least advantaged are bitter; they reject society's conception of justice and see themselves as oppressed. The second way is milder: we grow distant from political society and retreat into our social world. We feel left out; and, withdrawn and cynical, we cannot affirm the principles of justice in our thought and conduct over a complete life. Though we are not hostile or rebellious, those principles are not ours and fail to engage our moral sensibility.

One who supports the utility principle may say that the strains of commitment are excessive only when our share of social resources does not permit us to lead a decent human life, and to meet what in our society is seen as citizens' essential needs. The idea is that in virtue of our humanity—our

---

ternative to the difference principle. To this Waldron replies by formulating a distinct idea of the minimum as that of meeting the basic human needs essential for a decent life. He connects this idea with the strains of commitment. I accept his account as showing that my claim in *Theory* is mistaken. I also follow his lead in using that concept of a minimum in the text to go with the principle of restricted utility. This forces a revision of the argument against the utility principle.

common human needs—everyone is owed at least that much; and this not merely on the ground that it is politically prudent to eliminate the causes of unrest. It is claimed, though, that the argument from the strains of commitment requires no more than this. Once the two principles win out in the first comparison, the veil of ignorance with its attendant uncertainties does not require a higher minimum than one covering those essential needs.

38.4. This concept of the minimum is vague in that the guidelines it suggests do not specify a very definite minimum, which will in any case depend in part on society's level of wealth. But the concept itself is distinct from that in justice as fairness. For the difference principle requires a minimum that, together with the whole family of social policies, maximizes the life-prospects of the least advantaged over time. (We come back to some of the details of this in Part IV.)

Of course, it is possible that the social minimums specified by these two concepts will not be very far apart in practice. What is owed persons in virtue of their humanity and what is owed them as free and equal citizens (given the other social policies as adjusted by the difference principle) may be much the same. But put this matter aside for the moment, and ask the main question: namely, whether a social minimum covering only the needs essential for a decent life guarantees that the strains of commitment will not be excessive.

Let us grant that the minimum in the restricted utility principle will prevent those strains from being excessive in the first way. The least advantaged will not experience their condition as so miserable, or their needs so unmet, that they reject society's conception of justice and are ready to resort to violence to improve their condition. But is this sufficient to prevent the strains of commitment from being excessive in the second way? This requires that the least advantaged feel that they are a part of political society, and view the public culture with its ideals and principles as of significance to themselves.

In Part IV, I suggest that the concept of a minimum as covering the needs essential for a decent human life is a concept for a capitalist welfare state. It suffices to prevent the strains of commitment from being violated in the first way mentioned. But it seems inadequate to ensure that the strains of commitment are not violated in the second way. Moreover, when we take seriously the idea of society as a fair system of cooperation between citizens as free and equal—the outcome of the first comparison means that we are dealing with such a case—we hope to realize another conception of political society. We hope that even the situation of the least advantaged does not prevent them from being drawn into the public world and seeing themselves as full members of it, once they understand society's ideals and principles and recognize how the greater advantages achieved by others work to their good.

To this end, together with the other social policies it regulates, the difference principle specifies a social minimum derived from an idea of reciprocity. This covers at least the basic needs essential to a decent life, and presumably more. We suppose citizens to view themselves as free and equal, and to regard society as a fair system of social cooperation over time. They also think of distributive justice as regulating economic and social inequalities in life-prospects, inequalities affected by one's social class of origin, native endowments, and good fortune over the course of life.

We then say: if those who view themselves and their society in that way are not to withdraw from their public world but rather to consider themselves full members of it, the social minimum, whatever it may provide beyond essential human needs, must derive from an idea of reciprocity appropriate to political society so conceived. While a social minimum covering only those essential needs may suit the requirements of a capitalist welfare state, it is not sufficient for what in Part IV I call a property-owning democracy in which the principles of justice as fairness are realized.

## §39. Comments on Equality

39.1. Justice as fairness is an egalitarian view, but in what way? There are many kinds of equality and many reasons for being concerned with it. So let us review several of the reasons for regulating economic and social inequalities.[48]

(a) One reason is that, in the absence of special circumstances, it seems wrong that some or much of society should be amply provided for, while many, or even a few, suffer hardship, not to mention hunger and treatable illness. Urgent needs and wants go unfulfilled, while the less urgent ones of others are satisfied. But here it may not be inequality of income and wealth as such that bothers us; instead we may think that, unless there is real scarcity, all should have at least enough to meet their basic needs.

(b) A second reason for controlling economic and social inequalities is

48. For these various reasons, I am indebted to some notes of and discussion with T. M. Scanlon.

to prevent one part of society from dominating the rest. When those two kinds of inequalities are large, they tend to support political inequality. As Mill said, the bases of political power are (educated) intelligence, property, and the power of combination, by which he meant the ability to cooperate in pursuing one's political interests.[49] This power allows a few, in virtue of their control over the machinery of state, to enact a system of law and property that ensures their dominant position in the economy as a whole. Insofar as this domination is experienced as a bad thing, as making many peoples' lives less good than they might otherwise be, we are again concerned with the effects of economic and social inequality.

(c) A third reason brings us closer to what is wrong with inequality in itself. Significant political and economic inequalities are often associated with inequalities of social status that encourage those of lower status to be viewed both by themselves and by others as inferior. This may arouse widespread attitudes of deference and servility on one side and a will to dominate and arrogance on the other. These effects of social and economic inequalities can be serious evils and the attitudes they engender great vices.[50] But is the inequality wrong or unjust in itself?

It is close to being wrong or unjust in itself in that in a status system, not everyone can have the highest rank. Status is a positional good, as is sometimes said. High status assumes other positions beneath it; so if we seek a higher status for ourselves, we in effect support a scheme that entails others' having a lower status. And so we like to think that those with higher status normally earn or achieve their position in appropriate ways that yield compensating benefits for the general good. Fixed status ascribed by birth, or by gender or race, is particularly odious.

(d) Inequality can be wrong or unjust in itself whenever society makes use of fair procedures. Two examples are: fair, that is, open and workably competitive markets; and fair political elections. In these cases a certain equality, or a well-moderated inequality, is a condition of economic and political justice. Monopoly and its kindred are to be avoided, not simply for their bad effects, among them inefficiency, but also because without a special justification they make markets unfair. Much the same is true of elections influenced by the dominance of a wealthy few in politics.

49. See Mill's review of Tocqueville's *Democracy in America*, in *Collected Works*, 18:163.
50. The first great figure on this subject seems to have been Rousseau in his *Discourse on Inequality* (1755).

39.2. The last two ways in which inequality is unjust in itself suggest Rousseau's solution, followed (with modifications) in justice as fairness: namely, the fundamental status in political society is to be equal citizenship, a status all have as free and equal persons.[51] It is as equal citizens that we are to have fair access to the fair procedures on which the basic structure relies. The idea of equality is, then, of significance in itself at the highest level: it enters into whether political society itself is conceived as a fair system of social cooperation over time between persons seen as free and equal, or in some other way. It is from the point of view of equal citizens that the justification of other inequalities is to be understood.

All this enables us to say that in a society well ordered by the principles of justice as fairness, citizens are equal at the highest level and in the most fundamental respects. Equality is present at the highest level in that citizens recognize and view one another as equals. Their being what they are—citizens—includes their being related as equals; and their being related as equals is part both of what they are and of what they are recognized as being by others. Their social bond is their public political commitment to preserve the conditions their equal relation requires.

This equal relation at the highest level favors, when life-prospects are involved, a social minimum based on an idea of reciprocity over one that only covers the human needs essential to a decent human life. Here we see how the appropriate concept of a social minimum depends on the content of the public political culture, which in turn depends on how political society itself is conceived by its political conception of justice. The concept of the appropriate minimum is not given by the basic needs of human nature taken psychologically (or biologically) apart from any particular social world. Rather, it depends on the fundamental intuitive ideas of person and society in terms of which justice as fairness is laid out.

## §40. Concluding Remarks

40.1. This concludes our survey of the two fundamental comparisons, which belong to the first part of the argument for the two principles of justice (§25.5). We have still to take up the second part of the argument when we discuss in Part V the question of the stability of the well-ordered society of justice as fairness.

We should recognize, though, that the difference principle is not often

51. See Rousseau, *Social Contract* (1762).

expressly endorsed; indeed, it may prove to have little support in our public political culture at the present time. Nevertheless, I believe it worth studying: it has many desirable features and formulates in a simple way an idea of reciprocity for a political conception of justice. I think that in some form this idea is essential to democratic equality once we view society as a fair system of social cooperation between free and equal citizens from one generation to the next.

From the preceding account of the second fundamental comparison it is evident that, while I view the balance of the reasons as favoring the difference principle, the outcome is certainly less clear and decisive than in the first. The argument rests importantly on the great significance of certain features of the public political culture (for example, how it encourages the political virtues of mutual trust and cooperation) and not on plain and evident considerations of greater public good. We try to specify an idea of reciprocity appropriate to the relation between citizens as free and equal. This idea is more in keeping with the political convention of any reasonably just democratic society, a convention no political party normally dares openly to violate, namely, that everyone as a citizen should gain from its policies.

40.2. A final comment about method: in §23.4 we noted that we should try to present the parties' reasoning in the original position so as to show it to be fully deductive, a kind of moral geometry with all the rigor that name suggests, even though we grant our reasoning is highly intuitive and falls far short of that ideal.

This statement can be misleading unless it is carefully understood: the idea is that all the necessary premises for the argument from the original position, including the necessary psychology (beliefs, interests, and special attitudes), are included in the description we gave of it. Our aim is to show that the selection of the two principles is based on the premises explicitly set out in that description and not on further psychological or other suppositions. Otherwise the original position does not keep track of our assumptions and we don't know which ones we have to justify.

The ideal of rigorous deductive reasoning cannot, however, be fully attained, for at least two reasons. The first reason is that there are indefinitely many considerations that may be appealed to in the original position and each alternative conception of justice is favored by some considerations and disfavored by others. Unless we can close the list of possible considerations (which we cannot), it remains uncertain how the balance would turn out, all things tallied up. The best we can do is to say that these are the most im-

portant considerations and to trust that those we have not examined would
not upset the balance of these reasons.

A second reason the ideal cannot be fully attained is that the balance of
reasons itself rests on judgment, though judgment informed and guided by
reasoning. Of course, we can draw an indifference curve to depict how we
balance reasons.[52] But an indifference curve is merely a representation: it
does not ground the balance it depicts in further reasons; it merely depicts
(represents) the outcome of judgments already assumed to be made.


40.3. The best worked out political conception cannot overcome these
limits; nor are they defects, as they lie in the nature of our practical reason.
In political philosophy, as elsewhere, we must rely on judgment as to what
considerations are more and less significant, and when in practice to close
the list of reasons. Even when judgment is unanimous we may not be able
to articulate our reasons any further. By pulling together many smaller and
larger points, and shaping them into a perspicuous view by an organizing
fundamental idea within which other ideas can be seen to fit, we try slowly
to build up a reasonable political conception.

Whether such a conception serves its purpose can only be decided by
how well it identifies the more relevant considerations and helps us to balance them in the more important particular cases, especially those involving
the constitutional essentials and the basic questions of distributive justice.
If a conception seems, on due reflection (always the last appeal at any given
moment), to have cleared our understanding, made our considered convictions more coherent, and narrowed the disparities between the deeply held
conscientious convictions of those who affirm the basic principles of democratic institutions, its practical aim is achieved.

52. See the example at *Theory*, §7: 33.

# PART IV

# *Institutions of a Just Basic Structure*

## §41. Property-Owning Democracy: Introductory Remarks

41.1. We have completed our initial argument for the two principles of justice as given in the two fundamental comparisons (§§27–33, §§34–40). I now want to survey what would seem to be the main features of a well-ordered democratic regime that realizes those principles in its basic institutions. I outline a family of policies aimed at securing background justice over time, although I make no attempt to show that they will actually do so. This would require an investigation of social theory we cannot now undertake. The arguments and suggestions are rough and intuitive.

One reason for discussing these difficult matters is to bring out the distinction between a property-owning democracy,[1] which realizes all the main political values expressed by the two principles of justice, and a capitalist welfare state, which does not.[2] We think of such a democracy as an alterna-

1. The term is from J. E. Meade, *Efficiency, Equality, and the Ownership of Property* (London: G. Allen and Unwin, 1964), chap. 5 title.

2. This distinction is not sufficiently noted in *Theory*. An instructive discussion to which I am indebted is that of Richard Krouse and Michael McPherson, "Capitalism, 'Property-Owning Democracy,' and the Welfare State," in *Democracy and the Welfare State*, ed. Amy Gutmann (Princeton: Princeton University Press, 1988).

tive to capitalism.[3] Our survey is brief and most of the questions mentioned
are highly controversial, for example, those concerning public funding of
elections and political campaigns, different kinds of property ownership
and taxation. We cannot deal adequately with these intricate questions, and
my remarks are illustrative and highly tentative.

Another reason for reviewing these matters is to sketch in more detail the
kind of background institutions that seem necessary when we take seriously
the idea that society is a fair system of cooperation between free and equal
citizens from one generation to the next (§12.2). It is also important to trace
out, if only in a rough and ready way, the institutional content of the two
principles of justice. We need to do this before we can endorse these principles, even provisionally. This is because the idea of reflective equilibrium
involves our accepting the implications of ideals and first principles in particular cases as they arise. We cannot tell solely from the content of a political conception—from its principles and ideals—whether it is reasonable for
us. Not only may our feelings and attitudes as we work through its implications in practice disclose considerations that its ideals and principles must
be revised to accommodate, but we may find that our sentiments prevent us
from carrying it out. On reflection we cannot live with it.

41.2. Let us distinguish five kinds of regime viewed as social systems,
complete with their political, economic, and social institutions: (a) laissez-
faire capitalism; (b) welfare-state capitalism; (c) state socialism with a command economy; (d) property-owning democracy; and finally, (e) liberal
(democratic) socialism.

Regarding any regime four questions naturally arise. One is the question
of right: that is, whether its institutions are right and just. Another is the
question of design: that is, whether a regime's institutions can be effectively
designed to realize its declared aims and objectives. This implies a third
question: whether citizens, in view of their likely interests and ends as
shaped by the regime's basic structure, can be relied on to comply with just
institutions and the rules that apply to them in their various offices and positions.[4] The problem of corruption is an aspect of this. Finally, there is the
question of competence: whether the tasks assigned to offices and positions
would prove simply too difficult for those likely to hold them.

3. For a discussion of other alternatives, see *Alternatives to Capitalism,* ed. Jon Elster and
Karl Ove Moene (Cambridge: Cambridge University Press, 1989).
4. Economists call this problem that of incentive-compatibility.

What we would like, of course, are just and effectively designed basic institutions that effectively encourage aims and interests necessary to sustain them. Beyond this, persons should not confront tasks that are too difficult for them or that exceed their powers. Arrangements should be fully workable, or practicable. Much conservative thought has focused on the last three questions mentioned above, criticizing the ineffectiveness of the so-called welfare state and its tendencies toward waste and corruption. But here we focus largely on the first question of right and justice, leaving the others aside. We ask: what kind of regime and basic structure would be right and just, could it be effectively and workably maintained? This recognizes that the other questions still have to be faced.

41.3. When a regime works in accordance with its ideal institutional description, which of the five regimes satisfy the two principles of justice?

By the ideal institutional description of a regime I mean the description of how it works when it is working well, that is, in accordance with its public aims and principles of design. Here we assume that if a regime does not aim at certain political values, and has no arrangements intended to provide for them, then those values will not be realized. But while a regime may include institutions explicitly designed to realize certain values, it still may fail to do so. Its basic structure may generate social interests that make it work very differently than its ideal description.

For example, we can describe a basic structure professedly designed to realize fair equality of opportunity, but the social interests it generates may make that realization impossible. A regime's ideal description abstracts from its political sociology, that is, from an account of the political, economic, and social elements that determine its effectiveness in achieving its public aims. However, it seems safe to assume that if a regime does not try to realize certain political values, it will not in fact do so.

41.4. This assumption granted, we see from the ideal description of the first three kinds of regimes, (a) to (c) in 41.2, that each of them violates the two principles of justice in at least one way.

(a) Laissez-faire capitalism (the system of natural liberty (*Theory*, §12)) secures only formal equality and rejects both the fair value of the equal political liberties and fair equality of opportunity. It aims for economic efficiency and growth constrained only by a rather low social minimum (*Theory*, §17: 91f. on meritocracy).

(b) Welfare-state capitalism also rejects the fair value of the political liberties, and while it has some concern for equality of opportunity, the policies necessary to achieve that are not followed. It permits very large inequalities in the ownership of real property (productive assets and natural resources) so that the control of the economy and much of political life rests in few hands. And although, as the name "welfare-state capitalism" suggests, welfare provisions may be quite generous and guarantee a decent social minimum covering the basic needs (§38), a principle of reciprocity to regulate economic and social inequalities is not recognized.

(c) State socialism with a command economy supervised by a one-party regime violates the equal basic rights and liberties, not to mention the fair value of these liberties. A command economy is one that is guided by a general economic plan adopted from the center and makes relatively little use of democratic procedures or of markets (except as rationing devices).

This leaves (d) and (e) above, property-owning democracy and liberal socialism: their ideal descriptions include arrangements designed to satisfy the two principles of justice.

## §42. Some Basic Contrasts between Regimes

42.1. Both a property-owning democracy and a liberal socialist regime set up a constitutional framework for democratic politics, guarantee the basic liberties with the fair value of the political liberties and fair equality of opportunity, and regulate economic and social inequalities by a principle of mutuality, if not by the difference principle.

While under socialism the means of production are owned by society, we suppose that, in the same way that political power is shared among a number of democratic parties, economic power is dispersed among firms, as when, for example, a firm's direction and management is elected by, if not directly in the hands of, its own workforce. In contrast with a state socialist command economy, firms under liberal socialism carry on their activities within a system of free and workably competitive markets. Free choice of occupation is also assured.

42.2. To illustrate the content of the two principles of justice, we need not decide between a property-owning democracy and a liberal socialist regime. In each case, when their institutions work as described, the principles of justice can be realized. The first principle of justice includes a right to private personal property, but this is different from the right of private property in productive assets (§32.6).

When a practical decision is to be made between property-owning democracy and a liberal socialist regime, we look to society's historical circumstances, to its traditions of political thought and practice, and much
else. Justice as fairness does not decide between these regimes but tries to
set out guidelines for how the decision can reasonably be approached.

42.3. The contrast between a property-owning democracy and welfare-
state capitalism deserves closer examination, since they both allow private
property in productive assets. This may tempt us to think they are much
the same. They are not.[5]

One major difference is this: the background institutions of property-
owning democracy work to disperse the ownership of wealth and capital,
and thus to prevent a small part of society from controlling the economy,
and indirectly, political life as well. By contrast, welfare-state capitalism permits a small class to have a near monopoly of the means of production.

Property-owning democracy avoids this, not by the redistribution of income to those with less at the end of each period, so to speak, but rather by
ensuring the widespread ownership of productive assets and human capital
(that is, education and trained skills) at the beginning of each period, all
this against a background of fair equality of opportunity. The intent is not
simply to assist those who lose out through accident or misfortune (although that must be done), but rather to put all citizens in a position to
manage their own affairs on a footing of a suitable degree of social and economic equality.

The least advantaged are not, if all goes well, the unfortunate and un-
lucky—objects of our charity and compassion, much less our pity—but
those to whom reciprocity is owed as a matter of political justice among
those who are free and equal citizens along with everyone else. Although
they control fewer resources, they are doing their full share on terms recognized by all as mutually advantageous and consistent with everyone's self-
respect.

42.4. Note here two very different conceptions of the aim of the background adjustments over time. In welfare-state capitalism the aim is that
none should fall below a decent minimum standard of life, one in which
their basic needs are met, and all should receive certain protections against
accident and misfortune, for example, unemployment compensation and

5. As I have said, a serious fault of *Theory* is that it failed to emphasize this contrast.

medical care. The redistribution of income serves this purpose when, at the end of each period, those who need assistance can be identified. Yet given the lack of background justice and inequalities in income and wealth, there may develop a discouraged and depressed underclass many of whose members are chronically dependent on welfare. This underclass feels left out and does not participate in the public political culture.

In property-owning democracy, on the other hand, the aim is to realize in the basic institutions the idea of society as a fair system of cooperation between citizens regarded as free and equal. To do this, those institutions must, from the outset, put in the hands of citizens generally, and not only of a few, sufficient productive means for them to be fully cooperating members of society on a footing of equality. Among these means is human as well as real capital, that is, knowledge and an understanding of institutions, educated abilities, and trained skills. Only in this way can the basic structure realize pure background procedural justice from one generation to the next.

Under these conditions we hope that an underclass will not exist; or, if there is a small such class, that it is the result of social conditions we do not know how to change, or perhaps cannot even identify or understand. When society faces this impasse, it has at least taken seriously the idea of itself as a fair system of cooperation between its citizens as free and equal.

## §43. Ideas of the Good in Justice as Fairness

43.1. In what follows we focus on the regime of property-owning democracy and indicate how its basic structure tries to meet the two principles of justice. Before taking up these more institutional questions, however, we should review the various ideas of the good in justice as fairness as a political conception.[6] Doing this will help us to characterize important aspects of a property-owning democracy.

Now it may seem that the priority of right implies that justice as fairness can use only very thin, if not only purely instrumental, ideas of the good. But to the contrary: the right and the good are complementary; any conception of justice, including a political conception, needs both, and the priority of right does not deny this. That the right and the good are complementary is illustrated by this reflection: just institutions and the political virtues would serve no purpose—would have no point—unless those insti-

6. This section is drawn from "The Priority of Right and Ideas of the Good," *Philosophy and Public Affairs* 17 (Fall 1988): 251–276, reprinted in *Collected Papers*.

tutions and virtues not only permitted but also sustained conceptions of the good (associated with comprehensive doctrines) that citizens can affirm as worthy of their full allegiance. A conception of political justice must contain within itself sufficient space, as it were, for ways of life that can gain devoted support. If it cannot do this, that conception will lack support and be unstable. In a phrase, the just draws the limit, the good shows the point.

In justice as fairness, then, the general meaning of the priority of right is that admissible ideas of the good must fit within its framework as a political conception. Given the fact of pluralism, we must be able to assume: (1) that the ideas used are, or could be, shared by citizens generally regarded as free and equal; and (2) that they do not presuppose any particular fully (or partially) comprehensive doctrine.

Keep in mind that these restrictions are accepted so that justice as fairness can meet the liberal principle of legitimacy: namely, that when constitutional essentials and questions of basic justice are at stake, the exercise of coercive political power, the power of free and equal citizens as a collective body, is to be justifiable to all in terms of their free public reason.

43.2. Altogether, six ideas of the good appear in justice as fairness:

(i) The first is that of goodness as rationality, and in some form it is taken for granted by any political conception of justice. It supposes that citizens have at least an intuitive plan of life in the light of which they schedule their more important endeavors and allocate their various resources so as rationally to pursue their conceptions of the good over a complete life. This idea assumes that human existence and the fulfillment of basic human needs and purposes are good, and that rationality is a basic principle of political and social organization.

(ii) The second idea is that of primary goods (§17). It is designed to go with the aims of justice as fairness as a political conception: it specifies citizens' needs (as opposed to preferences, desires, and final ends) in accordance with the political conception of their status as free and equal persons.

(iii) The third idea of the good is that of permissible (complete) conceptions of the good (each associated with a comprehensive doctrine) (§17.4). The priority of right is sometimes introduced in this connection: in its more specific, as opposed to its general, meaning, that priority means that only those conceptions of the good are permissible the pursuit of which is compatible with the principles of justice—in the case of justice as fairness, with the two principles we have discussed.

(iv) The fourth idea of the good is that of the political virtues (§33.3). These virtues specify the ideal of a good citizen of a democratic regime. This is a political ideal but it presupposes no particular comprehensive doctrine and hence, although it is a (partial) conception of moral worth, it is consistent with the priority of right in both its meanings and can be incorporated into a political conception of justice.

There are two further ideas of the good. One of these is (v) the idea of the political good of a society well ordered by the two principles of justice. The other is (vi) the idea of the good of such a society as a social union of social unions.[7] The political good of a well-ordered society we consider in Part V. But note here that in showing how the preceding four ideas of the good fit within justice as fairness we relied on the fact that those ideas are built up in sequence. Starting with the idea of goodness as rationality (combined with the political conception of the person, the general facts of human life, and the normal structure of rational plans of life), we get the primary goods. Once we use these goods to specify the parties' aims in the original position, the argument from that position gives the two principles of justice. Permissible (complete) conceptions of the good are those the pursuit of which is compatible with those principles. Next, the political virtues are specified as those qualities of citizens' moral character important in securing a just basic structure over time.

43.3. In light of these ideas of the good, let us look at the two traditional views of civic humanism and classical republicanism. Now although justice as fairness is perfectly consistent with classical republicanism, it rejects civic humanism. To explain: in the strong sense, civic humanism is (by definition) a form of Aristotelianism: it holds that we are social, even political, beings whose essential nature is most fully achieved in a democratic society in which there is widespread and active participation in political life. This participation is encouraged not merely as possibly necessary for the protection of basic liberties but because it is the privileged locus of our (complete) good.[8] This makes it a comprehensive philosophical doctrine

7. See *Theory*, §79.

8. There doesn't seem to be a settled meaning for "civic humanism" and "classical republicanism." I adopt the meaning of a recognized writer and then stick with it. The definition of civic humanism used in the text is from Charles Taylor, *Philosophy and the Human Sciences* (Cambridge: Cambridge University Press, 1985), pp. 334f. Taylor is discussing Kant and attributes the view to Rousseau, and notes that Kant does not accept it.

and as such incompatible with justice as fairness as a political conception of justice.

As noted in §32, the equal basic liberties need not be equally provided for, nor are they all valued for the same reasons. Justice as fairness agrees with the strand of the liberal tradition (represented by Constant and Berlin) that regards the equal political liberties (the liberties of the ancients) as having in general less intrinsic value than, say, freedom of thought and liberty of conscience (the liberties of the moderns). By this is meant, among other things, that in a modern democratic society, taking a continuing and active part in public life generally has, and may indeed reasonably have, a lesser place in the conceptions of the (complete) good of most citizens. In a modern democratic society politics is not the focus of life as it was for native-born male citizens in the Athenian city-state.[9]

The political liberties can still be counted as basic even if they are only essential institutional means to protect and preserve other basic liberties. When politically weaker groups and minorities are denied the franchise and excluded from political office and party politics, they are likely to have their basic rights and liberties restricted if not denied. This suffices to include the political liberties in any fully adequate scheme of basic liberties. We do not assert that, for most persons, the political liberties are merely instrumental: we simply want to allow that not all the basic liberties are valued, or regarded as basic, for the same reasons.

43.4. Do not mistake civic humanism (as defined) for the truism that we must live in society to achieve our good.[10] Rather, civic humanism specifies the chief, if not the sole human good as our engaging in political life, often in the form associated historically with the city-state, taking Athens and Florence as exemplars.[11]

To reject civic humanism (in the sense defined) is not to deny that one of the great goods of human life is that achieved by citizens through engaging

9. But how far did this depend on the fact that nine-tenths of the population (women, aliens, and slaves) were excluded? Is it fair to say that as the Athenian ecclesia was an all-male club of the native born, of course they enjoyed politics as the exercise of their domination?

10. See *Theory*, §79: 458, for criticism of this utterly trivial interpretation of human sociability.

11. Recall the tendency of Rousseau's remarks in the *Social Contract*, bk. III, chap. 15, par. 1–4.

in political life. Yet the extent to which we make engaging in political life part of our complete good is up to us as individuals to decide, and reasonably varies from person to person.

Of course, complementing the good of political life, as Mill and Tocqueville emphasized, are the goods achieved in various (nonpolitical) associations which together constitute civil society, in Hegel's sense.[12] Citizens' claims in behalf of the associative goods do not override but must always respect the principles of justice and the freedom and opportunities they guarantee. This means that membership in all associations is voluntary at least in this sense: even when born into them, as in the case of religious traditions, citizens have a right to leave them unmolested by the coercive powers of the government. Furthermore, no association comprises all of society.

43.5. Classical republicanism, on the other hand, is the view that the safety of democratic liberties, including the liberties of nonpolitical life (the liberties of the moderns), requires the active participation of citizens who have the political virtues needed to sustain a constitutional regime (§33).[13] The idea is that unless there is widespread participation in democratic politics by a vigorous and informed citizen body moved in good part by a concern for political justice and public good, even the best-designed political institutions will eventually fall into the hands of those who hunger for power and military glory, or pursue narrow class and economic interests, to the exclusion of almost everything else. If we are to remain free and equal citizens, we cannot afford a general retreat into private life.

Between classical republicanism, so understood, and the liberalism represented by Constant and Berlin, there is no fundamental opposition, for the question is to what degree citizens' engaging in politics is needed for the safety of basic liberties, and how the requisite participation is best achieved. Here there may be differences in weighing competing political values; but this is importantly a matter of political sociology and institutional design. Since classical republicanism does not involve a comprehensive doctrine, it is also fully compatible with political liberalism, and with justice as fairness as a form thereof.

It remains to add that justice as fairness does not deny (any more than Constant or Berlin denies) that some will find, and indeed, given their gifts

12. See Hegel, *The Elements of the Philosophy of Right,* §§182–256.

13. Machiavelli's *Discourses* is sometimes taken as illustrating classical republicanism as defined in the text. See Quentin Skinner, *Machiavelli* (Oxford: Oxford University Press, 1981). A third term, "civic republicanism," means something else again. See below, §44, n. 16.

and aims, should find their good importantly in political life; thus for them this life is a central part of their complete good. It is to the good of society that this be so, in the same way that it is generally beneficial for people to develop their different and complementary talents and engage in mutually advantageous schemes of cooperation. The idea of division of labor (rightly viewed) applies here as elsewhere.[14]

## §44. Constitutional versus Procedural Democracy

44.1. A property-owning democracy has been described as a constitutional regime and not as what we may call a procedural democracy. A constitutional regime is one in which laws and statutes must be consistent with certain fundamental rights and liberties, for example, those covered by the first principle of justice. There is in effect a constitution (not necessarily written) with a bill of rights specifying those freedoms and interpreted by the courts as constitutional limits on legislation.

By contrast, a procedural democracy is one in which there are no constitutional limits on legislation and whatever a majority (or other plurality) enacts is law, provided the appropriate procedures, the set of rules that identify law, are followed.[15] While these rules specify the required democratic procedures, these procedures themselves impose no limits on the content of legislation. They do not, for example, forbid the legislature to deny equal political rights to certain groups, or to limit freedom of thought and speech. Or if it is insisted that these political rights are part of the meaning of democracy, there is no bar to legislation denying freedom of nonpolitical thought and speech, or denying liberty of conscience, or the many liberties implicit in the rule of law, such as the writ of habeas corpus.

44.2. Can anything be said in favor of a constitutional regime over a procedural democracy? Or is the question of which is preferable simply a question of political sociology, and thus a matter of which is most likely to

14. See *Theory,* §79: 463f.

15. Here we touch upon a difficult question: the point is that there must be some basic norms in the light of which the actions of this collection of people (the members of parliament, say) are law, and not something else. What identifies these people as members of parliament? What identifies these statements as laws, and not as resolutions, or proposals, or indeed just a rehearsal of a play? And so on. Clearly some basic norms are presupposed in any legal system, what Hart would call "rules of recognition." See his *Concept of Law,* esp. chaps. 5–6.

result in just legislation given the historical circumstances of a particular people with their traditions of political thought and practice? Some have thought that if a people is truly democratic in spirit, a constitution with a bill of rights is unnecessary; while if a people is not democratic, such a constitution cannot make it so. But this latter view overlooks the possibility that certain features of a political conception importantly affect the political sociology of the basic institutions that realize it. More exactly, we must consider how that sociology may be affected by the educational role of a political conception of justice such as justice as fairness with its fundamental ideas of person and society.

In §35 we noted the three levels of what we called the publicity condition and said that, when all three levels are achieved in a well-ordered society, the political conception has an educational role. Those who grow up in such a society will in good part form their conception of themselves as citizens from the public political culture and from the conceptions of person and society implicit in it. They will see themselves as having certain basic rights and liberties, freedoms they can not only claim for themselves but freedoms they must also respect in others. Doing this belongs to their conception of themselves as sharing the status of equal citizenship.

It would seem, then, that the political sociology of a constitutional regime will differ from that of a procedural democracy. The conceptions of person and society are more fully articulated in the public charter of the constitution and more clearly connected with the basic rights and liberties it guarantees. Citizens acquire an understanding of the public political culture and its traditions of interpreting basic constitutional values. They do so by attending to how these values are interpreted by judges in important constitutional cases and reaffirmed by political parties. If disputed judicial decisions—there are bound to be such—call forth deliberative political discussion in the course of which their merits are reasonably debated in terms of constitutional principles, then even these disputed decisions, by drawing citizens into public debate, may serve a vital educational role.[16] We are led to articulate fundamental political values for ourselves, and so to form a conception of the reasons relevant when the constitutional essentials are at stake.

16. The importance of deliberative political discussion is a theme of what is sometimes called "civic republicanism." For an informative discussion of this kind of republicanism, see Cass Sunstein, "Beyond the Republican Revival," *Yale Law Journal* 97 (July 1988): 1539–1590.

This public forum of principle[17] is a distinctive feature of a constitutional regime with some form of judicial review. Of course, it has its dangers: courts may fail in their task and make too many unreasonable decisions not easily corrected. Legislators may leave to courts too many matters that legislation should handle. Here the historical conditions of a people become relevant, but this does not affect the point at issue: namely, that the greater educational role of a political conception in a constitutional regime may alter its political sociology so as to favor it over procedural democracy.

44.3. The point may be developed this way. Consider J. S. Mill's philosophy. The unity of Mill's view depends on a few psychological principles, among them the principles of dignity, individuality, and the increasing desire to live in unity with others. Mill connects his conception of utility with the permanent interests of humankind as progressive beings. It is plausible, he thinks, that in the conditions of the modern world, following his principles of justice and liberty is an effective if not the best way to realize those permanent interests.

But what happens should these psychological principles fail to hold, or should they not be sufficiently strong with respect to other psychological influences? From commonsense knowledge and ordinary experience, Mill's principles may seem an excessively optimistic view of our nature. The idea behind the educational role of a political conception of justice suitable for a constitutional regime is that by being embedded in political institutions and procedures, that conception may itself become a significant moral force in a society's public culture. This embedding is done in various ways: by incorporating the basic rights and liberties that limit legislation into a constitution, and by having the judiciary interpret the constitutional force of those freedoms in the first instance. That is, while the courts' decisions are binding on the present case, and while they deserve due respect from other branches of government as precedents, they are not as such binding as general political rules.[18] They may legitimately be questioned in the public forum of principle by citizens and political parties. To spell this out we need

17. The phrase is Ronald Dworkin's in "The Forum of Principle," in *A Matter of Principle* (Cambridge, Mass.: Harvard University Press, 1985).

18. See *Abraham Lincoln: A Documentary Portrait through His Speeches and Writings*, ed. Don E. Fehrenbacher (New York: New American Library, 1964), pp. 88–93, 113–117, 138ff.

an account of the appropriate scope and limits of judicial review, which we cannot go into here.[19]

The point, though, is clear: the political conception supporting a constitutional regime need not be as general as Mill's conception of utility nor rely, as Mill's does, for its more specific content on a quite definite human psychology. Rather, like justice as fairness, it may have far more definite normative content as expressed by its fundamental conceptions of person and society, and by the way these conceptions are developed to yield certain principles of justice. We then conjecture that a basic structure in the public political culture in which these fundamental conceptions and principles are embedded has a different political sociology than that of a procedural democracy: those conceptions may acquire a significant educational role that fashions an effective political influence on the side of the principles of justice. A constitutional regime may be more likely to realize those principles and the ideals of free public reason and deliberative democracy. As we shall see in Part V, a further reason for this is that when these principles and ideals are realized, if only in part, the idea of the good of political society is also realized in part and is experienced by citizens as such.

## §45. The Fair Value of the Equal Political Liberties

45.1. Now let us turn to the fair value of the equal political liberties that enable citizens to participate in public life. The idea of their fair value is introduced in an attempt to answer this question: how shall we meet the familiar objection, often made by radical democrats and socialists (and by Marx), that the equal liberties in a modern democratic state are in practice merely formal? While it may appear, the objection continues, that citizens' basic rights and liberties are effectively equal—all have the right to vote, to run for political office and to engage in party politics, and so on—social and economic inequalities in background institutions are ordinarily so large that those with greater wealth and position usually control political life and enact legislation and social policies that advance their interests.[20]

---

19. One main part of this account would be a rendering of the basic constitutional freedoms that courts should protect. What these might be is suggested by §§13, 30, 32–33. Note that these freedoms include those going beyond procedural arrangements of democracy, for example, liberty of conscience and fair equality of opportunity, and various elements of the rule of law such as the right of habeas corpus, to mention a few important ones.

20. This and the next section attempt to meet the kind of objection raised by Norman Daniels in "Equal Liberty and Unequal Worth of Liberty," in *Reading Rawls,* ed. Norman Daniels (New York: Basic Books, 1975).

To discuss this question, distinguish between the basic liberties and the worth of these liberties as follows: these liberties are the same for all citizens (are specified in the same way) and the question of how to compensate for a lesser liberty does not arise. But the worth, that is, the usefulness of these liberties, which is estimated by the index of primary goods, is not the same for all (*Theory,* §32: 179). The difference principle, in maximizing the index available to the least advantaged, maximizes the worth to them of the equal liberties enjoyed by all. Yet some have more income and wealth than others, and so more all-purpose material means for realizing their ends.

45.2. This distinction between the equal liberties and their worth is simply a definition. It settles no important question; nor does it answer the objection that in a modern democratic state the political liberties may be in practice merely formal. To meet that objection justice as fairness treats the political liberties in a special way. We include in the first principle of justice a proviso that the equal political liberties, and *only* these liberties, are to be guaranteed their fair value (*Theory,* §36: 197ff.). To explain:

(i) This guarantee means that the worth of the political liberties to all citizens, whatever their economic or social position, must be sufficiently equal in the sense that all have a fair opportunity to hold public office and to affect the outcome of elections, and the like. This idea of fair opportunity parallels that of fair equality of opportunity in the second principle.

(ii) When the principles of justice are adopted in the original position, it is understood that the first principle includes this proviso and that the parties take this into account in their reasoning. The requirement of the fair value of the political liberties, as well as the use of primary goods, is part of the meaning of the two principles of justice.

45.3. I cannot consider here how this fair value is best realized in political institutions. I simply assume that there are practicable institutional ways of doing this compatible with the central range of application of the other basic liberties. Reforms to that end are likely to involve such things as the public funding of elections and restrictions on campaign contributions; the assurance of a more even access to public media; and certain regulations of freedom of speech and of the press (but not restrictions affecting the content of speech). Here there may arise a conflict of equally significant basic liberties and some adjustments may need to be made.

These adjustments cannot be rejected simply because they infringe on the freedoms of speech and of the press; these liberties are no more absolute than the political liberties with their guaranteed fair value.[21] In adjusting these basic liberties one aim is to enable legislators and political parties to be independent of large concentrations of private economic and social power in a private-property democracy, and of government control and bureaucratic power in a liberal socialist regime. This is to further the conditions of deliberative democracy and to set the stage for the exercise of public reason, an aim which (as we saw in §44) justice as fairness shares with civic republicanism.[22] These are all important questions and the flourishing of constitutional democracy depends on finding a workable answer to them.

45.4. Note two features of the guarantee of the fair value of the political liberties:

(a) First, it secures for each citizen a fair and roughly equal access to the use of a public facility designed to serve a definite political purpose, namely, the public facility specified by the constitutional rules and procedures which govern the political process and control the entry into positions of political authority. These rules and procedures are to be a fair process, framed so far as possible to yield just legislation.[23] The valid claims of each citizen are held within certain standard limits by the idea of a fair and equal access to the political process as a public facility.

(b) Second, this public facility has limited space, as it were. Without a guarantee of the fair value of the political liberties, those with greater means can combine together and exclude those who have less. The difference principle is presumably not sufficient to prevent this. The limited space of the public political forum, so to speak, allows the usefulness of the political liberties to be far more subject to citizens' social position and economic means than the usefulness of other basic liberties. Therefore, we add the requirement of fair value for the political liberties.

## §46. Denial of the Fair Value for Other Basic Liberties

46.1. The idea of fair value of the political liberties raises another question: namely, why not secure fair value for all the basic liberties? This proposal of a wide guarantee of fair value for all basic liberties carries the idea

---

21. See "The Basic Liberties and Their Priority," where *Buckley v. Valeo* is discussed at pp. 72–79.

22. On the meaning of "civic republicanism" see §44.2, n. 16.

23. *Theory*, §31: 173ff.

of equality further than the two principles. The idea of this wide guarantee is, I think, either irrational, or superfluous, or socially divisive. For consider how it might be understood:

(a) If that guarantee means that income and wealth are to be distributed equally, it is irrational: it does not allow society to meet the requirements of social organization and efficiency. If it means that a certain level of income and wealth is to be assured to everyone in order to express the ideal of the equal worth of the basic liberties, it is superfluous, given the difference principle.

(b) If the wider guarantee means that income and wealth are to be distributed according to the content of certain interests regarded as central to citizens' plans of life, for example, the religious interest, then it is socially divisive. To illustrate: some persons may count among their religious duties going on pilgrimages, or building magnificent cathedrals or temples. To guarantee the equal worth of religious liberty would mean, then, that society is to devote social resources to these citizens rather than to others whose understanding of their religious duties calls for far fewer material requirements. The latter's religious needs, as it were, are less. It seems clear that trying to maintain the equal worth (thus understood) of all basic liberties will surely lead to deep religious controversy, if not civil strife.

46.2. Similar consequences follow, I believe, whenever a political conception makes citizens' basic claims to social resources (the claims to which the difference principle applies) depend on the determinate final ends and loyalties that belong to their complete conception of the good.[24] Given the fact of reasonable pluralism, the basis of social unity is best founded on a public conception of justice that judges citizens' claims to social resources in terms of a partial conception of the good rooted in a view of the objective needs of citizens regarded as free and equal. This leads to the idea of primary goods. At least with regard to the constitutional essentials, and the all-purpose means needed for a fair opportunity to take advantage of our basic freedoms, justice as fairness rules out claims based on various wants and aims arising from people's different and incommensurable conceptions of the good.

In doing so, it excludes certain perfectionist values from the family of po-

24. To illustrate this point *Theory* discusses briefly the principle of proportionate satisfaction at §77: 446f. A fuller discussion is in "Fairness to Goodness," pp. 551f, reprinted in *Collected Papers*, 281f.

litical values in terms of which questions of constitutional essentials and the basic questions of distributive justice are to be settled. It also puts in question whether society can allocate great public resources to pure science—to mathematics and theoretical physics, say—or to philosophy, or to the arts of painting and music, solely on the grounds that their study and practice realizes certain great excellences of thought, imagination, and feeling. No doubt their study does this,[25] but it is far better to justify the use of public funds to support them by reference to political values. Some public support of art and culture and science, and funding museums and public performances, is certainly vital to the public political culture: to a society's sense of itself and its history, and an awareness of its political traditions. But a large fraction of the social product for the advancement of mathematics and science requires a basis in advancing the good of citizens generally, say by the expected benefits to public health and preserving the environment, or to the needs of (justified) national defense.

Some will find this subordinate place of perfectionist values a serious objection to political liberalism and its idea of public reason. I shall not, however, discuss the question further here. I think this subordinate place is acceptable once we see that the exclusion applies to questions of the constitutional essentials and to basic questions of justice. The perfectionist idea is that some persons have special claims because their greater gifts enable them to engage in the higher activities that realize perfectionist values. It does not follow that perfectionist values can never be appealed to in any form, say in suitably circumscribed questions legislators must consider, or on certain matters of policy.[26] The main point is that there should be a good-faith commitment not to appeal to them to settle the constitutional essentials and basic matters of justice. Fundamental justice must be achieved first. After that a democratic electorate may devote large resources to grand projects in art and science if it so chooses.

25. Perfectionism in one form holds that these values are so great as to justify society's allocating to them whatever is necessary to sustain them, barring certain severe adverse consequences.

26. For example, a bill may come before the legislature that allots public funds to preserve the beauty of nature in certain places (national parks and wilderness areas). While some arguments in favor may rest on political values, say the benefits of these areas as places of general recreation, political liberalism with its idea of public reason does not rule out as a reason the beauty of nature as such or the good of wildlife achieved by protecting its habitat. With the constitutional essentials all firmly in place, these matters may appropriately be put to a vote.

## §47. Political and Comprehensive Liberalism: A Contrast

47.1. It is a long-standing objection to liberalism that it is hostile to certain ways of life and biased in favor of others; or that it favors the values of autonomy and individuality and opposes those of community and of associational allegiance. In reply, observe first that the principles of any reasonable political conception must impose restrictions on permissible comprehensive views, and the basic institutions those principles require inevitably encourage some ways of life and discourage others, or even exclude them altogether.

The substantive question, then, concerns how the basic structure (required by a political conception) encourages and discourages certain comprehensive doctrines and their associated values, and whether the way this happens is just. Considering this question will explain the sense in which the state, at least as concerns constitutional essentials, is not to do anything intended to favor any particular comprehensive view.[27] At this point the contrast between political and comprehensive liberalism is clear and fundamental.[28]

27. [The aims of the basic institutions and public policy of justice as fairness can be said to be neutral with respect to comprehensive doctrines and their associated conceptions of the good. Neutrality of aim means that those institutions and policies are neutral in the sense that they can be endorsed by citizens generally as within the scope of a public political conception. Neutrality of aim contrasts with procedural neutrality, understood by reference to a procedure that can be legitimated, or justified, without appealing to moral values at all, but at most to neutral values such as impartiality, consistency, and the like. Justice as fairness is not procedurally neutral. Clearly, its principles of justice are substantive and express far more than procedural values, as do its political conceptions of society and person, which are represented in the original position. See *Political Liberalism*, lect. V, §5, esp. 191–192.]

28. The next several paragraphs are adapted from my reply in "Fairness to Goodness," §VI, to an objection raised by Thomas Nagel in his review of *Theory* entitled "Rawls on Justice," *Philosophical Review* 83 (April 1973): 226–229. In an instructive discussion that I can only briefly summarize here, Nagel argues that the setup of the original position in *Theory*, although it is ostensibly neutral between different conceptions of the good, is not actually so. He thinks this is because the suppression of knowledge (by the veil of ignorance) required to bring about unanimity is not equally fair to all parties. The reason is that primary goods, on which the parties base their selection of principles of justice, are not equally valuable in pursuit of all conceptions of the good. Moreover, he says that the well-ordered society of justice as fairness has a strong individualistic bias, and one that is arbitrary because objectivity between conceptions of the good is not established. The reply in the text above supplements that in "Fairness to Goodness" in two ways. It makes clear first, that the conception of the person used in arriving at a workable list of primary goods is a political

47.2. There are at least two ways in which comprehensive doctrines may be discouraged: those doctrines and their associated ways of life may be in direct conflict with the principles of justice; or else they may be admissible but fail to gain adherents under the political and social conditions of a just constitutional regime. The first case is illustrated by a conception of the good requiring the repression or degradation of certain persons on, say, racial, or ethnic, or perfectionist grounds, for example, slavery in ancient Athens or in the antebellum South. Examples of the second case may be certain forms of religion. Suppose that a particular religion, and the conception of the good belonging to it, can survive only if it controls the machinery of state and is able to practice effective intolerance. This religion will cease to exist in the well-ordered society of political liberalism. No doubt there are such cases; and such doctrines may endure, but always among relatively small segments of society.

The question is this: if, in a just constitutional regime, some conceptions will die out and others only barely survive, does this by itself imply that its political conception of justice fails to be neutral between them? Given the connotations of "neutral," perhaps it does fail, and this is a difficulty with that term. But the important question surely is whether the political conception is arbitrarily biased against these views, or better, whether it is just or unjust to the persons whose conceptions they are, or might be. Without further explanation, it would not appear to be unjust to them, for social influences favoring some doctrines over others cannot be avoided on any view of political justice. No society can include within itself all ways of life. We may indeed lament the limited space, as it were, of social worlds, and of ours in particular; and we may regret some of the inevitable effects of our culture and social structure. As Isaiah Berlin long maintained (it was one of his fundamental themes), there is no social world without loss: that is, no social world that does not exclude some ways of life that realize in special ways certain fundamental values. The nature of its culture and institutions proves too uncongenial.[29] But these inevitable exclusions are not to be mistaken for arbitrary bias or for injustice.

---

conception; and second, that justice as fairness itself is a political conception of justice. Once we understand justice as fairness and the conceptions that belong to it in this way, we can make a more forceful reply to Nagel's objection, provided of course it is accepted that neutrality of influence is impracticable.

29. See Berlin's essay "The Pursuit of the Ideal," in *The Crooked Timber of Humanity*, esp. pp. 11–19. See also his "Two Concepts of Liberty"(1958), reprinted in *Four Essays on Liberty* (New York: Oxford University Press, 1969), pp. 167ff. A similar view is often attrib-

47.3. The objection must go further and hold that the well-ordered society of political liberalism fails to establish, in ways that existing circumstances allow—circumstances that include the fact of reasonable pluralism—a just basic structure within which permissible ways of life have a fair opportunity to maintain themselves and to gain adherents over generations. But if a comprehensive conception of the good is unable to endure in a society securing the familiar equal basic liberties and mutual toleration, there is no way to preserve it consistent with democratic values as articulated by the idea of society as a fair system of cooperation among citizens viewed as free and equal. This raises, but does not of course settle, the question of whether the corresponding way of life is viable under other historical conditions, and whether its passing is to be regretted.[30]

Historical experience shows that many ways of life pass the test of enduring and gaining adherents over time in a democratic society; and if numbers are not the measure of success (and why should they be?), many pass that test with equal success: different groups with distinctive traditions and ways of life find different comprehensive views fully worthy of their alle-

---

uted to Max Weber; see for example the essays "Politics as a Vocation" (1918) in *From Max Weber: Essays in Sociology,* ed. H. H. Gerth and C. Wright Mills (New York: Oxford University Press, 1946); and "The Meaning of 'Ethical Neutrality' in Sociology and Economics," in *Max Weber on the Methodology of the Social Sciences,* trans. and ed. Edward A. Shils and Henry A. Finch (New York: Free Press, 1949). However, the differences between Berlin's and Weber's views are marked. I can't go into this here except to say I believe that Weber's view rests on a form of value skepticism and voluntarism; political tragedy arises from the conflict of subjective commitments and resolute wills. Whereas for Berlin the realm of values is objective: the point is rather that the full range of values is too extensive to fit into any one social world. Not only are they incompatible with one another, imposing conflicting requirements on institutions despite their being objective; but there exists no family of workable institutions that can allow sufficient space for them all. That there is no social world without loss is rooted in the nature of values and the world. Much human tragedy reflects that. A just liberal society may have far more space than other social worlds but it can never be without loss.

30. Thus we may often want to say that the passing of certain ways of life is to be lamented. It is too optimistic to say that only unworthy ways of life lose out in a just constitutional regime. It will be objected by those who affirm the conceptions that cannot flourish that political liberalism does not allow sufficient space for them. But there is no criterion for what counts as sufficient space except that of a reasonable and defensible political conception of justice itself. The idea of sufficient space is metaphorical and has no meaning beyond that shown in the range of comprehensive doctrines that the principles of such a conception permit and that citizens can affirm as worthy of their full allegiance. The objection may still be raised that the political conception fails to identify the right space, but this is simply the question of which is the most reasonable political conception.

giance. Thus whether political liberalism is arbitrarily biased against certain conceptions and in favor of others turns on whether, given the fact of reasonable pluralism and the other historical conditions of the modern world, realizing its principles in institutions specifies fair background conditions wherein different conceptions of the good can be affirmed and pursued. Political liberalism is unjustly biased against certain comprehensive conceptions only if, say, individualistic conceptions alone can endure in a liberal society, or they so predominate that associations affirming values of religion or community cannot flourish, and further, if the conditions leading to this outcome are themselves unjust.

47.4. An example may clarify this point: various religious sects oppose the culture of the modern world and wish to lead their common life apart from its foreign influences. A problem now arises about their children's education and the requirements the state can impose. The liberalisms of Kant and Mill may lead to requirements designed to foster the values of autonomy and individuality as ideals to govern much if not all of life. But political liberalism has a different aim and requires far less. It will ask that children's education include such things as knowledge of their constitutional and civic rights, so that, for example, they know that liberty of conscience exists in their society and that apostasy is not a legal crime, all this to ensure that their continued religious membership when they come of age is not based simply on ignorance of their basic rights or fear of punishment for offenses that are only considered offenses within their religious sect. Their education should also prepare them to be fully cooperating members of society and enable them to be self-supporting; it should also encourage the political virtues so that they want to honor the fair terms of social cooperation in their relations with the rest of society.

Here it may be objected that requiring children to understand the political conception in these ways is in effect, though not in intention, to educate them to a comprehensive liberal conception. Doing the one may lead to the other, if only because once we know the one we may of our own accord go on to the other. It must be granted that this may indeed happen in the case of some. And certainly there is some resemblance between the values of political liberalism and the values of the comprehensive liberalisms of Kant and Mill.[31] But the only way this objection can be answered is to set out the great differences in both scope and generality between political and com-

31. And see Joseph Raz in *The Morality of Freedom* (Oxford: Oxford University Press, 1986), esp. chaps. 14 and 15, to mention a contemporary example.

prehensive liberalism as I have specified them. The unavoidable consequences of reasonable requirements for children's education may have to be accepted, often with regret. I would hope, however, that the account of political liberalism provides a sufficient reply to the objection.

In meeting the objection that political liberalism is wrongly hostile to certain ways of life and biased in favor of others, it is fundamental that, beyond the requirements already described, justice as fairness does not seek to cultivate the distinctive virtues and values of the liberalisms of autonomy and individuality, or indeed of any other comprehensive doctrine. For in that case it ceases to be a form of political liberalism. Justice as fairness honors, as far as it can, the claims of those who wish to withdraw from the modern world in accordance with the injunctions of their religion, provided only that they acknowledge the principles of the political conception of justice and appreciate its political ideals of person and society. Observe here that we try to answer the question of children's education entirely within the political conception. The state's concern with their education lies in their role as future citizens, and so in such essential things as their acquiring the capacity to understand the public culture and to participate in its institutions, in their being economically independent and self-supporting members of society over a complete life, and in their developing the political virtues, all this from within a political point of view.

## §48. A Note on Head Taxes and the Priority of Liberty

48.1. A brief note on head taxes will help to clarify the priority of liberty as well as the sense in which the difference principle expresses an agreement to regard the distribution of native endowments as a common asset (§21).[32]

Recall the precept cited by Marx, which he thinks will be satisfied in the final stage of communist society: "From each according to his abilities, to each according to his needs."[33] If we take this as a precept of justice, it may seem that the difference principle could satisfy it once society imposed a head tax (lump sum tax) on native endowments and required the better endowed to pay a higher tax. In this way, inequalities in income and wealth in people's life-prospects would be greatly reduced if not eliminated.

There are two decisive objections to this proposal. The first might seem merely practical but it cuts deeper. It is this: there may be no measure of na-

---

32. I draw on my "Reply to Alexander and Musgrave," §VII.
33. Karl Marx, *Critique of the Gotha Program* (1873), §1.

tive endowments (as opposed to realized endowments) sufficiently accurate for us to have confidence that we can justify such a coercive tax. Moreover, once established, the tax is public knowledge and people will have a strong incentive to conceal their endowments, as well as a strong incentive not to realize them until after the age at which the tax is imposed. And when would that be?

Again, as we have seen (in §16.2), native endowments such as intelligence and various natural abilities (to sing and to dance) are not fixed assets with constant capacity. They are, as such, merely potential, and their actual realization depends on social conditions, among which are the social attitudes directly concerned with their training, encouragement, and recognition. A usable measure of native endowments seems out of the question, even in theory.

48.2. For our purposes, however, the relevant difficulty is that a head tax would violate the priority of liberty. It would force the more able into those occupations in which earnings were high enough for them to pay off the tax in the required period of time; it would interfere with their liberty to conduct their life within the scope of the principles of justice. They might have great difficulty practicing their religion, for example; and they might not be able to afford to enter low-paying, though worthy, vocations and occupations.

The point is clear and brings out a further aspect in which our native endowments are ours and not society's: namely, that we cannot be subject to a head tax to equalize the advantages our endowments might confer. That would violate our basic liberties. The difference principle does not penalize the more able for being fortunately endowed. Rather, it says that to benefit still further from that good fortune we must train and educate our endowments and put them to work in socially useful ways that contribute to the advantages of those who have less.[34]

## §49. Economic Institutions of a Property-Owning Democracy

49.1. In §§15–16 we noted various reasons for focusing on the basic structure as the primary subject of justice. We need not review them here;

---

34. Here we see how the meaning of the difference principle is determined in part by its ranking as subordinate to the first principle of justice. That meaning is not given by taking it in isolation.

but let us recall one main reason: namely, that if the basic structure can be effectively regulated by relatively simple and clear public principles of justice so as to maintain background justice over time, then perhaps most things can be left to citizens and associations themselves, provided they are put in a position to take charge of their own affairs and are able to make fair agreements with one another under social conditions ensuring a suitable degree of equality. The basic structure is to secure citizens' freedom and independence, and continually to moderate tendencies that lead, over time, to greater inequalities in social status and wealth, and in the ability to exert political influence and to take advantage of available opportunities. This raises a question about how far the present generation is bound to respect the claims of its successors.[35] The principle of just savings addresses this question.

49.2. The relation between the difference principle and the principle of just saving (*Theory*, §44) is this. The principle of just saving holds between generations, while the difference principle holds within generations. Real saving is required only for reasons of justice: that is, to make possible the conditions needed to establish and to preserve a just basic structure over time. Once these conditions are reached and just institutions established, net real saving may fall to zero. If society wants to save for reasons other than justice, it may of course do so; but that is another matter.

A feature of the difference principle is that it does not require continual economic growth over generations to maximize upward indefinitely the expectations of the least advantaged measured in terms of income and wealth. As we have said (§18.3), that would not be a reasonable conception of justice. We certainly do not want to rule out Mill's idea of a society in a just stationary state where (real) capital accumulation may cease.[36] A property-owning democracy should allow for this possibility. We saw that what the difference principle does require is that during an appropriate interval of time the differences in income and wealth earned in producing the social product be such that if the legitimate expectations of the more advantaged were less, those of the less advantaged would also be less. Society is on the upward-rising part or at the top of the OP curve.[37] Permissible inequalities (thus defined) satisfy that condition and are compatible with a social prod-

---

35. *Theory*, §44: 251.

36. See Mill, *Principles of Political Economy*, bk. IV, chap. VI.

37. See the distinction at *Theory*, §13: 68, between perfectly just schemes and those just throughout.

uct of a steady-state equilibrium in which a just basic structure is supported and reproduced over time.

49.3. As for the adoption of a just savings principle, we proceed as follows. To preserve the present-time-of-entry interpretation of the original position (§25.2), the question of savings must be dealt with by constraints that hold between citizens as contemporaries. Since society is to be a fair system of cooperation between generations over time, a principle governing savings is required. We must not imagine a (hypothetical and nonhistorical) direct agreement between all generations, so we say the parties are to agree to a savings principle subject to the condition that they must want all previous generations to have followed it. They are to ask themselves how much (what fraction of the social product) they are prepared to save at each level of wealth as society advances, should all previous generations have followed the same schedule.[38]

The correct principle, then, is one the members of any generation (and so all generations) would adopt as the principle they would want preceding generations to have followed, no matter how far back in time. Since no generation knows its place among the generations, this implies that all later generations, including the present one, are to follow it. In this way we arrive at a savings principle that grounds our duties to other generations: it supports legitimate complaints against our predecessors and legitimate expectations about our successors.[39]

49.4. With a savings principle adopted, the following remarks indicate some of the kinds of taxation by which economic and social background justice might be preserved over time (*Theory*, §43: 245–249).

First, consider bequest and inheritance: we borrow from Mill (and oth-

38. A schedule is a rule stating a fraction of social product to be saved at any given level of wealth.

39. This account of how the just savings principle is derived differs from *Theory*, §44. There it is not required that the parties must want previous generations to have followed the savings rule they adopt as contemporaries. So taking the parties to be mutually disinterested, nothing constrains them to make any savings at all. To meet this difficulty, *Theory* assumes they care for their descendants. While this is not an unreasonable stipulation, it has certain difficulties. It also changes the motivation assumption (of mutual disinterest) in order to get a savings principle. The account in the text, which follows a suggestion made to me by Thomas Nagel and Derek Parfit in 1972, avoids this, and seems simpler. It was stated independently later by Jane English in her "Justice between Generations," *Philosophical Studies* 31 (1977): 98.

ers) the idea of regulating bequest and restricting inheritance. To do this an estate itself need not be subject to tax, nor need the total given by bequest be limited. Rather the principle of progressive taxation is applied at the receiver's end. Those inheriting and receiving gifts and endowments pay a tax according to the value received and the nature of the receiver. Individuals and corporate bodies of certain kinds (educational institutions and museums, say) may be taxed at different rates. The aim is to encourage a wide and far more equal dispersion of real property and productive assets.

Second, the progressive principle of taxation might not be applied to wealth and income for the purposes of raising funds (releasing resources to government), but solely to prevent accumulations of wealth that are judged to be inimical to background justice, for example, to the fair value of the political liberties and to fair equality of opportunity. It is possible that there need be no progressive income taxation at all.

Third, income taxation might be avoided altogether and a proportional expenditure tax adopted instead, that is, a tax on consumption at a constant marginal rate. People would be taxed according to how much they use of the goods and services produced and not according to how much they contribute (an idea that goes back to Hobbes). Such a proportional tax can allow for all the usual exemptions. By taxing only total expenditures above a certain income, the tax can be adjusted to allow for an appropriate social minimum.

The difference principle might, then, roughly be satisfied by raising and lowering this minimum and adjusting the constant marginal rate of taxation. The principle cannot be satisfied exactly, but society may publicly aim at its approximate, or its good-faith, satisfaction. No fine-tuning is possible anyway. The above policies involve only various kinds of taxation and so do not require direct interference by government with individual and associational decisions or particular transactions.

49.5. I comment on two worries sometimes raised about the difference principle. The first is whether it requires us, on every policy matter, to consider how it affects the prospects of the least advantaged. The principle has seemed objectionable to many if it does require this. Clearly this difficulty may be pressed against any principle applicable to the basic structure. A useful reply is this: we are to proceed by selecting a few instruments, as we may call them, that can be adjusted so as to meet the difference principle, once the whole family of policies is given. As indicated above, given the equal basic liberties (with the fair value of the political liberties), fair equality of opportunity, and the like, perhaps the difference principle can be roughly satisfied by adjusting upward or downward the level of income exempt from the proportional income tax. Here that level serves as the instrument. Doing this frees us from having to consider the difference principle on every question of policy.

A second worry is whether the fulfillment of the difference principle should be affirmed in a society's constitution. It seems that it should not, for this risks making it a constitutional essential which the courts are to interpret and enforce, and this task is not one they can perform well. Whether that principle is met requires a full understanding of how the economy works and is extremely difficult to settle with any exactness, although it may often be clear that it is not satisfied. Still, if there is sufficient agreement on the principle, it might be accepted as one of society's political aspirations in a preamble that lacks legal force (as with the U.S. Constitution).

What should be a constitutional essential is an assurance of a social minimum covering at least the basic human needs, as specified in §38.3–4. For it is reasonably obvious that the difference principle is rather blatantly violated when that minimum is not guaranteed. This meets the desideratum that the fulfillment, or lack of it, of a constitutional essential should be fairly obvious, or at any rate, a matter open to public view that courts should be reasonably competent to assess.[40]


## §50. The Family as a Basic Institution

50.1. The aims of the following comments about the family are modest: they merely indicate why the principles of justice apply to the family, but they do not indicate in any detail what those principles require. Before doing this, I comment that the family is part of the basic structure, the reason being that one of its essential roles is to establish the orderly production and reproduction of society and of its culture from one generation to the next. Recall that a political society is always regarded as a scheme of cooperation over time indefinitely; the idea of a future time when its affairs are to be wound up and society disbanded is foreign to our conception of society. Reproductive labor is socially necessary labor. Accepting this, essential to

40. This endorses Frank Michelman's view in his discussion "The Supreme Court, 1968 Term—Foreword: On Protecting the Poor through the Fourteenth Amendment," *Harvard Law Review* 83 (1969): 7–59. See also his "Welfare Rights in a Constitutional Democracy," *Washington University Law Quarterly* (1979): 659–693.

the role of the family is the arrangement in a reasonable and effective way of the raising and caring for children, ensuring their moral development and education into the wider culture.[41] Citizens must have a sense of justice and the political virtues that support just political and social institutions. Moreover, the family must fulfill this role in appropriate numbers to maintain an enduring society. Still, no particular form of the family (monogamous, heterosexual, or otherwise) is so far required by a political conception of justice so long as it is arranged to fulfill these tasks effectively and does not run afoul of other political values.[42]

These necessities limit all arrangements of the basic structure, including efforts to achieve fair equality of opportunity. The family imposes constraints on ways in which this can be done, and the two principles are stated to try to take those constraints into account. Here the difference principle is relevant, for when it is met, those with lesser opportunity can accept more easily the constraints the family and other social conditions impose.[43] I cannot pursue these complexities here, but assume that as children we grow up in a small intimate group in which elders (normally our parents) have a certain moral and social authority.[44]

50.2. It may be thought that the principles of justice do not apply to the family and that therefore they cannot secure equal justice for women and their children.[45] This is a misconception. It may arise as follows: the primary subject of justice is the basic structure of society understood as the arrangement of society's main institutions into a unified system of social cooperation over time. The principles of political justice are to apply directly to this structure, but they are not to apply directly to the internal life of the many associations within it, the family among them. Thus, it may be asked

41. *Theory*, §§70–76.

42. Note that this observation sets the way in which justice as fairness deals with the question of gay and lesbian rights and duties, and how they affect the family. If these rights and duties are consistent with orderly family life and the education of children, they are, ceteris paribus, fully admissible.

43. See *Theory*, §77: 448.

44. Some think that the lexical priority of fair equality of opportunity over the difference principle is too strong, and that either a weaker priority or a weaker form of the opportunity principle would be better, and indeed more in accord with fundamental ideas of justice as fairness itself. At present I do not know what is best here and simply register my uncertainty. How to specify and weight the opportunity principle is a matter of great difficulty and some such alternative may well be better.

45. See Susan Moller Okin, *Justice, Gender, and the Family* (New York: Basic Books, 1989), chap. 5, e.g., pp. 90–93.

how, if those principles do not apply directly to the internal life of families, they can ensure equal justice for wives along with their husbands.

We mentioned this question earlier (§4.2), but it needs further discussion. Note that much the same question arises in regard to all associations, whether they be churches and universities, professional and scientific associations, business firms and labor unions. The family is not peculiar in this respect. To illustrate: it is clear that the two principles of justice (as with other liberal principles) do not require ecclesiastical governance to be democratic. Bishops and cardinals need not be elected; nor are the benefits attached to a church's hierarchy of offices to satisfy the difference principle. This illustrates how the principles of political justice do not apply directly to the internal life of a church, nor is it desirable, or consistent with liberty of conscience or freedom of association, that they should.

On the other hand, the principles of political justice do impose certain essential constraints that bear on ecclesiastical governance. As we saw (§4.2), churches cannot practice effective intolerance since, as the principles of justice require, public law does not recognize heresy and apostasy as crimes, and its members are always at liberty to leave their faith. Thus, although the principles of justice do not apply directly to the internal life of churches, they do protect the rights and liberties of their members by the constraints to which all churches and associations are subject.

This is not to deny that there are appropriate conceptions of justice that apply directly to most if not all associations and groups, as well as to the various kinds of relationships among individuals. Yet these conceptions of justice are not political conceptions. In each case, what is the appropriate conception is a separate and additional question, to be considered anew in any particular instance, given the nature and role of the association, group, or relation at hand.

50.3. Now consider again the family. Here the formula is the same: political principles do not apply directly to its internal life but they do impose essential constraints on the family as an institution and guarantee the basic rights and liberties and fair opportunities of all its members. This they do, as I have said, by specifying the basic claims of equal citizens who are members of families. The family as part of the basic structure cannot violate these freedoms. Since wives are equally citizens with their husbands, they have all the same basic rights and liberties and fair opportunities as their husbands; and this, together with the correct application of the other principles of justice, should suffice to secure their equality and independence.

To put the point another way, we distinguish between the point of view of people as citizens and their point of view as members of families and of other associations.[46] As citizens we have reasons to impose the constraints specified by the political principles of justice on associations; while as members of associations we have reasons for limiting those constraints so that they leave room for a free and flourishing internal life appropriate to the association in question. Here again we see the need for the division of labor between different kinds of principles. We wouldn't want political principles of justice to apply directly to the internal life of the family. It is hardly sensible that as parents we be required to treat our children in accordance with political principles. Here those principles are out of place. Certainly parents should follow some conception of justice (or fairness) and due respect in regard to each of their children, but, within certain limits,[47] this is not for political principles to prescribe. Of course, the prohibition of abuses and the neglect of children, and much else, will, as constraints, be a vital part of family law. But at some point society has to trust to the natural affection and goodwill of parents.[48]

Beyond the above considerations founded on the equality of women, the principles of justice also impose constraints on the family on behalf of children who are society's future citizens and have claims as such. As we have

46. I borrow this thought from Joshua Cohen. See his review, "Okin on Justice, Gender, and Family," in the *Canadian Journal of Philosophy* 22 (June 1992): 263–286.

47. The point here is that the treatment of children must be such as to support the family's role in upholding a constitutional regime. Suppose, for example, that primogeniture, or singling out the first son or daughter as always especially favored, were to undercut the family's role in that respect. Then it should be reconsidered.

48. Michael Sandel, in his *Liberalism and the Limits of Justice* (Cambridge: Cambridge University Press, 1982), on p. 33, considers the situation in which the harmonious family comes to be wrought with dissension. The affections and openness of previous times give way to the demands of fairness and rights. He imagines that past good feelings are replaced by an unexceptionable integrity and judiciousness, so that no injustice prevails. "Parents and children reflectively equilibrate, dutifully if sullenly, abide by the two principles of justice, and even manage to achieve the conditions of stability and congruence, so that the good of justice is realized within their household." One mistake here is that he supposes the two principles to hold generally for all associations, whereas they hold only for the basic structure. Another mistake is that he seems to take justice as fairness as saying that the establishment of full justice would restore the moral character of the family. This last, justice as fairness does not say. Some conception of justice is indeed viewed as appropriate for the family, as for other associations and cases of local justice. Yet such a conception—usually a different one for each kind of association—is necessary, but by no means sufficient, to restore the moral character of the family. The fundamental role of basic justice must not be taken for more than it is.

noted, a long and historic injustice to women is that they have borne, and continue to bear, a disproportionate share of the task of raising, nurturing, and caring for their children. When they are even further disadvantaged by the law of divorce, this burden makes them highly vulnerable.[49] These injustices bear harshly not only on women but also on their children and they tend to undermine children's capacity to acquire the political virtues required of future citizens in a viable democratic regime.[50] Mill held that the family in his day was a school for male despotism: it inculcated habits of thought and ways of feeling and conduct incompatible with democracy.[51] If so, the principles of justice enjoining democracy can plainly be invoked to reform it.

50.4. Thus, when political liberalism distinguishes between political justice that applies to the basic structure and other conceptions of justice that apply to the various associations within that structure, it does not regard the political and the nonpolitical domains as two separate, disconnected spaces, as it were, each governed solely by its own distinct principles. Even if the basic structure alone is the primary subject of justice, principles of justice still put essential restrictions on the family and all other associations. The adult members of families and other associations are equal citizens first: that is their basic position. No institution or association in which they are involved can violate their rights as citizens.

A domain so-called, or a sphere of life, is not, then, something already given apart from principles of justice. A domain is not a kind of space, or place, but rather is simply the result, or upshot, of how the principles of political justice are applied, directly to the basic structure and indirectly to the associations within it. The principles defining the equal basic liberties and fair opportunities of citizens always hold in and through all so-called domains. The equal rights of women and the claims of their children as future citizens are inalienable and protect them wherever they are. And as we have seen, gender distinctions limiting those rights and liberties are excluded (§18.4–6). So the spheres of the political and the public, and of the not-public and the private, take their shape from the content and application of the conception of justice and its principles. If the so-called private sphere is a space alleged to be exempt from justice, then there is no such thing.

49. See Okin's discussion, *Justice, Gender, and the Family,* chap. 7.
50. On these virtues, see Part V, §§57, 59.
51. J. S. Mill, *The Subjection of Women* (1868), in *Collected Works,* vol. XXI, chap. 2.

50.5. More generally, since property-owning democracy aims for full equality of women, it must include arrangements to achieve that. If a basic, if not the main, cause of women's inequality is their greater share in the bearing, nurturing, and caring for children in the traditional division of labor within the family, steps need to be taken either to equalize their share or to compensate them for it. How best to do this in particular historical conditions is not for political philosophy to decide. But a now common proposal is that as a norm or guideline, the law should count a wife's work in raising children (when she bears that burden as is still common) as entitling her to an equal share in the income her husband earns during their marriage. Should there be a divorce, she should have an equal share in the increased value of the family's assets during that time.[52]

Any departure from this norm would require a special and clear justification. It seems intolerable that a husband may depart the family, taking his earning power with him and leaving his wife and children far less advantaged than before. Forced to fend for themselves, their economic position is often precarious. A society that permits this does not care about women, much less about their equality, or even about their children who are its future. Indeed, is it a political society at all?[53]

50.6. Okin in her critical though not unsympathetic discussion of *Theory* has said that there is implicit in it a potential critique of the family and gender-structured social institutions. This critique can be developed, she thinks, first, from the fact that the parties in the original position do not know the sex of those they represent; and second, from the fact that the family and the gender system, as part of the basic structure, are to be subject to the scrutiny of its principles.[54]

I should like to think that Okin is right. The crucial question may be: what precisely is covered by gender-structured institutions? How are their lines drawn? If we say the gender system includes whatever social arrangements adversely affect the equal basic liberties and opportunities of women, as well as of those of their children as future citizens, then surely that sys-

---

52. For an instructive discussion of this proposal and other related questions concerning the equality of women, see Okin, *Justice, Gender, and the Family*, chaps. 7–8.

53. I have in mind here the fact that a political society is a system of cooperation from one generation to the next. Note that in the text I have assumed that the traditional division of labor in the family is common and have addressed only that situation in order to indicate what the principles of justice seem to require.

54. Okin, *Justice, Gender, and the Family*, pp. 101, 105.

tem is subject to critique by the principles of justice. The question then becomes whether the fulfillment of these principles suffices to remedy the system's faults. This depends in part on social theory and human psychology, and much else. It cannot be settled by a conception of justice alone and I shall not try to reflect further on the matter here.

I conclude by remarking that I have appealed to only a few values of public reason covered by the political conception of justice. Among these values are the equality of women, the equality of children as future citizens, and finally, the value of the family in securing the orderly production and reproduction of society and of its culture from one generation to the next, and so in a just democratic society, its value in cultivating and encouraging the attitudes and virtues supporting such institutions. In other cases, further political values can be appealed to.

## §51. The Flexibility of an Index of Primary Goods

51.1. In order to illustrate the practical use of an index of primary goods and the flexibility such an index provides, I discuss in some detail an objection Sen has raised to such an index: namely, that it is bound to be too inflexible to be fair.[55] Discussing this will clarify the idea of primary goods by noting their connection with Sen's important idea that interpersonal comparisons must be based, in part at least, on a measure of what he calls a person's "basic capabilities."

Sen's objection rests on two points. The first is that to use an index of these goods is, in effect, to work in the wrong space, and so involves a misleading metric: that is, primary goods themselves should not be viewed as the embodiment of advantage, since in fact advantage depends on a relation between persons and goods. An acceptable basis of interpersonal comparisons, the objection continues, must rest, at least in good part, on a measure of a person's basic capabilities.

To explain: Sen holds that utilitarianism is mistaken in viewing goods solely as satisfying individuals' desires and preferences. He thinks that the relation of goods to basic capabilities is also essential: goods make it possible for us to do certain basic things, for example, dressing and feeding our-

55. Sen's objection was first stated in "Equality of What?" *Tanner Lectures on Human Values*, vol. 1 (Salt Lake City: University of Utah Press, 1979), reprinted in *Choice, Welfare, and Measurement* (Cambridge, Mass.: MIT Press, 1982), pp. 365–366. This objection is further elaborated in his *Inequality Reexamined* (Cambridge, Mass.: Harvard University Press, 1992); see especially chap. 5.

selves, moving from place to place unassisted, holding a position or pursuing an occupation, and taking part in politics and the public life of our
community. By abstracting from the relation of goods to basic capabilities
and focusing on primary goods, Sen thinks an index of primary goods focuses on the wrong thing.

51.2. In reply, it should be stressed that the account of primary goods
does take into account, and does not abstract from, basic capabilities:
namely, the capabilities of citizens as free and equal persons in virtue of
their two moral powers. It is these powers that enable them to be normal
and fully cooperating members of society over a complete life and to maintain their status as free and equal citizens. We rely on a conception of citizens' capabilities and basic needs, and the equal rights and liberties are
specified with these moral powers in mind. As we have seen (§32), those
rights and liberties are essential conditions for the adequate development
and full exercise of those powers in certain fundamental cases of great significance. We say:

(i) The equal political liberties, and freedom of speech and freedom of
assembly and the like, are necessary for the development and exercise of
citizens' sense of justice and are required if citizens are to make rational
judgments in the adoption of just political aims and in the pursuit of effective social policies.

(ii) The equal civil liberties, liberty of conscience and freedom of association, and free choice of occupation and the like, are necessary for the development and exercise of citizens' capacity for a conception of the good:
that is, the capacity to form, to revise and rationally to pursue what one
views as worthwhile in human life, as understood in the light of a (fully or
partially) comprehensive religious, philosophical, or moral doctrine.

(iii) Income and wealth are general all-purpose means required to
achieve a wide range of (permissible) ends, whatever they may be, and in
particular, the end of realizing the two moral powers and advancing the
ends of the (complete) conceptions of the good that citizens affirm or
adopt.

These remarks locate the role of primary goods within the framework of
justice as fairness as a whole. Attending to this framework, we see that it
does recognize the fundamental relation between primary goods and persons' basic capabilities. In fact, the index of those goods is drawn up by
asking what things, given the basic capabilities included in the (normative)
conception of citizens as free and equal, are required by citizens to maintain

their status as free and equal and to be normal, fully cooperating members of society. Since the parties know that an index of primary goods is part of the principles of justice, included in their meaning, they will not accept those principles unless that index secures what they think is required to protect the essential interests of the persons they represent.

51.3. So far, we have made an important background assumption: namely, that with respect to the kinds of needs and requirements that political justice should take into account, citizens' needs and requirements are sufficiently similar for an index of primary goods to serve as a suitable and fair basis for interpersonal comparisons in matters of political justice.

If this background assumption does indeed hold, Sen might accept the use of primary goods, at least in many instances.[56] His objection rests on the further point that the relevant needs and requirements of normal and fully cooperating members of society are in fact sufficiently different so that the two principles of justice with an index of primary goods are bound to be too inflexible to yield a fair way of adjusting to these differences. In reply, I shall try to show that in drawing up an index of primary goods we have considerable flexibility.

To begin, I put aside the more extreme cases of persons with such grave disabilities that they can never be normal contributing members of social cooperation. I consider instead only two kinds of cases, both within what I shall call the normal range, that is, the range of differences in citizens' needs and requirements compatible with everyone's being a normal and cooperating member of society. They will illustrate the flexibility of the two principles in dealing with those differences.

51.4. The first kind of case concerns the differences in the development and exercise of the two moral powers and in realized native endowments, differences above the minimum essentials required to be a fully cooperating member of society. For example, the judicial virtues are excellences of the moral power of a sense of justice and there is, let's suppose, considerable variation in the capacity for those virtues. These powers involve intellect and imagination, the capacity to be impartial and to take a wider and more inclusive view, as well as a certain sensitivity to the concerns and circumstances of others.

The two principles of justice incorporate the concept of pure back-

56. See Sen, "Equality of What?" in *Choice, Welfare, and Measurement*, p. 368.

ground procedural justice and not that of allocative justice (§14). The differences in citizens' moral powers do not, as such, lead to corresponding differences in the allocation of primary goods, including the basic rights and liberties. Rather, the basic structure is arranged to include the requisite institutions of background justice so that citizens have available to them the general all-purpose means to train and educate their basic capabilities, and a fair opportunity to make good use of them, provided their capabilities lie within the normal range. It is left to citizens as free and equal persons, secure in their basic rights and liberties and able to take charge of their own life, to avail themselves of the opportunities guaranteed to all on a fair basis.

Consider the differences in the capacity for the judicial virtues mentioned above: within the normal range, these differences do not affect the way the two principles apply to citizens as free and equal. All still have the same basic rights and liberties and fair opportunities, and all are covered by the guarantees of the difference principle. Of course, those with a greater capacity for the judicial virtues have, other things equal, a greater chance of holding positions of authority with the responsibilities that call for the exercise of those virtues. Over the course of a life, they may have higher expectations of primary goods, and their greater capacities, properly trained and exercised, may be differently rewarded depending on the plans they make and on what they do. (These last remarks assume a more or less well-ordered society; as always we work within ideal theory, unless otherwise noted.)

But the particular distribution that results does not come about by following principles of justice (either allocative or procedural) that use a measure of basic capabilities. A scientific (as opposed to a normative) measure of the full range of these capabilities is impossible as a matter of practice, if not theoretically as well. In justice as fairness, adjusting to these differences in capabilities proceeds by way of an ongoing social process of pure background procedural justice in which qualifications suitable for particular offices and positions play a distributive role. But, as always, no differences in basic capabilities (within the normal range) affect persons' equal basic rights and liberties. The claim of justice as fairness is that in a well-ordered society such an ongoing social process would not lead to political injustice.

51.5. I now turn to the second kind of case, namely, the differences in citizens' needs for medical care. These cases are characterized as ones in which citizens fall temporarily—for a period of time—below the minimum essential capacities for being normal and fully cooperating members of society. As a first step in working out a conception of political justice we may abstract entirely (as we have done) from illness and accident, and view the fundamental question of political justice as simply that of specifying the fair terms of cooperation between citizens as free and equal. But I hope that justice as fairness can not only help with that question but also be extended to cover differences in need to which illness and accident give rise. To attempt this extension we interpret the assumption that citizens are normally cooperating members of society over a complete life to allow that they may be seriously ill or suffer from severe accidents from time to time.

In making this extension we rely on three features of the index of primary goods that give the two principles of justice a certain flexibility in adjusting to the differences among citizens in their need for medical care.

First, these goods are not specified in full detail by considerations available in the original position. This is obvious with respect to both the basic rights and liberties, and the other primary goods. It suffices, for example, that in the original position the general form and content of the basic rights and liberties can be outlined and the grounds of their priority understood. The further specification of those rights and liberties is left to the constitutional, legislative, and judicial stages as more information is made available, and particular social conditions can be taken into account. In outlining the general form and content of basic rights and liberties, we must make their special role and central range of application sufficiently clear so that at each later stage the process of specification is guided in a suitable way.

Second, the primary goods of income and wealth are not to be identified only with personal income and private wealth. For we have control, or partial control, over income and wealth not only as individuals but also as members of associations and groups. Members of a religious sect have some control over church property; members of a faculty have some control over a university's wealth viewed as a means for carrying out their aims of scholarship and research. As citizens we are also the beneficiaries of the government's providing various personal goods and services to which we are entitled, as in the case of health care, or of its providing public goods (in the economist's sense), as in the case of measures ensuring public health (clean air and unpolluted water, and the like). All of these items can (if necessary) be included in the index of primary goods.[57]

Third, the index of primary goods is an index of expectations of these goods over the course of a complete life. These expectations are viewed as

57. These points are made in my "Fairness to Goodness," §III.

attached to the relevant social positions within the basic structure. This enables the two principles to allow for differences in need arising from illness and accident over the normal course of a complete life. Individuals' expectations of primary goods (their index) can be the same ex ante, while the goods they actually receive are different ex post, depending on the various contingencies—in this case, on the illnesses and accidents that befall them.

51.6. Given this background, I indicate—here I cannot do more than that—how the two principles apply to the medical and health needs of citizens as normal cooperating members of society whose capacities for a time fall below the minimum.

This matter is to be decided at the legislative stage (*Theory,* §31) and not in the original position or constitutional convention, since the practicable application of the two principles to this case depends in part on information about the prevalence of various illnesses and their severity, the frequency of accidents and their causes, and much else. At the legislative stage this information is available, and hence the policies to protect public health and to provide medical care can be taken up there.

Since the index of primary goods is specified in terms of expectations, considerable flexibility in adjusting to citizens' various needs is a feature of the two principles of justice. For simplicity, let us focus on the least-advantaged group and assume that information is available concerning its members' likely medical needs in the aggregate and the cost of covering them at various levels of treatment and care. Within the guidelines of the difference principle, provisions can be made for covering these needs up to the point where further provision would lower the expectations of the least advantaged. This reasoning parallels that in fixing a social minimum (*Theory,* §44: 251f.). The only difference is that now the expectation of an assured provision of health care at a certain level (calculated by estimated cost) is included as part of that minimum. Once again, the same expectations ex ante are compatible with widely divergent benefits received depending on differences in need ex post.

Observe that what sets an upper bound to the fraction of the social product spent on medical and health needs are the other essential expenditures society must make, whether these are paid for by private or public funds. For example, an active and productive workforce must be sustained, children must be raised and properly educated, part of the annual product must be invested in real capital and another part counted as depreciation, and provision must be made for those who are retired, not to mention the requirements of national defense and a (just) foreign policy in a world of nation-states. The representatives of citizens who view these claims from the point of view of the legislative stage must strike a balance between them in allocating society's resources.

Here we see the great significance of regarding citizens as having a public (political) identity over a complete life, and viewing them as normal and fully cooperating members of society over that life. Their representatives at the legislative stage must consider how the two principles are to be further specified given the general information now available. Of course, regarding citizens in this way does not single out a precise answer. As always we have at best only guidelines for deliberation. But the representatives of citizens must view all the various claims mentioned above—including those we make in all phases of life from childhood to old age—from the point of view of one person who is to live through all phases of life. The idea is that the claims of those in each phase derive from how we would reasonably balance those claims once we viewed ourselves as living through all phases of life.

The preceding comments view the question of medical care under the guidelines of the difference principle. This may give the mistaken impression that provision of medical care is merely to supplement the income of the least advantaged when they cannot cover the costs of the medical care they may prefer. To the contrary: as already emphasized, provision for medical care, as with primary goods generally, is to meet the needs and requirements of citizens as free and equal. Such care falls under the general means necessary to underwrite fair equality of opportunity and our capacity to take advantage of our basic rights and liberties, and thus to be normal and fully cooperating members of society over a complete life.

This conception of citizens enables us to do two things: first, to estimate the urgency of different kinds of medical care, and second, to specify the relative priority of claims of medical care and public health generally with respect to other social needs and requirements. Thus, regarding the first, treatment that restores persons to good health, enabling them to resume their normal lives as cooperating members of society, has great urgency—more exactly, the urgency specified by the principle of fair equality of opportunity; whereas cosmetic medicine, say, is not offhand a need at all. By regarding the strength of claims to medical care as tied to maintaining our capacity to be a normal member of society and restoring that capacity once it falls below the minimum required, a guideline is provided (as the preceding discussion outlines) for balancing the costs of such care against the other claims on the social product covered by the two principles of justice. I shall not, however, pursue further these difficult and complicated matters.[58]

51.7. To conclude: In reply to the objection that an index of primary goods is too inflexible to be fair, I have made two main points:

First, that the idea of primary goods is closely connected with the conception of citizens as having certain basic capabilities, among the most important being the two moral powers. What those goods are depends on the fundamental intuitive idea of citizens as persons with those powers, and with a higher-order interest in their development and exercise. This accords with Sen's view that basic capabilities must be taken into account not only in making interpersonal comparisons but in laying out a reasonable political conception of justice.

Second, that in order to show the flexibility allowed by the use of primary goods, we must distinguish between two kinds of cases. The first case concerns differences among citizens' capabilities within the normal range but above the minimum essentials required to be a fully cooperating member of society. These differences are accommodated by an ongoing social process of pure background procedural justice. In this kind of case, no measure of citizens' differences in capabilities is necessary; nor does a workable measure seem possible.

The second kind of case involves those in which because of illness and accident citizens fall for a time below the minimum essentials. Here we rely on the fact that the index of primary goods is to be more definitely specified at the legislative stage and, as always, in terms of expectations. These features allow it to be flexible enough to meet differences in medical needs arising from illness and accident. Important here is the use of the conception of the citizen as a cooperating member of society over a complete life, which enables us to ignore differences in capabilities and endowments above the minimum. That conception directs us to restore, or in an appropriate way to make good, our capabilities when by illness and accident we fall below the minimum and are unable to play our part in society.

This rather simple distinction between the two cases—of differences above and below the minimum essentials—is an example of the kind of

58. For an instructive discussion, see Norman Daniels, "Health-Care Needs and Distributive Justice," *Philosophy and Public Affairs* 10 (Spring 1981): 146–179. This is worked out further in Daniels's *Just Health Care* (Cambridge: Cambridge University Press, 1985). See chaps. 1–3.

practicable distinction that is, I believe, vital to any political conception that has some chance of being the focus of an overlapping consensus in a democratic regime. Our aim is to avoid difficulties, to simplify when simplification is possible, and to keep in touch with common sense.[59]

51.8. This concludes our survey of the main institutions of a property-owning democracy. Included among them are other important arrangements:

(a) Provisions for securing the fair value of the political liberties, although what these are in detail was not examined (§45).

(b) So far as practicable, provisions for realizing fair equality of opportunity in education and training of various kinds.

(c) A basic level of health-care provided for all (§51).

Note also that Mill's idea of worker-managed cooperative firms is fully compatible with property-owning democracy, since such firms are not owned or controlled by the state. We come to this now in our brief comparison with Marx.

## §52. Addressing Marx's Critique of Liberalism

52.1. We look at Marx's views mainly from one perspective: his critique of liberalism. We try to meet those of his criticisms that most clearly require an answer. For example:

(a) To the objection that some of the basic rights and liberties, those he

59. The more extreme cases I have not considered, but this is not to deny their importance. I take it as obvious, and accepted by common sense, that we have a duty towards all human beings, however severely handicapped. The question concerns the weight of these duties when they conflict with other basic claims. At some point, then, we must see whether justice as fairness can be extended to provide guidelines for these cases; and if not, whether it must be rejected rather than supplemented by some other conception. It is premature to consider these matters here. Justice as fairness is presented mainly as an attempt to get a clear and uncluttered view of what in the tradition of democratic political thought has been the fundamental question of political philosophy, namely, what principles of justice are most appropriate to specify the fair terms of cooperation when society is viewed as a system of cooperation between citizens regarded as free and equal persons, and as normal and fully cooperating members of society over a complete life (§2.3). A method enabling us to discuss this question in a manageable way is surely worth looking for. I don't know how far justice as fairness can be successfully extended to cover the more extreme kinds of cases. If Sen can work out a plausible view for these, it would be an important question whether, with certain adjustments, it could be included in justice as fairness when suitably extended, or else adapted to it as an essential complementary part.

connects with the rights of man (and which we have labeled the liberties of the moderns), express and protect the mutual egoisms of citizens in the civil society of a capitalist world, we reply that in a well designed property-owning democracy those rights and liberties, properly specified, suitably express and protect the higher-order interests of citizens as free and equal. And while a right to property in productive assets is permitted, that right is not a basic right but subject to the requirement that, in existing conditions, it is the most effective way to meet the principles of justice.

(b) To the objection that the political rights and liberties of a constitutional regime[60] are merely formal, we reply that, by the fair value of the political liberties (working with the other principles of justice) all citizens, whatever their social position, may be assured a fair opportunity to exert political influence.

(c) To the objection that a constitutional regime with private property secures only the so-called negative liberties, we reply that the background institutions of a property-owning democracy, together with fair equality of opportunity and the difference principle, give adequate protection to the so-called positive liberties.[61]

(d) To the objection against the division of labor under capitalism, we reply that the narrowing and demeaning features of the division should be largely overcome once the institutions of a property-owning democracy are realized (*Theory*, §79: 463f.).

While the idea of property-owning democracy tries to meet legitimate objections of the socialist tradition, the idea of the well-ordered society of justice as fairness is quite distinct from Marx's idea of a full communist society. A full communist society seems to be one beyond justice in the sense that the circumstances that give rise to the problem of distributive justice are surpassed and citizens need not be, and are not, concerned with it in everyday life. Justice as fairness, by contrast, assumes that given the general facts of the political sociology of democratic regimes (such as the fact of reasonable pluralism), the principles and political virtues falling under justice will always play a role in public political life. The evanescence of justice, even of distributive justice, is not possible, nor, I think, is it desirable (but I shall not discuss this).

60. In *On the Jewish Question* (1843), Marx distinguishes between the rights of man and the political liberties. The latter he greatly values and he thinks that in some form they will be honored under communism; but a role for the former would seem to disappear.

61. On the distinction between negative and positive liberties, see Isaiah Berlin, "Two Concepts of Liberty."

52.2. Of course, Marx would say that, even accepting the ideal of property-owning democracy, such a regime generates political and economic
forces that make it depart all too widely from its ideal institutional description. He would say that no regime with private property in the means of
production can satisfy the two principles of justice, or even do much to realize the ideals of citizen and society expressed by justice as fairness.

This is a major difficulty and must be faced. But even if it is in good part
true, the question is not yet settled. We must ask whether a liberal socialist
regime does significantly better in realizing the two principles. Should it do
so, then the case for liberal socialism is made from the standpoint of justice
as fairness. But we must be careful here not to compare the ideal of one
conception with the actuality of the other, but rather to compare actuality
with actuality, and in our particular historical circumstances.

52.3. Marx would raise another objection, namely, that our account of the
institutions of property-owning democracy has not considered the importance of democracy in the workplace and in shaping the general course of
the economy. This is also a major difficulty. I shall not try to meet it except
to recall that Mill's idea of worker-managed firms[62] is fully compatible with
property-owning democracy. Mill believed that people would much prefer
to work in such firms; this would enable the firms to pay lower wages while
being highly efficient. In due course these firms would increasingly win out
over capitalist firms. A capitalist economy would gradually disappear and
be peacefully replaced by worker-managed firms within a competitive economy.

Since this has not happened, nor does it show many signs of doing so,
the question arises whether Mill was wrong about what people prefer, or
whether worker-managed firms have not had a fair chance to establish
themselves. If the latter is the case, should such firms be granted subsidies,
at least for a time, so that they can get going? Would there be advantages
from doing this that could be justified in terms of the political values expressed by justice as fairness, or by some other political conception of justice for a democratic regime? For example, would worker-managed firms be
more likely to encourage the democratic political virtues needed for a constitutional regime to endure? If so, could greater democracy within capitalist firms achieve much the same result? I shall not pursue these questions. I
have no idea of the answers, but certainly these questions call for careful ex-

62. See Mill, *Principles of Political Economy,* bk. IV, chap. 7.

amination. The long-run prospects of a just constitutional regime may depend on them.

## §53. Brief Comments on Leisure Time

53.1. In elaborating justice as fairness we assume that all citizens are normal and fully cooperating members of society over a complete life. We do this because for us the question of the fair terms of cooperation between citizens so regarded is fundamental and to be examined first. Now this assumption implies that all are willing to work and to do their part in sharing the burdens of social life, provided of course the terms of cooperation are seen as fair.

But how is this assumption expressed in the difference principle? The index of primary goods, as discussed so far, makes no mention of work, and the least advantaged are those with the lowest index. Are the least advantaged, then, those who live on welfare and surf all day off Malibu?

53.2. This question can be handled in two ways: one is to assume that everyone works a standard working day; the other is to include in the index of primary goods a certain amount of leisure time, say sixteen hours per day if the standard working day is eight hours. Those who do no work have eight extra hours of leisure and we count those eight extra hours as equivalent to the index of the least advantaged who do work a standard day. Surfers must somehow support themselves.[63]

Of course, if leisure time is included in the index, society must make sure that opportunities for fruitful work are generally available. We cannot discuss the complicated issues involved here. The point is that we can include leisure time in the index should this be workable and the best way to express the idea that all citizens are to do their part in society's cooperative work.

If necessary we can also include in the index realized native endowments and even states of consciousness like physical pain. However, for the sake of having an objective measure and relying on information that is readily available and easy to comprehend, it is much better not to include such goods in the index. But leisure time has a reasonably objective measure and is open to view. It also meets the essential condition that primary goods must not presuppose any particular comprehensive doctrine.

63. See, "The Priority of the Right and Ideas of the Good," p. 257, n. 7.

# PART V

# The Question of Stability

## §54. The Domain of the Political

54.1. In this last part we take up the question of the stability of justice as fairness and how its stability connects with the good of a political society well ordered by it. Our aim is to complete the argument for the two principles of justice. Recall that earlier (§25.5) we split the argument from the original position into two parts. In the first part, in which the principles of justice are provisionally chosen, the parties assume that the persons they represent are not moved by the special psychologies (or attitudes), as we called them. That is, the parties ignore persons' inclinations to be envious or spiteful, or to have a will to dominate or a tendency to be submissive, or to be peculiarly averse to uncertainty and risk. This assumption greatly simplifies the parties' reasoning in selecting principles, as is clear in the case of social and economic inequalities where the role of envy and spite cannot be ignored. Special attitudes aside, the parties can reason in terms of the fundamental interests of those they represent.

Yet these attitudes are important in human life and must be considered at some point. Here a difficulty arises: there seems to be no way of knowing in general, apart from considering at least the broad features of the main institutions of the existing basic structure, how liable people are to those propensities. So in carrying out the idea of the original position, how are we to direct the parties to proceed?

54.2. The second part of the argument concerns the question of the stability of justice as fairness. This is the question whether justice as fairness is able to generate sufficient support for itself (§25.5).[1] The parties are to ask whether people who grow up in a society well ordered by the two principles of justice—the principles adopted in the first part of the argument—acquire a sufficiently strong and effective sense of justice so that they normally comply with just arrangements and are not moved to act otherwise, say, by social envy and spite, or by a will to dominate or a tendency to submit. If they do acquire a sufficiently strong sense of justice and are not swayed to the contrary by those special attitudes, then the outcome of the first part of the argument is confirmed and the argument for the two principles is complete.

By splitting the argument into two parts, we postpone the discussion of the special psychologies until the principles of justice are selected on the basis of the fundamental interests of persons as free and equal citizens. Once that is done those principles, when realized in the basic structure, provide the institutional background the parties need to estimate how likely it is that citizens who grow up within that background will be swayed by destabilizing special attitudes. This two-part argument removes the difficulty.

Together with the discussion of the special psychologies, the second part must take up the question whether in view of the general facts that characterize a democracy's political culture, and in particular the fact of reasonable pluralism, the political conception can be the focus of an overlapping consensus.[2] We will consider how the question of stability leads to the idea of an overlapping consensus on a political conception of justice. The social unity of a constitutional regime is seen to rest on such a consensus and this enables us to complete the discussion of stability—so far as we can go into it here—by giving a brief account of a reasonable moral psychology and of the good of political society.

54.3. We begin by recalling the idea of the domain of the political and of justice as fairness as a free-standing view. It is clear from the three features of a political conception (§9.1) that justice as fairness is such a conception

---

1. Note that stability as defined here is a property of a conception of justice, and not a property of a scheme of institutions. The latter is a different though not unrelated topic.

2. [See *Political Liberalism*, p. 141.]

and is not applied moral philosophy. Its principles, standards, and values are not the result of applying an already elaborated and independent religious, philosophical, or moral doctrine, comprehensive in scope and general in range. Rather, it formulates a family of highly significant (moral) values that properly apply to the basic structure of society. These are the political values: they arise in virtue of certain special features of the political relationship, as distinct from other relationships.

The political relationship we characterize as having at least two significant distinctive features.

First, it is a relationship of persons within the basic structure of society, a structure of basic institutions we enter only by birth and exit only by death (or so we may appropriately assume).[3] Political society is closed, as it were; and we do not, and indeed cannot, enter or leave it voluntarily.

Second, political power is, of course, always coercive power backed by the state's machinery for enforcing its laws. But in a constitutional regime political power is also the power of equal citizens as a collective body: it is regularly imposed on citizens as individuals, some of whom may not accept the reasons widely believed to justify the general structure of political authority (the constitution); or when they do accept that structure, they may not regard as well grounded many of the laws enacted by the legislature to which they are subject.

Political liberalism holds, then, that there is a distinctive domain of the political identified by these features (among others) to which certain values, specified in an appropriate way, characteristically apply. So understood, the political is distinct from the associational, say, which is voluntary in ways that the political is not; it is also distinct from the familial and the personal, which are affectional, again in ways the political is not. (The associational, the familial, and the personal are simply three examples of the nonpolitical; there are others.)

54.4. Taking the political as a distinctive domain, let us say that a political conception formulating its basic characteristic values is a free-standing view. This means two things: first, that it is framed to apply in the first in-

---

3. The appropriateness of this assumption rests in part on a point made in §26.5: namely, that the right of emigration does not make the acceptance of political authority voluntary in the way that freedom of thought and liberty of conscience make the acceptance of ecclesiastical authority voluntary. This brings out a further feature of the domain of the political, one that distinguishes it from the associational.

stance to the basic structure of society alone;[4] and second, that it formulates the characteristic political values without drawing on, or mentioning, independent nonpolitical values. A political conception does not deny that there are other values applying to the associational, the familial, and the personal; nor does it say that political values are entirely separate from, or unrelated to, those values. In §11 we introduced the idea that the problem of stability in a democratic society leads us to specify a political conception of justice and the domain of the political so as to make it possible for a political conception to be the focus of an overlapping consensus: that is, to gain the support of at least the reasonable comprehensive doctrines that endure and gain adherents over time. Otherwise, the institutions of a constitutional regime will not be secure.

Thus as a form of political liberalism, justice as fairness holds that, with regard to the constitutional essentials and questions of basic justice, and given the existence of a reasonably well ordered constitutional regime, the family of basic political values expressed by its principles and ideals have sufficient weight to override all other values that may normally come into conflict with them. It also holds, again with respect to constitutional essentials, that so far as possible, questions about those essentials are best settled by appeal to those political values alone. It is on those questions that agreement among those who affirm opposing comprehensive doctrines is most urgent.

54.5. These convictions clearly imply some relation between political and other values. Thus if it is said that outside the church there is no salvation,[5] and hence a constitutional regime cannot be accepted, we must make some reply. From the point of view of political liberalism, the appropriate reply is that such a doctrine is unreasonable:[6] it proposes to use the public's political power—a power in which all citizens have an equal share—forcibly to impose a view affecting constitutional essentials about which many citizens as reasonable persons, given what we have called the burdens of judgment (§11.4–5), are bound to differ uncompromisingly.

This reply does not say that the doctrine *extra ecclesia nulla salus* is not true. Rather, it says that it is unreasonable of any citizen, or citizens as

4. The extension of justice as fairness to the just relations between nation-states is discussed in *The Law of Peoples*.

5. So said Boniface VIII in his famous bull *Unam Sanctam* of 1302.

6. For clarity on this point I owe thanks to Wilfried Hinsch and Peter de Marneffe.

members of an association, to insist on using the public's (coercive) political power—the power of citizens as equals—to impose what they view as the implications of that doctrine upon other citizens. A reply from within a comprehensive view—the kind of reply we should like to avoid in discussing constitutional essentials—might say that the doctrine is untrue and rests on a misapprehension of the divine nature. If we do reject as unreasonable the state's enforcing a doctrine, we may of course also regard that doctrine as untrue. There may be no way to avoid implying its lack of truth, even when considering constitutional essentials.

Note, however, that in saying it is unreasonable to enforce a doctrine, it is not necessary that we also reject it as incorrect. Quite the contrary: it is vital to the idea of political liberalism that we may with perfect consistency hold that it would be unreasonable to use political power to enforce our own comprehensive religious, philosophical, or moral view, which we must, of course, affirm as true or reasonable (or as not unreasonable).

## §55. The Question of Stability

55.1. We said that the argument for the two principles is presented in two parts. In the first part the parties' aim is to select the principles that best secure the good of the persons they represent, their fundamental interests, leaving aside the special psychologies. Only with the principles of justice provisionally on hand do the parties take up, in the second part, the question of stability. They now consider the special psychologies by checking whether those who grow up under just institutions (as the principles adopted specify them) will develop a sufficiently firm sense of justice with respect to those attitudes and inclinations. This aspect of the question is addressed in *Theory*, where §§80–81 illustrate the kind of discussion needed. I would not change them substantially for our purposes. What is said below in §§59–60 supplements that account.

More important for us, now that justice as fairness is seen as a political conception, is that the parties must also consider whether the principles adopted, and the conception to which they belong, can gain the support of the diversity of reasonable comprehensive doctrines bound to exist in a well-ordered democratic society. It is at this point that we introduce the idea of an overlapping consensus: a consensus in which the same political conception is endorsed by the opposing reasonable comprehensive doctrines that gain a significant body of adherents and endure from one generation to the next.

In describing the second part of the argument, let us agree that a political conception must be practicable, fall under the art of the possible. This contrasts with a moral conception that is not political: a moral conception may condemn the world and human nature as too corrupt to be moved by its precepts and ideals.

55.2. There are, however, two ways in which a political conception may be concerned with stability.[7] In one we suppose that stability is a purely practical matter: if a conception fails to be stable, it is futile to try to realize it. Perhaps we think there are two separate tasks: one is to work out a political conception that seems sound, or reasonable, at least to us; the other is to find ways to bring others who may now reject it to share it, or failing that, to act in accordance with it, if need be prompted by penalties enforced by state power. As long as the means of persuasion or enforcement can be found, the conception is viewed as stable; it is not utopian in the pejorative sense.

But as a liberal conception, justice as fairness is concerned with stability in a different way. Finding a stable conception is not simply a matter of avoiding futility. Rather, what counts is the kind of stability, the nature of the forces that secure it. The idea is that, given certain assumptions specifying a reasonable human psychology and the normal conditions of human life, those who grow up under just basic institutions—institutions that justice as fairness itself enjoins—acquire a reasoned and informed allegiance to those institutions sufficient to render them stable. Put another way: citizens' sense of justice, given their character and interests as formed by living under a just basic structure, is strong enough to resist the normal tendencies to injustice. Citizens act willingly to give one another justice over time. Stability is secured by sufficient motivation of the appropriate kind acquired under just institutions.

The kind of stability required of justice as fairness is based, then, on its being a liberal political view, one that aims to be acceptable to citizens as reasonable and rational, as well as free and equal, and so as addressed to their public reason. We have seen how this feature of liberalism connects with the feature of political power in a constitutional regime: namely, that it is the power of equal citizens as a collective body. It follows that if justice as fairness were not expressly designed to gain the reasoned support of citi-

7. In this and the next several paragraphs I am indebted to helpful discussions with T. M. Scanlon.

zens who affirm reasonable though conflicting comprehensive doctrines—the existence of such conflicting doctrines being a feature of the kind of public culture that conception itself sustains—it would not be liberal.

55.3. The point, then, is that, as a liberal conception, justice as fairness must not only avoid futility, but also the explanation of why it is practicable must be of the right kind. The problem of stability is not that of bringing others who reject a conception to share it, or to act in accordance with it, by workable sanctions, if necessary, as if the task were to find ways to impose that conception once we are convinced it is sound. Rather, as a liberal political conception, justice as fairness is not reasonable in the first place unless it generates its own support in a suitable way by addressing each citizen's reason, as explained within its own framework.[8] Only so is it an account of political legitimacy as opposed to an account of how those who hold political power can satisfy themselves in the light of their own convictions that they are acting properly. A liberal conception of political legitimacy aims for a public basis of justification and appeals to free public reason, and hence to citizens viewed as reasonable and rational.

55.4. The idea of an overlapping consensus was not used in *Theory*.[9] That work never discusses whether justice as fairness is meant as a comprehensive moral doctrine or as a political conception of justice. In one place (*Theory*, §3: 15) it says that if justice as fairness succeeds reasonably well, a next step would be to study the more general view suggested by the name "rightness as fairness." There is, though, no mention of the distinction between a political conception and a comprehensive doctrine. The reader might reasonably conclude that justice as fairness is set out as part of a comprehensive view that might be developed later were success to invite.

This conclusion is supported by the account of a well-ordered society in Part III of *Theory*. There the members of any well-ordered society, whether it be that of justice as fairness or of some other view, accept not only the same conception of justice but also the same comprehensive doctrine of which that conception is a part, or from which it can be derived. See, for

8. The force of the phrase "within its own framework" as used in the text is expressed by the two parts of the argument from the original position. Both parts are carried out within the same framework and subject to the same conditions included in the original position as a device of representation.

9. The term is used once, *Theory*, §59: 340, but for a different purpose than my present one.

example, the discussion of the relative stability of justice as fairness and utilitarianism (*Theory, §76*). In the latter case, the members of the associated well-ordered society are said to affirm the utilitarian view, which is by its nature (unless expressly restricted) a comprehensive doctrine (*Theory, §76*: 436–440).

55.5. As we said in §11.1, the idea of an overlapping consensus[10] is used to enable us to think of the well-ordered society of justice as fairness in a more realistic way. Given the free institutions that conception enjoins, we can no longer assume that citizens generally, even if they accept justice as fairness as a political conception, also accept the particular comprehensive view to which it might seem in *Theory* to belong.

We now assume that citizens hold two distinct views; or perhaps better, their overall view has two parts: one part can be seen to be, or to coincide with, a political conception of justice; the other part is a (fully or partially) comprehensive doctrine to which the political conception is in some manner related. The political conception may be simply a part of, or an adjunct to, a partially comprehensive view; or it may be endorsed because it can be derived within a fully articulated comprehensive doctrine. It is left to citizens individually to decide for themselves in what way their shared political conception is related to their more comprehensive views.

Thus we now say: a society is well ordered by justice as fairness so long as, first, citizens who affirm reasonable comprehensive doctrines generally endorse justice as fairness as giving the content of their political judgments; and second, unreasonable comprehensive doctrines do not gain enough currency to compromise the essential justice of basic institutions. This is a better and no longer utopian way of thinking of the well-ordered society of justice as fairness. It corrects the view in *Theory,* which fails to allow for the condition of pluralism to which its own principles lead.

Moreover, because justice as fairness is a free-standing political conception (§54.3) that articulates fundamental political and constitutional values, endorsing it involves far less than is contained in a comprehensive doctrine. Taking such a well-ordered society as the aim of reform and change seems not altogether impracticable: under the reasonably favorable conditions that make a constitutional regime possible, that aim is a reasonable guide and may be in good part realized. By contrast, a free democratic society well ordered by any comprehensive doctrine, religious or secular, is surely

---

10. The idea is first introduced in "Justice as Fairness: Political Not Metaphysical," §VI.

utopian in the pejorative sense. Achieving it would in any case require the oppressive use of state power. This is as true of the liberalism of rightness as fairness, as it is of the Christianity of Aquinas or Luther.

## §56. Is Justice as Fairness Political in the Wrong Way?

56.1. We now check that the idea of an overlapping consensus does not make justice as fairness political in the wrong way. Everyday ideas about consensus politics and how to achieve consensus have misleading connotations. We need to be clear that these connotations are not involved in our very different idea of an overlapping consensus.

For a political conception to avoid being political in the wrong way, it must formulate a free-standing view of the very great (moral) values applying to the political relationship. It must also set out a public basis of justification for free institutions in a manner accessible to public reason. By contrast, a political conception is political in the wrong way when it is framed as a workable compromise between known and existing political interests, or when it looks to particular comprehensive doctrines presently existing in society and then tailors itself to win their allegiance.

56.2. Our use of the idea of an overlapping consensus arises thus: we suppose a constitutional democratic regime to be reasonably just and workable, and worth defending. Yet given the fact of reasonable pluralism, how can we frame our defense of it so that it might win wide support and thus achieve sufficient stability?

To this end, we do not look to the comprehensive doctrines that in fact exist and then draw up a political conception that strikes some kind of balance of forces between them. To illustrate: in specifying a list of primary goods,[11] say, we could proceed in two ways. We could look at the various comprehensive doctrines actually found in society and develop an index of such goods that is near to those doctrines' center of gravity, so to speak. That is, we would seek a kind of average of what those who affirmed those views would demand by way of institutional rights and claims and all-purpose means. Doing this might seem the best way to ensure that the index provides the basic elements necessary to advance the conceptions of the

---

11. The idea of primary goods is introduced in *Political Liberalism*, lect. II, §5.3, and discussed in some detail in lect. V, §§3-4.

good associated with existing doctrines and thus to improve the likelihood of actually securing an overlapping consensus.

56.3. This is not how justice as fairness proceeds; and to do so would make it political in the wrong way. Instead, it elaborates a political conception as a free-standing view working from the fundamental idea of society as a fair system of cooperation and its companion ideas. Our hope is that this idea, with its index of primary goods arrived at from within it, can be the focus of a reasonable overlapping consensus. We leave aside comprehensive doctrines that now exist, have existed, or might exist. The thought is not that primary goods are fair to comprehensive conceptions of the good associated with such doctrines by striking a fair balance among them, but rather that it is fair to free and equal citizens as those persons whose conceptions of the good they are.

The problem is how to frame a conception of justice for a constitutional regime such that those who support, or who might be brought to support, that kind of regime might also endorse the political conception, despite differences in their comprehensive views. This leads to the idea of a political conception of justice, starting from the fundamental ideas of a democratic society and presupposing no particular wider doctrine. We put no doctrinal obstacles to its winning the support of a reasonable and enduring overlapping consensus.

## §57. How Is Political Liberalism Possible?

57.1. The question now arises as to how, as we have specified it, political liberalism is possible. That is, how can the values of a distinctive domain of the political—a subdomain of the realm of all values—normally outweigh whatever values may conflict with them? Or, put another way: how can we affirm a comprehensive doctrine as true or reasonable and yet hold that it would not be reasonable to use the state's power to require others' acceptance of it or compliance with the special laws it might sanction?

The answer to this question has two complementary parts. The first part says that the characteristic values of the political are very great values and hence not easily overridden: these values govern the basic framework of social life—the very groundwork of our existence[12]—and specify the fundamental terms of political and social cooperation. In justice as fairness some

---

12. The phrase is from J. S. Mill, *Utilitarianism,* chap. 5, par. 25.

of these great values are the values of justice expressed by the principles of justice for the basic structure: the values of equal political and civil liberty, fair equality of opportunity, and economic reciprocity as well as the social bases of citizens' self-respect.

Other great values fall under the values of public reason (§26), and are expressed in the guidelines for public inquiry and in the steps taken to secure that such inquiry is free and public, informed and reasonable. These values include not only the appropriate use of the fundamental concepts of judgment, inference, and evidence, but also the virtues of reasonableness and fair-mindedness as shown in adhering to the criteria and procedures of commonsense knowledge and the methods and conclusions of science when not controversial, and in respecting the precepts governing reasonable political discussion.

57.2. Together, the values of justice and of public reason express the liberal ideal that since political power is the coercive power of citizens as a corporate body—a power in which each has an equal share—this power is to be exercised, at least when constitutional essentials and questions of basic justice are at stake, only in ways that all citizens may reasonably be expected to endorse.

As we have seen, political liberalism tries, so far as possible, to present the account of these values as those of a distinctive domain—the political— as a free-standing view; and as values that can be understood and affirmed without presupposing any particular comprehensive doctrine. It is left to citizens individually as part of their liberty of conscience to settle how they think the great values of the political domain are related to the other values they accept. We hope that in political practice we can thereby firmly ground the constitutional essentials in political values alone and that these values will provide a workable shared basis of public justification.

57.3. The second part of the answer as to how political liberalism is possible complements the first. This second part says that the history of religion and philosophy shows that there are many reasonable ways in which the wider realm of values can be understood so as to be either congruent with, or supportive of, or else not in conflict with, the values appropriate to the special domain of the political as specified by a political conception of justice. History tells of a plurality of not unreasonable comprehensive doctrines and this makes an overlapping consensus possible. How this can happen is shown by a model case of an overlapping consensus.

This model case contains three views: one view affirms the political conception because its religious doctrine and account of free faith lead to a principle of toleration and support the basic liberties of a constitutional regime; the second view affirms the political conception on the basis of a comprehensive liberal moral doctrine such as that of Kant or J. S. Mill. The third is but a loosely articulated doctrine covering a large family of nonpolitical values in addition to the political values of a constitutional regime; and it holds that under the reasonably favorable conditions that make democracy possible, those political values normally outweigh whatever nonpolitical values may conflict with them. Only the first two views—the religious doctrine and the liberalisms of Kant and Mill—are quite general and comprehensive; the third is loose and not systematic, although under reasonably favorable conditions it is normally adequate for questions of political justice. The first two more fully articulated and systematic views agree with the judgments of the third in these matters.

57.4. When is a comprehensive doctrine reasonable? Without giving a full definition, a reasonable doctrine must recognize the burdens of judgment (§11.4–5) and so, among other political values, that of liberty of conscience. To explain: we have distinguished between the reasonable and the rational (§2.2; §23.2–3). These two ideas, we said, are essential elements in the idea of society viewed as a fair system of cooperation among citizens regarded as free and equal. In general, reasonable persons are ready to propose certain principles (as specifying fair terms of cooperation), as well as to comply with those principles even at the expense of their own interests as circumstances require, when others are moved to do likewise. Further, where the claims of those cooperating are similarly based in relevant respects, as when all have the status of free and equal citizens, there is no reason for any of them to accept principles that assign them lesser basic rights than the rest. Those who insist on imposing such principles on others, moved say by their greater power or stronger bargaining position, are being unreasonable, yet given their interests, they may be perfectly rational. Everyday speech reflects this contrast between the reasonable and the rational.

Turning to the present case, we view democratic citizens not only as free and equal but as reasonable and rational, all having an equal share in the corporate political power of society, and all equally subject to the burdens of judgment. There is, therefore, no reason why any citizen, or association of citizens, should have the right to use the state's power to favor a comprehensive doctrine, or to impose its implications on the rest. Given the grounds for the priority of liberty (§30), no citizen when fairly represented could grant to others the political authority to do that, and the parties as representatives reason accordingly. Any such authority is therefore without reason, contrary to persons' fundamental interests in developing and exercising their moral powers and in pursuing their particular (permissible) conceptions of the good. Reasonable comprehensive doctrines recognize this fact and with it that all have an equal liberty of conscience.

## §58. An Overlapping Consensus Not Utopian

58.1. It may be objected that the idea of an overlapping consensus is utopian: that is, that there are not sufficient political, social, or psychological forces either to bring about an overlapping consensus (when one does not exist), or to render one stable (should one exist). Here we can only touch on this intricate question, and I merely outline one way in which such a consensus on a liberal political conception much like justice as fairness might come about and its stability be made secure.

Let us suppose that at a certain time, as a result of various historical contingencies, the principles of a liberal conception—say those of justice as fairness—have come to be accepted as a mere modus vivendi, and that existing political institutions meet their requirements. This acceptance has come about, we may assume, in much the same way that the acceptance of the principle of toleration as a modus vivendi came about following the Reformation: at first reluctantly, but nevertheless as providing the only alternative to endless and destructive civil strife. Here I use the phrase "modus vivendi" in the usual way, as may be illustrated by a treaty between two states whose national interests put them at odds. In negotiating a treaty, each state would be wise and prudent to make sure that the treaty is drawn up in such a way that it is public knowledge that it is not advantageous for either state to violate it. Both states, however, are ready to pursue their goals at the expense of the other, and should conditions change they may do so.

That the same may be true of toleration is clear from the example of Catholics and Protestants in the sixteenth century. At that time, both held that it was the duty of the ruler to uphold the true religion and to repress the spread of heresy and false doctrine. In this case, the acceptance of the principle of toleration would indeed be a mere modus vivendi: should either faith become dominant, the principle of toleration would no longer be followed. What is essential for an overlapping consensus is stability with respect to the distribution of power: this requires that the political conception be affirmed by citizens irrespective of the political strength of their comprehensive view.

58.2. Our question, then, is this: how might it happen that over generations the initial acquiescence in justice as fairness as a modus vivendi could develop into a stable and enduring overlapping consensus? At this point a certain looseness in our comprehensive views, as well as their being not fully, but only partially comprehensive, may be particularly significant.[13] Let us ask: how far in practice does the allegiance to a political conception actually depend on its derivation from a comprehensive view? Consider three possibilities: (a) the political conception is derived from the comprehensive doctrine; (b) it is not derived from but is compatible with that doctrine; and last, (c) the political conception is incompatible with it.

In everyday life we have not usually decided, or even thought much about, which of these cases hold. To decide among them would raise highly complicated questions; and in practice we may not need to decide among them. Most people's religious, philosophical, and moral doctrines are not seen by them as fully general and comprehensive; generality and comprehensiveness admit of degree, and so does the extent to which a view is articulated and systematic. There is lots of slippage, so to speak, many ways for the political conception to cohere loosely with a (partially) comprehensive view, and many ways within the limits of a political conception to allow for the pursuit of different (partially) comprehensive doctrines.

This suggests that many if not most citizens come to affirm the public political conception without seeing any particular connection, one way or the other, between it and their other views. Hence it is possible for them first to affirm that conception on its own and to appreciate the public good it accomplishes in a democratic society. Should an incompatibility later be recognized between the political conception and their comprehensive doctrines, then they might very well adjust or revise the latter rather than reject the political conception. Note that here we distinguish between the initial allegiance to, or appreciation of, the political conception and the later adjustment or revision of comprehensive doctrines to which that allegiance or appreciation leads when inconsistencies arise. These adjustments or revisions we may suppose to take place slowly over time as the political conception shapes comprehensive views to cohere with it.

13. Here I elaborate an idea of Samuel Scheffler's stated in conversation.

58.3. We now ask: in virtue of what political values might justice as fairness gain allegiance to itself? An allegiance to institutions and to the conception that regulates them may, of course, be based in part on long-term self- and group-interests, custom and traditional attitudes, or simply on the desire to conform to what is expected and normally done. Widespread allegiance may also be encouraged by institutions securing for all citizens the political values included under what Hart calls the minimum content of natural law.[14] But here we are concerned with the further bases of allegiance generated by a liberal conception of justice.

At this point we simply recall §33, where we said that a liberal conception, in effectively regulating basic political institutions, meets the three essential requirements of a stable constitutional regime. First, it fixes, once and for all, the content of basic rights and liberties, takes those guarantees off the political agenda, and puts them beyond the calculus of social interests. Second, its form of reasoning is relatively clear and perspicuous, and reasonably reliable in its own terms;[15] and third, its conception of free public reason encourages the cooperative political virtues.

We conjecture, then, that as citizens come to appreciate what a liberal conception achieves, they acquire an allegiance to it, an allegiance that becomes stronger over time. They come to think it both reasonable and wise to affirm its principles of justice as expressing political values that, under the reasonably favorable conditions that make democracy possible, normally outweigh whatever values may oppose them. With this we have an overlapping consensus.

58.4. That an overlapping consensus is quite different from a modus vivendi is clear from the model case in §57.3: the case where the political conception is the focus of a consensus containing a religious doctrine of free faith, a liberalism of the kind of Kant or Mill, and a rather unsystematic view that includes a wide range of nonpolitical values along with the political values of justice as fairness. In this example, note two features: first, the

14. See Hart's *The Concept of Law,* pp. 189–195, for what he calls the minimum content of natural law. I assume that a liberal conception includes (as do many other familiar conceptions) this minimum content; and so in the text I focus on the bases of the allegiance such a conception generates in virtue of the distinctive content of its principles.

15. Here the phrase "in its own terms" means that we are not at present concerned with whether the conception in question is true, or reasonable (as the case may be), but with how easily its principles and standards can be correctly understood and reliably applied in public discussion.

focus of consensus, the political conception of justice, is itself a moral conception. And second, it is affirmed on moral grounds, that is, it includes conceptions of society and of citizens as persons, as well as principles of justice, and an account of the cooperative virtues through which those principles are embodied in human character and expressed in public life.

An overlapping consensus, therefore, is not merely a consensus on accepting certain authorities, or on complying with certain institutional arrangements, based on a contingent, or historical, convergence of self- or group-interests. All three views in the model case support from within themselves the political conception: each recognizes its concepts, principles, and virtues as the shared content through which their several views coincide. The fact that those who affirm the political conception start from within their own comprehensive view, and hence organize their doctrine using different premises and grounds, does not make their affirming it any less religious, philosophical, or moral, as the case may be.

The preceding two features of an overlapping consensus (moral focus and moral grounds) connect with a third and essential feature, that of stability: that is, those who affirm the various views supporting the political conception will not withdraw their support of it should the relative strength of their view in society increase and eventually become dominant. So long as the three views are affirmed and not revised, the political conception will still be supported regardless of shifts in the distribution of political power; this in contrast with the case of Catholic and Protestant in the sixteenth century. Each view supports the political conception on its merits. The test for this is whether the consensus is stable with respect to changes in the distribution of power among views. This feature of stability highlights a basic contrast between an overlapping consensus and a modus vivendi, the stability of which does depend on that distribution.

## §59. A Reasonable Moral Psychology

59.1. We have just seen how an initial acquiescence in a liberal conception of justice as a modus vivendi may change over time into a stable overlapping consensus. This real possibility is all we need show in reply to the objection that the idea of such a consensus is utopian. However, to confirm this possibility, I sketch, necessarily only briefly, the main psychological assumptions underlying the preceding account of how political allegiance is generated. This leads to what we may think of as a reasonable moral psychology; indeed, a psychology of the reasonable itself. This name is appropriate since the idea of reciprocity appears both as a principle giving its content and as a disposition to answer in kind. And recall that the basis of equality at the highest level (§39.2) is simply the capacity to be both reasonable and rational. In short: the reasonable generates itself and answers itself in kind. It is not alone among dispositions is this respect. What makes it unique is its tie with reason.

The assumptions of this psychology essentially state that persons are capable of being reasonable and rational, and of engaging in fair social cooperation. Thus:

(1) In line with the (political) conception of the person with the two moral powers, citizens have a capacity for a conception of the good and a capacity to acquire conceptions of justice and to act as these conceptions require. In short, they have a capacity to be both reasonable and rational.

(2) When they believe that institutions or social practices are just, or fair (as specified, say, by principles they would themselves, when fairly represented, be prepared to propose or to acknowledge), citizens are ready and willing to do their part in those arrangements provided they have sufficient assurance that others will also do theirs. This belongs to the reasonable as we have specified it beginning in §2.2.

(3) When others with evident intention[16] do their part in just or fair institutions, citizens tend to develop trust and confidence in them. This tendency to answer in kind, to answer others' being fair to us with our being fair to them, and the like, is an element of the psychology of the reasonable. In the account in *Theory* of the three-stage development of the morality of principles (as it is called there), the psychological laws for each stage exhibit this reciprocity of disposition.[17]

(4) The trust and confidence (noted in (3)) grow stronger and more complete as the success of shared cooperative arrangements is sustained over a longer time; and they also grow stronger and more complete when the basic institutions framed to secure fundamental interests (for example, the basic rights and liberties) are more willingly and steadfastly recognized in public political life.

16. The idea of evident intention as used here is from Rousseau's *Emile*, see *Theory*, §70, n. 9.

17. See *Theory*, §70: 405f.; §71: 411f.; §72: 414f.; §75: 433. The moral psychology behind the assumptions as described in the text is given in considerably more detail in *Theory*, chap. VIII, §§70–72, 75–76. I simply refer to those sections as I would not change them substantially. What is essential is to see their role in (the second part of) the argument for the principles of justice as a whole.

(5) We may also suppose that everyone recognizes what I have called the historical and social conditions of modern democratic societies: (i) the fact of reasonable pluralism and (ii) the fact of its permanence, as well as (iii) the fact that this pluralism can be overcome only by the oppressive use of state power. These conditions are a shared historical situation. In this situation it is unreasonable not to recognize (iv) the fact of the burdens of judgment and to acknowledge that all are equally subject to them together with the full consequences of this (§57.4).

(6) Also part of the historical and social conditions of democracy are (v) the fact of moderate scarcity and (vi) the fact of there being numerous possibilities of gains from well-organized social cooperation, provided it can be established on fair terms. These last two facts and the four general facts specify the circumstances of political justice (§24).

59.2. We can now enlarge upon our answer to the question: how might an overlapping consensus on a liberal conception of justice develop from its acceptance as a mere modus vivendi? Recall our assumption that the comprehensive doctrines of most people are not fully comprehensive, and that this allows scope for the development of an independent allegiance to a liberal conception once the way it works is appreciated. This independent allegiance in turn leads people to act with evident intention in accordance with liberal arrangements, since they have reasonable assurance (founded in part on past experience) that others will also comply with them. Gradually over time, as the success of political cooperation continues, citizens come to have increasing trust and confidence in one another.

The discovery of a new social possibility: the possibility of a reasonably harmonious and stable pluralist and democratic society, may follow from this success of liberal institutions. Before the successful practice of toleration in societies with liberal institutions there was no way of knowing of that possibility. It may seem more natural to believe, as centuries-long acceptance of intolerance appeared to confirm, that social unity and concord require agreement on a general and comprehensive religious, philosophical, or moral doctrine. Intolerance was seen as a condition of social order and stability.[18] The weakening of that belief helps to clear the way for free institutions.

To conclude: precisely because it is not general and comprehensive, a

---

18. Hume remarks on this in par. 6 of "Liberty of the Press" (1741). See also A. G. Dickens, *The English Reformation* (Glasgow: Fontana Press, 1967), pp. 440f.

political conception of justice (taking justice as fairness as an example) may encourage the eventual development of a mere modus vivendi into an over-lapping consensus. The conception's limited scope together with the loose-ness of our comprehensive doctrines allows leeway for it to gain an initial allegiance to itself and thereby to shape those doctrines accordingly as con-flicts arise, a process that takes place gradually over generations (assuming a reasonable moral psychology). Religions that once rejected toleration may come to accept it and to affirm a doctrine of free faith; the comprehensive liberalisms of Kant and Mill, while viewed as suitable for nonpublic life and as possible bases for affirming a constitutional regime, are no longer pro-posed as political conceptions of justice. On this account an overlapping consensus is not a happy coincidence, even if aided, as it no doubt must be, by great historical good fortune. Rather, it is in part the work of society's public tradition of political thought in developing a practicable political conception of justice.

## §60. The Good of Political Society

60.1. Having understood how the question of stability calls for the idea of an overlapping consensus, we now take up an aspect of stability con-nected with the good of a political society well ordered by the two princi-ples of justice. This good is realized by citizens, both as persons and as a corporate body, when they act to uphold a just constitutional regime.[19]

Let us begin by examining the objection that because it is not based on a comprehensive religious, philosophical, or moral doctrine, justice as fair-ness abandons the ideal of a political community and views society as so many distinct individuals, or distinct associations, cooperating solely to pursue their own personal, or associational, advantage without having any final ends in common. (Here a final end is understood as an end valued or wanted for its own sake and not solely as a means to something else.) It is sometimes objected that, as a contract doctrine, justice as fairness is an in-dividualistic view and sees political institutions as purely instrumental to individual or associational ends, as the institutions of, let's say, a private so-ciety. In this case, political society itself is not a good, but at best a means to individual or associational good.

In reply, justice as fairness does indeed abandon the ideal of political

19. This good is the fifth conception of the good so far discussed. For the preceding four, see §43.2. On the sixth conception of the good see note 22.

community if by that ideal is meant a political society united on one (partially or fully) comprehensive religious, philosophical, or moral doctrine. That conception of social unity is excluded by the fact of reasonable pluralism. It is no longer a political possibility for those who accept the basic liberties and the principle of toleration that is basic to democratic institutions. We must view social unity in a different way: as deriving from an overlapping consensus on a political conception of justice. As we have seen, in such a consensus this political conception is affirmed by citizens who hold different and conflicting comprehensive doctrines, and they affirm it from within their own distinct views.

60.2. Recall (from §3) that to say a society is well ordered by a conception of justice means three things: (1) that it is a society in which all citizens accept, and acknowledge before one another that they accept, the same principles of justice; (2) that its basic structure, its main political and social institutions and the way they hang together as one system of cooperation, is publicly known, or with good reason believed, to satisfy those principles; and (3) that citizens have a normally effective sense of justice, that is, one that enables them to understand and to apply the principles of justice, and for the most part to act from them as their circumstances require. Social unity so understood is the most desirable conception of unity available to us: it is the limit of the practical best.

A well-ordered society, as thus specified, is not, then, a private society; for citizens do have final ends in common. While it is true that they do not affirm the same comprehensive doctrine, they do affirm the same political conception; and this means that they share one basic political end, and one with high priority: namely, the end of supporting just institutions and giving one another justice accordingly, not to mention the other ends they must also share and realize through their political cooperation. Moreover, in a well-ordered society the end of political justice is among citizens' most basic aims by reference to which they express the kind of person they want to be.[20]

From this last remark it follows that a political society is a community if

---

20. If we use the term "identity" in a manner now common, we can say that the shared final end of giving one another justice may be part of citizens' identity. See Amy Gutmann, "Communitarian Critics of Liberalism," *Philosophy and Public Affairs* 14 (Summer 1985): 308–322. At p. 311n, Gutmann is surely right in saying that our commitment to treat other citizens as equals, and therefore to respect their freedom of religion, say, may be just as elemental a part of our identity as our affirming a particular religion and fulfilling its practices.

we now mean by a community a society, including a political society, the members of which—in this case citizens—share certain final ends to which they give very high priority, so much so that in stating before themselves the kind of person they want to be they count their having these ends as essential. Of course, nothing turns on these definitions of community alone; they are simply verbal stipulations. What is vital is that the well-ordered society specified by the political conception of justice characterizes citizens as having shared final ends of the requisite kind.

60.3. Together with other assumptions made, these shared final ends provide the basis for the good of a well-ordered society. We regard citizens as having the two moral powers, and the basic rights and liberties of a constitutional regime are to assure that everyone can adequately develop these powers and exercise them fully over the course of a complete life as they so decide. Under normal circumstances, then, we suppose those moral powers to be developed and exercised within institutions of political freedom and liberty of conscience, and their exercise to be supported and sustained by the social bases of self-respect.

These matters granted, the well-ordered society of justice as fairness is a good in two ways. In the first way it is a good for persons individually, and this for two reasons. One reason is that the exercise of the two moral powers is experienced as good. This is a consequence of the moral psychology used in justice as fairness.[21] That their exercise may be an important good, and will be one for many people, is clear from the central role of these powers in the political conception of persons as citizens. We view citizens, for the purposes of political justice, as normal and fully cooperating members of society over a complete life, and thus as having the moral powers that enable them to assume this role. In this context we might say: part of the essential nature of citizens (within the political conception) is their having the two moral powers that are the root of their capacity to engage in fair social cooperation. A second reason political society is a good for citizens is that it secures for them the good of justice and the social bases of mutual- and self-respect. Thus, in securing the equal basic rights, liberties and fair opportunities, political society guarantees persons public recognition of their status as free and equal. In securing these things political society answers to their fundamental needs.

21. In *Theory* this psychology uses the so-called Aristotelian principle (see §65); other views might adopt different principles to reach much the same conclusion.

The good involved in the exercise of the moral powers and in the public recognition of persons' status as citizens belongs to the political good of a well-ordered society and not to that of a comprehensive doctrine. Repeatedly we must insist on this distinction, even though a comprehensive doctrine may endorse this good from within its own point of view. Otherwise we lose sight of the path justice as fairness must follow if it is to gain the support of an overlapping consensus. As we have stressed, the priority of right does not mean that ideas of the good must be avoided; that is impossible (§43.1). Rather, it means that the ideas used must be political ideas: they must be tailored to meet the restrictions imposed by the political conception of justice and fit into the space it allows.

60.4. A well-ordered political society is also good in a second way. For whenever there is a shared final end, the achievement of which calls on the cooperation of many, the good realized is social: it is realized through citizens' joint activity in mutual dependence on the appropriate actions being taken by others. Establishing and successfully maintaining reasonably just (though of course always imperfect) democratic institutions over a long period of time, perhaps gradually reforming them over generations, though not, to be sure, without lapses, is a great social good and appreciated as such. This is shown by the fact that a democratic people esteem it as one of the significant achievements of their history.

That there should be such political and social goods is no more mysterious than that members of an orchestra, or players on a team, or even both teams in a game, should take pleasure and a certain (proper) pride in a good performance, or in a good play of the game, one they will want to remember.[22] No doubt the requisite conditions become more difficult to satisfy as societies become larger and the social distance between citizens becomes greater, but these differences, as great and inhibiting as they may be, do not affect the psychological principle involved in realizing the good of justice in a well-ordered political society. Moreover, this good can be highly significant even when the conditions for realizing it are quite imperfect; and the sense of its loss can also be highly significant. A democratic people's pride in distinguishing themselves from nondemocratic peoples makes this clear, as does their concern to distance themselves from periods of their history in which injustice may have prevailed. But these reflections I shall not

22. Here I hint at the idea of the good of political society as a social union of social unions. See §43.2 and *Theory*, §79.

pursue. We need not establish how great a good is political good, only that it is a significant good, and one that fits within the political conception.

To see this, recall the public character of this good. For at the stage of the morality of principles ((3) of §59.1 above), each citizen of a well-ordered society recognizes the others as also affirming the principles of justice. Hence each also recognizes that all citizens give high priority to the end of cooperating politically with one another on terms that the representative of each would endorse in a situation in which they are all fairly represented as free and equal, and reasonable and rational (*Theory*, §72: 418f.). Put another way, citizens want to cooperate politically with one another in ways that satisfy the liberal principle of legitimacy: that is, on terms that can be publicly justified to all in the light of shared political values.

It remains only to point out the relation between citizens' seeing their political society as good and its stability. The more they see their political society as good for themselves both as a corporate body and as individuals, and the greater their appreciation of the political conception in securing the three essentials of a stable regime, the less they will be prompted by the special attitudes of envy, spite, the will to dominate, and the temptation to deprive others of justice. As this was put in *Theory:* the question is whether the just and the good are congruent. *Theory*, §86, argues that those who grow up in a society well ordered by justice as fairness, who have a rational plan of life, and who also know, or reasonably believe, that everyone else has an effective sense of justice, have sufficient reason founded on their good (rather than on justice) to comply with just institutions. This is not to say that they do not also have reasons of justice so to act.

A well-ordered society is stable, then, because citizens are satisfied, all things considered, with the basic structure of their society. The considerations that move them are not perceived threats or dangers from outside forces but are given in terms of the political conception they all affirm. For in the well-ordered society of justice as fairness, the just and the good (as specified by that political conception) fit together in such a way that citizens who count as part of their good being reasonable and rational and being seen by others as such, are moved by reasons of their good to do what justice requires. Among these reasons is the good of political society itself in the ways we have discussed.

# Index

Abortion, 117

Abstract conceptions: role of, 8

Allocative justice: defined, 50; incompatible with justice as fairness, 50; and utilitarianism, 50; vs. background justice, 50–51, 170–171. *See also* Fair system of cooperation

Aquinas, St. Thomas, 188

Aristotelianism, 142–143

Aristotelian principle, 200n

Associations: vs. political society, 4, 11, 20, 94, 182; bound indirectly by principles of justice, 10–11, 164–166; nonpublic reason of, 92; membership voluntary, 93, 144, 182

Background justice, 10, 54, 118; vs. allocative justice, 50–51, 170–171; to ensure fairness over time, 51–55, 139–140, 156; and institutional division of labor, 54; and contingencies in life-prospects, 55–57; as ideal social process, 57; limits to unequal distributions not specified, 68. *See also* Basic structure of society; Ideal social process view

Barry, Brian, 43n5, 69n37, 71

Basic liberties. *See* Equal basic liberties

Basic structure of society: defined, 4, 8–9, 10, 199; as primary subject of justice, 10, 12, 39–40, 52, 163, 182–183; as fundamen-

tal idea, 10, 14; and background justice, 10, 159; includes family, 10, 162–166; no sharp boundaries of, 11, 57; and overlapping consensus, 12; and first feature of political conception, 12, 26–27, 33; two roles, 48, 49; requires regulation over time, 52–55; profound influence on citizens, 55–57; assessed from certain standard points of view, 65

Bentham, Jeremy, 50

Berlin, Isaiah: no social world without loss, 36n26, 154n; his liberalism, 143, 144; negative vs. positive liberties, 177n61

Boniface VIII, 183n5

Broome, John, 69n37

Buchanan, Allen, 58n24

Buchanan, James, 16n, 97

Burdens of judgment, 35–37, 183, 191, 197

Capabilities, basic vs. primary goods, 168–170

Capitalism: conflicts with justice as fairness, 8n; welfare-state vs. property-owning democracy, 8n, 135–136, 139–140; violates two principles of justice, 136–137; does not recognize principle of reciprocity, 138; and worker-managed firms, 178

Catholics vs. Protestants in sixteenth century, 192, 195

Children. *See* Education; Family

Circumstances of justice: objective, 84; subjective, 84; reasonably favorable conditions, 101; and historical and social conditions of democratic societies, 197

Citizens: as free and equal, 4, 5, 18–24; taking seriously freedom and equality of, 4, 79, 140; abstract conception of, 8; equality of, 18, 20, 21, 49, 87, 132, 146, 196; fundamental interests and moral powers of, 18–21, 45, 85, 112–114, 169, 192, 200; conception of comes from public political culture, 19; political not metaphysical conception of, 19; freedom of has two aspects, 21–24; public vs. moral identity, 22–23, 199–200; and changes of moral identity, 22–23; as self-authenticating sources of claims, 23–24; can play a role in social life, 24; conception of is normative not biological or psychological, 24; affirm two distinct views, 33, 187; equality of requires difference principle, 49, 71, 76; do not suffer from special psychologies, 88–89, 202; equality of in social contract tradition vs. utilitarianism, 96; fundamental interests of secured by two principles, 102–110, 170, 200; fundamental interests vs. actual preferences, 107, 141; fundamental interests have priority, 110; fundamental interests and basic liberties, 112–113, 200; and principle of restricted utility, 122; and medical care, 173–175; have public identity over a complete life, 174; share certain final ends, 199–200, 202; and good of political society, 200–202; have sufficient reason to comply with just institutions, 202. *See also* Moral powers, two; Primary goods

Citizenship, ideal of, 92, 117

Civic humanism, 142–144

Civic republicanism, 146n, 150

Civility, duty of, 90, 92, 117. *See also* Virtues

Classical republicanism, 142–144

Cohen, Joshua, 43n3, 53n20, 58n24, 100n21, 165n46

Community vs. democratic society, 3, 198–200. *See also* Political society

Comprehensive doctrines: reasonable pluralism of, 9, 15, 25, 32, 60; defined, 14, 19; vs. political conception, 14, 181–182; and public justification, 28–29; fully vs. partially, 33, 60, 197; and public reason, 90, 117; freely accepted, 93; and constitutional essentials, 153–154, 184; when unreasonable, 183; not distinguished in *Theory*, 186–187; when reasonable, 191–192. *See also* Kant, Immanuel; Mill, J. S.; Overlapping consensus; Political conception of justice; Political liberalism; Utilitarianism

Conscription, 47

Considered judgments: defined, 29; made at all levels of generality, 30; use in selecting principles of justice, 41–42. *See also* Original position; Reflective equilibrium

Constant, Benjamin, 2, 143, 144

Constitution: guided by first principle of justice, 46. *See also* Constitutional essentials

Constitutional essentials: examples of, 28; settled by appeal to political conception of justice, 28, 32, 41, 183, 190; and political legitimacy, 41; and basic liberties, 46, 151; covered by first principle, 47; includes social minimum, 47–48; vs. difference principle, 48–49, 162; and loyal opposition, 49; vs. institutions of distributive justice, 49; and public reason, 91; and abortion, 117; and perfectionist values, 152; and comprehensive views, 153–154, 184

Dahl, Robert A., 13n12

Daniels, Norman, 148n20, 175

Dasgupta, Partha, 47n

Deductive reasoning: used in original position, 17, 82, 133–134; not used to spell out central organizing idea, 25

De Marneffe, Peter, 91n, 183n6

Democracy: constitutional vs. procedural, 145–148; deliberative, 148, 150; in the workplace, 178. *See also* Democratic regime; Democratic society; Property-owning democracy

Democratic regime: must have support of different comprehensive doctrines, 34; its power as power of citizens, 40, 90, 93–94

Democratic society: not a community, 3, 198–200; not a fixed natural order, 6; not justified by religious doctrines, 6; as a system of social cooperation, 6; four general facts about, 33–35; historical and social conditions of, 197; possibility of as pluralist and harmonious, 197. *See also* Oppression, fact of; Political society; Public political culture; Reasonable pluralism, fact of

Desert. *See* Entitlements; Native endowments

Deservingness. *See* Entitlements

Dickens, A. G., 197

Difference principle: stated, 42–43, 59–60, 64, 123; does not rely on maximin rule, 43n3, 94–95, 96; set within prior principle, 43, 46n10, 61, 67–68, 71, 78, 158n; revisions to, 43–44; not a constitutional essential, 48–49, 162; a form of reciprocity, 49, 60, 62, 64, 76–77, 96, 123–124, 126, 130, 133; sense in which egalitarian, 49, 68–69; applies to institutions, 51; and entitlements, 52, 74–75; and expectations of primary goods, 59; simplest form of, 59n26, 65, 69; as principle of distributive justice, 61–62; does not require continual economic growth, 63, 159; identifying relevant positions, 65–66; special form of, 65–66; counterexamples, 66–72; limits to inequalities not specified, 68; depends on rough continuum of basic structures, 70; expresses concern for all members of society, 71; and distribution of native endowments, 75–76; role of permissible inequalities, 78; arguments for not decisive, 95, 133; vs. principle of restricted utility, 119–130; three reasons why acceptable to more advantaged, 125–126; and social minimum, 129–130; may have little support in our public culture, 133; and worth of liberties, 149; and fair value of liberties, 151; and head taxes, 157–158; vs. principle of just savings, 159;

and taxation, 161–162; and the family, 163; and medical care, 173–174. *See also* Inequalities

Distributive justice: vs. constitutional essentials, 49; problem of, 50; vs. allocative justice, 50; and background procedural justice, 52. *See also* Background justice; Difference principle

Dreze, Jean, 47n

Dworkin, Ronald, 17n, 68n

Education: and wide role of political conception, 56–57, 122, 125–126, 146–148, 156; of children, 156–157, 163, 166, 173

Elections, 131, 136, 149

Elster, Jon, 11

English, Jane, 160n39

Entitlements: and background justice, 50–51; respected by difference principle, 52; specified by public rules, 72; vs. moral desert, 73, 77–79; and deservingness, 73–74; and legitimate expectations, 73–75, 77–79; presuppose deliberate acts of will, 75; authorize effective inequalities, 77; express principle of reciprocity, 77; address serious income inequalities, 77–78; fully adequate, 78

Envy. *See* Special psychologies

Equal basic liberties: as constitutional essentials, 28; and first principle of justice, 42; no priority to liberty as such, 44; specified by list, 44; list drawn up in two ways, 45; guaranteed by a constitution, 46; priority of, 46–47, 64, 105, 111, 115, 158, 192; and conscription, 47; and role of basic structure, 48; not absolute, 104; must be adjusted, 104, 111, 150; restriction vs. regulation of, 111; are truly essential, 112–114; regulation of by two conflicting criteria, 112–113; and two fundamental cases, 112–113; wide guarantee of fair value rejected, 150–152

Equality: conflict with liberty, 2; taking seriously, 4, 79, 140; of women, 11, 117, 167; and original position, 20; and difference principle, 49, 71, 76; and veil of ignorance, 87; and utilitarianism, 96; and first

Equality *(continued)*
    fundamental comparison, 96, 123; and
    fair system of cooperation, 96, 132, 167;
    and reciprocity, 123. *See also* Citizens;
    Fair equality of opportunity

Fair agreement, idea of. *See* Original position
Fair equality of opportunity: and associations, 11; meaning of, 43–44; and liberal
    equality, 44; not a constitutional essential, 47; and distribution of wealth, 51, 53;
    essential to background justice, 52; prevents more advantaged from exploiting
    their market power, 67; and property-owning democracy, 139, 176; and taxation, 161; lexically prior to difference
    principle, 163; and the family, 163–166;
    and medical care, 174; as great value, 190
Fair system of cooperation: as fundamental
    idea, 14; vs. allocative justice, 50, 95–96;
    and background institutions, 52; and social contract tradition, 95–96; includes
    idea of reciprocity, 96; relation to idea of
    equality, 96, 132, 167; and difference
    principle, 133; realized in property-owning democracy, 140; and ideas of the reasonable and rational, 191
Fair terms of cooperation, 6; specified by
    principles of justice, 7, 172; and idea of
    well-ordered society, 8; settled by agreement, 14–15; specified in original position, 16
Fair value of political liberties. *See* Political
    liberties
Family: as part of basic structure of society,
    10, 162–166; bound indirectly by principles of justice, 10–11, 163–167; and equality between men and women, 11, 163–
    168; no particular form of required, 163
Federalists, debates with Anti-Federalists, 1
Fellner, William, 98n
First fundamental comparison: quite conclusive, 95; compares two principles with
    principle of average utility, 95–96, 119;
    gives reasoning for first principle, 95–96;
    and equality, 96, 123; little support to dif-

ference principle, 96, 119; more
    fundamental than second comparison,
    97; argument stated, 97–98; avoids difficult points in theory of probability, 101;
    secures basic rights and liberties, 102–
    110, 119–120; controversial points in, 110
Four-stage sequence, 48, 112, 114, 172, 173–
    174
Freedom: outer limit of, 4, 92. *See also* Citizens
Freedom of association, 113
Free speech, 111–112, 113–114, 149–150
Fundamental ideas, 5–6, 14; sequence of,
    24–25; not justified by intrinsic reasonableness, 26; used to formulate political
    conception of justice, 27. *See also* Basic
    structure of society; Citizens; Fair system
    of cooperation; Original position; Public
    justification; Well-ordered society
Fundamental interests. *See* Citizens

Gauthier, David, 16n, 97
Gay and lesbian rights, 163n42
Gender: and difference principle, 64–66.
    *See also* Women
Gibbard, Allan, 107n
Global justice: vs. justice of basic structure,
    11; and Kant's view, 13; nature of, 13; and
    domestic justice, 13–14
Good: conception of defined, 19; permissible conceptions of, 61, 141, 153–154, 169;
    as rationality, 141–142; of political virtues,
    142; of a society, 142; of society as social
    union of social unions, 142, 201n; six
    conceptions of, 198n; congruence with
    the just, 202. *See also* Primary goods
Gutmann, Amy, 199n

Harsanyi, J. C., 97n, 100n22
Hart, H. L. A.: reply to, 42n; on minimum
    content of natural law, 56n, 145n15, 194;
    his criticism of account of liberties in
    *Theory*, 112
Head taxes, 157–158
Health care. *See* Medical care
Hedonism, 105
Hegel, G. W. F., 3, 34n, 144

Hinsch, Wilfried, 183n6
Hobbes, Thomas, 1, 82n2, 161
Howe, R., 108–110
Hume, David, 56n, 197n
Hurley, S. L., 106n

Ideal social process view: and institutional division of labor, 54; vs. historical process view, 54; and background justice, 57
Ideal theory: defined, 13; vs. nonideal theory, 13, 66; as main concern, 65–66; excludes use of rigid designators, 69
Inequalities: most fundamental, 40–41; principle regulating, 42–43; in life-prospects affected by three contingencies, 55; of race and gender, 64–66; permitted when effective, 67–69, 77, 78; reasons for regulating, 130–132
Inquisition: not an accident, 34
Institutional division of labor, 54
International law. *See* Global justice
Interpersonal comparisons: and primary goods, 60; and basic capabilities, 175
Intrinsic reasonableness, 26n21, 30, 31
Intuitionism: as a comprehensive doctrine, 14, 28; and conception of political justice, 97

Judicial review, 148
Justice as fairness: companion fundamental ideas, 5; practical aim of, 5, 29, 134; and public political culture, 5, 122, 148; central idea of, 5–6; as focus of overlapping consensus, 12; as realistically utopian, 13; as a political conception not a comprehensive doctrine, 14, 19, 182; explanation of name, 16; as form of contract doctrine, 16n; uses idea of public justification, 29; support of overlapping consensus not guaranteed, 37; question it answers, 39–40, 41; its primary subject, 39–40; a form of political liberalism, 40; uses three points of view, 45n; vs. allocative justice, 50; an ideal social process view, 54; and desert, 72–74; not part of theory of rational choice, 82n2; not utilitarian, 107–109; as egalitarian, 130–132; relies on norma-

tive conception vs. psychology, 148; neutrality of aim vs. procedural neutrality, 153n27; role of primary goods in, 169–170; as free-standing view, 181–183, 187–190; concern with stability, 185; not political in the wrong way, 188–189; abandons ideal of political community based on shared comprehensive doctrine, 198–199; social unity derives from an overlapping consensus, 199. *See also* Political conception of justice; Political philosophy; Stability
Justice between generations. *See* Just savings, principle of
Justice between peoples. *See* Global justice
Just savings, principle of, 159–161

Kant, Immanuel: on orientation in political philosophy, 3n2; on world government, 13; comprehensive doctrine of, 33, 34, 156, 191, 194, 198; and priority of the right, 81–82; rejects civic humanism, 142n8
Kelly, Erin, 12n, 22n
Kripke, Saul, 59n26
Krouse, Richard, 135n2

Laden, Anthony, 108n
Law of peoples. *See* Global justice
Least advantaged: defined, 59; identified by income and wealth, 59, 59n26, 65; not a rigid designator, 59n26, 69, 72; position in well-ordered society quite satisfactory, 99–100; two reactions to excessive strains of commitment, 128; are owed reciprocity, 139
Legitimate expectations. *See* Entitlements
Leisure time, 179
Liberal principle of legitimacy. *See* Political legitimacy
Libertarian, objections, 83. *See also* Buchanan, James; Gauthier, David; Nozick, Robert
Liberties: of the moderns vs. the ancients, 2, 2n, 143; negative vs. positive, 177
Liberty: conflict with equality, 2. *See also* Citizens; Principles of justice

Liberty of conscience: and Wars of Religion, 1; and associations, 11, 182n; as constitutional essential, 28; and moral powers, 45, 113, 169; as primary good, 58; and restrictions on, 104–105, 111–112; and utilitarianism, 115; to overcome ideology, 122; more valuable than political liberties, 143; and education, 156; and burdens of judgment, 191; as fundamental interest, 192

Lincoln, Abraham, 29, 147n18

Local justice, principles of: defined, 11; constrained by principles for the basic structure, 11–12

Locke, John: on toleration, 1; on liberty vs. equality, 2; social contract doctrine of, 16, 16n; on constituent vs. ordinary power, 46n9; ideal historical process view vs. ideal social process view, 52–54

Luther, Martin, 188

Machiavelli, Niccolò, 144

Markets, 131

Marx, Karl, 31, 157; on ideology, 4n, 79, 121–122, his critique of liberalism, 148, 176–179

Maximin rule: not used to argue for difference principle, 43n3, 94–95, 96; not general principle of rational decision, 97n; defined, 97–98; applies under three conditions, 98–99; as heuristic device, 99; and third condition, 101–104; forces parties to focus on fundamental interests, 103n27

McClennen, E. F., 126n

McPherson, Michael, 135n2

Meade, J. E., 135n1

Media, access to, 149

Medical care: right to, 11; and primary goods, 60n28; differences in citizens' need for, 171–172; and legislative stage, 173; as part of social minimum, 173, 176; and difference principle, 173–174; and the handicapped, 176n59

Michelman, Frank, 162n

Mill, J. S.: comprehesive doctrine of, 33, 34, 156, 191, 194, 198; idea of society in a just stationary state, 64, 159; objection to Bentham, 119; on bases of political power, 131; on associative goods, 144; reliance on psychological principles, 147–148; on regulating bequest and inheritance, 160–161; on family, 166; on worker-managed cooperative firms, 176, 178; on political values, 189n

Modus vivendi, 89n, 192, 194–195; may change over time into an overlapping consensus, 33, 192–193, 197–198

Montesquieu, Charles de, 1

Moral desert vs. entitlements, 72–73. *See also* Entitlements

Moral personality. *See* Citizens; Moral powers

Moral persons. *See* Citizens

Moral powers, two: defined, 18–19, 196; companion powers, 24; and basic liberties, 45, 112–113, 169; two fundamental cases, 45, 112–114, 169; developed within basic structure, 57; and primary goods, 58, 170–175; and fundamental interests, 85; and property rights, 114; and basic capabilities, 169–170; differences in exercise and development of, 170; as good, 200. *See also* Citizens

Moral psychology: and political virtues, 117; and question of stability, 181, 195–198; and the reasonable, 195–198. *See also* Original position; Special psychologies

Moral realism, 14–15

Murrell, Peter, 118n

Nagel, Thomas, 153n28, 160n39

Native endowments: not fixed natural assets, 56–57, 158; our place in distribution of not deserved, 74–75, 78; question of ownership does not arise, 75; distribution of regarded as common asset, 75–76, 124; distribution of to be regulated by difference principle, 76; and head taxes, 157–158; differences in, 170

Natural rights doctrine: as a political conception, 9

Neutrality: of aim in justice as fairness, 153n27; of aim vs. procedural, 153n27; vs. bias, 154

Nozick, Robert, 32n; contract view of, 16n, 53n19; objections to justice as fairness, 52n, 83n, 97

Okin, Susan Moller, 163n45, 166n49, 167
Oppression, fact of, 34, 84, 187–188, 197
Original position, 10; as fundamental idea, 14–15; and conditions for fair agreements, 14–15, 80; and veil of ignorance, 15, 18; generalizes idea of social contract, 16; vs. Locke, 16; question it answers, 16, 79; eliminates bargaining advantages, 16, 87; hypothetical and nonhistorical, 16–17; and deductive reasoning, 17, 82, 133–134; as device of representation, 17–18, 30, 80, 85, 86; models our considered convictions, 18, 30; models equality of citizens, 20; leads to view of distribution of endowments as common asset, 76; keeps track of assumptions, 81; vs. arguments in economics and social theory, 81; aim of, 81, 83; similarity to Kant's categorical imperative, 81–82; necessary psychology included, 83, 133; parties are artificial persons, 83; principles chosen from list, 83, 95; aims of parties as trustees, 84–85, 102, 105, 106–107, 108–110; parties not self-interested, 85; and concept of the right, 85–86; and publicity condition, 86; we may enter at any time, 86, 160; parties not moved by special psychologies, 87, 88; argument has two parts, 88, 180–181, 184, 186n8; second part concerns psychology of citizens, 88–89, 181; includes agreement on standards of public reason, 89–90; role of idea of agreement, 102–103; parties must weigh strains of commitment, 103–104, 110, 128–129; parties not especially averse to uncertainty, 106–107, 109–110; fundamental interests take priority, 110; does not fully specify primary goods, 172, 174. *See also* First fundamental comparison; Second fundamental comparison; Veil of ignorance

Overlapping consensus: justice as fairness as focus of, 12, 181, 183, 189; related to idea of public justification, 26, 29, 32, 37, 121; meaning of, 32, 184; why introduced, 32, 187, 188; most reasonable basis of social unity, 32, 199; and features of political conception, 33; not designed as balance between existing comprehensive doctrines, 37, 61, 188–189; and primary goods, 60; citizens have their own further grounds for, 121, 190, 201; and need for simplification, 175–176; and stability, 181, 183, 195; and liberalism, 185–186; not used in *Theory*, 186; and model case, 190–191; vs. modus vivendi, 192–193, 194–195; not utopian, 192–195; how it might come about, 193–195, 197–198; not a happy coincidence, 198. *See also* Justice as fairness; Modus vivendi; Political conception of justice

Pareto efficiency, 61n29
Parfit, Derek, 69n37, 160n39
Patterson, Orlando, 24n
Peffer, R. G., 44n7
Perfectionism: as a comprehensive doctrine, 14; and conception of justice, 97; and constitutional essentials, 151–152
Permissible conceptions of the good. *See* Good
Person, conception of. *See* Citizens
Phelps, E. S., 123n
Pluralism. *See* Reasonable pluralism, fact of
Political, domain of, 181–183, 190
Political conception of justice: and agreement, 9; as most reasonable basis of social unity, 9, 32, 84, 199; must fulfill public role, 9, 89; first feature: applies to basic structure, 12, 26–27, 33; vs. a comprehensive doctrine, 19; second feature: does not presuppose accepting any particular comprehensive doctrine, 26–29, 33, 37, 182, 187, 189; third feature: drawn from public political culture, 27, 29, 33, 34–35, 148; to resolve constitutional essentials, 28, 32, 41, 183, 190; three features allow an overlapping consensus, 33; has support of an overlapping consensus of irreconcilable comprehensive doctrines, 34, 36–37, 37; not designed as

Political conception of justice *(continued)*
  balance between existing comprehensive
  doctrines, 37, 61; and distribution of
  wealth, 53; wide role of, 56; and primary
  goods, 58–60, 141, 170; belongs to a
  moral conception, 78, 195; its educational role, 122, 125–126, 146–148; must
  take into account economic efficiency,
  123; influence on public political culture,
  132, 146–147; practical aim of, 134;
  whether reasonable, 136; as free-standing, 181–183, 188–190; not discussed in
  *Theory,* 186; many ways to cohere with
  comprehensive doctrines, 190, 193, 198.
  *See also* Justice as fairness; Political philosophy
Political judgments: subject of reasonable
  disagreement, 36
Political justice, fundamental question of,
  7–8, 172
Political legitimacy: problem of, 40–41; liberal principle of, 41, 84, 89–92, 141, 202;
  and two roles of basic structure, 48; and
  stability, 125, 186
Political liberalism: and comprehensive
  doctrines, 28; defined, 40; how arises,
  40–41; compatible with classical republicanism, 144; vs. comprehensive liberalism, 153–157; not arbitrarily biased, 153–
  157; how possible, 189–192
Political liberties: and moral powers, 45,
  112, 169; their fair value, 46, 148–150, 161,
  176, 177; and distribution of wealth, 51;
  essential to background justice, 52; and
  argument for in first fundamental case,
  112–113; less valuable than liberty of conscience, 143; not merely formal, 148–149,
  177; as great values, 189–190
Political philosophy: practical role of, 1–2,
  28–29, 32, 185; and orientation, 3; and
  reconciliation, 3, 4n, 37–38, 76; as ideological, 4n; as realistically utopian, 4;
  fundamental question of, 7–8, 13, 172,
  176n; part of domain of the moral, 14;
  not applied moral philosophy, 14, 182;
  cannot show superiority of any comprehensive doctrine, 84

Political power: as coercive power of citizens, 40, 90, 93–94, 94n15, 182, 183–184,
  185, 190
Political relationship: its special features,
  40, 182
Political society: not a community or an association, 3, 4, 11, 20–21, 94, 182, 198–
  200; as a fair system of cooperation between free and equal citizens, 4, 8; not
  voluntary, 4, 20, 40, 93–94, 94n14, 182; as
  well-ordered, 8–9; fundamental status in
  is equal citizenship, 132; good of, 198–
  202; as social union of social unions,
  201n
Political values: two kinds, 91; examples of,
  117; to justify use of public funds, 152;
  apply to basic structure, 182; used to settle constitutional essentials, 183, 190; relation to nonpolitical values, 183–184,
  190; not easily overridden, 189, 194
Primary goods: defined, 57–58, 60, 88; five
  kinds, 58–59; part of political conception, 58–60, 141, 170; shares of specified
  by index, 59; given by reference to objective features, 59–60, 116, 151, 179; belong
  to a partial conception of the good, 60;
  and interpersonal comparisons, 60; two
  ways to specify, 61, 188–189; problem
  they solve, 88, 169–170; and worth of political liberties, 149; objections to, 153,
  168–169; do not abstract from basic capabilities, 169–176; flexibility of index of,
  170–176; differences in expectations of,
  171; income and wealth not identified
  only with personal income and private
  wealth, 172; not specified fully in original
  position, 172, 175; index is of expectations over a complete life, 172–173; and
  leisure time, 179; fair to free and equal
  citizens, 189. *See also* Moral powers, two
Principles of justice: role of, 7–8; do not apply directly to associations or the family,
  10–11, 73, 163–164; and considered convictions, 41–42; to regulate inequalities,
  41–42; content of two, 42–43; revisions
  to, 43–45; priority of first principle
  (equal liberties), 46–47, 64, 105, 111, 115,

192; express political values, 48; should be reasonably simple, 78; publicity of, 78, 86, 116; not derived from rationality alone, 82n2; chosen from list, 83, 95; general and universal, 86; argument for them has two parts, 88, 180–181, 184, 186n8; agreement on them has two parts, 89; their stability, 89, 115–117; values characterizing, 91; secure citizens' fundamental interests, 103–104, 170, 200; foster political virtues, 116–117; their institutional content, 136; compatible with property-owning democracy and liberal socialism, 138–139; and fair value of political liberties, 149; priority of liberty and head taxes, 158. *See also* Background justice; Constitutional essentials; Difference principle; Equal basic liberties; First fundamental comparison; Second fundamental comparison

Priority of liberty. *See* Principles of justice

Private sphere: if exempt from justice then no such thing, 166

Procedural justice. *See* Background justice

Property, right to, 114–115, 177

Property-owning democracy: vs. capitalist welfare state, 8n, 135–136, 139–140; and background justice, 51; and social minimum, 130; satisfies two principles, 138–139; vs. liberal socialism, 138–139; realizes fair system of cooperation, 140; as constitutional regime, 145, 150; its economic institutions, 158–162; capital accumulation may cease, 159; aims for full equality of women, 167; and fair equality of opportunity, 176; compatible with worker managed firms, 178

Psychology. *See* Moral psychology; Reasonable

Public justification: as fundamental idea, 8, 14, 26; and overlapping consensus, 26, 29, 32, 37, 121; is addressed to others who disagree with us, 27; not simply valid argument from given premises, 27; must be acceptable on due reflection, 27; proceeds from some consensus, 27; meaning of, 27, 91n; and public reason,

27, 186, 188; aims to preserve social cooperation on footing of mutual respect, 28; political vs. comprehensive ideas of, 28–29; practical aim of reasonable agreement, 28–29, 32; and public political culture, 29; distinguished from mere agreement, 29; and educational role of political conception, 56–57, 122, 125–126, 146–148, 156; and priority of liberties, 105; encourages political virtues, 117; three levels of in well-ordered society (full publicity), 121–122, 146

Public political culture: and fundamental ideas of justice as fairness, 5, 6, 19, 21, 25, 122, 148; contains a variety of possible organizing ideas, 25; as source of political conception of justice and public justification, 27, 29, 33, 34–35, 78; and political will, 101; role of in first fundamental comparison, 118; and citizens' self-conceptions, 122, 146; and political virtues, 126; to determine content of social minimum, 132; influence of political conception on, 132, 146–147; and normativity of political conception, 148; and support of art, 152; overlapping consensus as feature of, 185–186

Public reason: and public justification, 26–27, 186, 188; defined, 27, 41, 91–92; and liberal principle of legitimacy, 48, 141; part of original agreement, 89–90; reasonable comprehensive doctrines can be introduced, 90; wide vs. inclusive view, 90n12; not specified by comprehensive doctrines or disputed economic theories, 90, 117; holds for constitutional essentials vs. most legislative questions, 91; values of, 91–92, 168; vs. nonpublic reason, 92; how content may vary, 93; conditions for its possibility, 112–113, 116; and restrictions on free speech, 113–114; and political virtues, 116–118, 194; and abortion, 117; and constitutional regime, 148; and stability of justice as fairness, 185–186; its great values, 190

Pure procedural background justice. *See* Background justice

Rabinowitz, Joshua, 58n24

Race, 64–66

Rational: idea of, 6, 87; vs. the reasonable, 6–7, 7n, 81, 191; idea of not explicitly defined, 82; and special psychologies, 87

Raz, Joseph, 156n

Realistic utopia, 4, 13

Reasonable: idea of, 3n3, 6–7, 82, 196; vs. the rational, 6–7, 7n, 81, 191; as moral idea, 7; idea of not explicitly defined, 82; and political conception of justice, 136; vs. unreasonable doctrines, 183, 191–192; vs. true, 189; psychology of, 195–198

Reasonableness. *See* Reasonable; Virtues

Reasonable pluralism, fact of, 3–4, 40, 84; as permanent condition, 4, 33–34, 36, 197; and reconciliation, 5; rules out comprehensive doctrines as basis for agreement, 9, 15, 25, 32, 60; means democratic society cannot be a community, 21; and overlapping consensus, 32, 60, 188, 190; how it comes about, 35; need not imply philosophical skepticism, 36; no agreement on moral desert, 73, 77; and priority of liberties, 115; and ideas of the good, 141; and basis of social unity, 151, 199; and whether political liberalism is biased, 155–156; not acknowledged in *Theory*, 187

Reciprocity, 6, 49n; difference principle as form of, 49, 60, 62, 64, 76–77, 96, 123–124, 126, 130, 133; and equal-justice lines, 62; utilitarianism violates requirements of, 63, 96, 117, 122; entitlements express principle of, 77; situated between impartiality and mutual advantage, 77; and social contract tradition vs. utilitarianism, 95–96; and second fundamental comparison, 96, 122–124; between efficiency and equality, 123; and capitalism, 138; least advantaged are owed, 139; as great value, 189–190; as both principle and disposition, 196

Reflective equilibrium: idea of connects with public justification, 26–29; and consistency of considered judgments, 29–30; and intrinsic reasonableness of our judgments, 30; narrow vs. wide, 30–31; gen-

eral and full, 31; nonfoundationalist, 31; testing counterexamples to justice as fairness, 66–72; and practical aim of political conception, 134; and reasonableness of political conception, 136. *See also* Considered judgments; Intrinsic reasonableness

Reformation, 192

Regimes: five kinds, 136; four questions about, 136–137; ideal institutional description of, 137, 178

Right: priority of, 82, 141; and political ideas of the good, 201

Rightness as fairness, 186, 188

Risk aversion. *See* Special psychologies

Risk vs. uncertainty, 106

Roemer, J., 108–110

Rousseau, J. J., 196n16; on inequalities, 131n50, 132; his civic humanism, 2, 142n8, 143n11

St. Augustine, 34n

Sandel, Michael, 165n48

Scanlon, T. M., 7n, 58n24, 91n, 130n, 185n

Scheffler, Samuel, 58n24, 193n

Schelling, Thomas, 123n

Second fundamental comparison: less conclusive, 95, 133; gives reasoning for difference principle, 95–96; and reciprocity, 96, 122–124; compares two principles with principle of restricted utility, 120; and publicity, 120–122; and stability, 124–126

Self-respect, social bases of: as primary good, 59; vs. self-respect as an attitude, 60; and property rights, 114

Sen, Amartya, 7n, 47n; objection to primary goods, 168–169; reply to, 169–176

Sense of justice: involves an intellectual power, 29. *See also* Citizens; Moral powers, two

Sibley, W. M., 7n

Sidgwick, Henry, 50, 99; principle of equity, 87

Skinner, Quentin, 144n13

Social contract tradition: its idea of society, 95; vs. utilitarianism, 95–96

Social cooperation: fair terms of, 6; idea of, 6; and rational advantage, 6; vs. socially coordinated activity, 6; well-ordered society specifies idea of, 9; idea of as sequence of fundamental ideas, 24–25; idea of not understood through deductive argument, 25; various ways of fixing terms of, 25; maintained by public agreement on constitutional essentials, 28. *See also* Fair system of cooperation

Socialism, 114, 136, 150, 178; command economy violates two principles, 138; liberal is compatible with two principles, 138–139

Social unity, basis of. *See* Political conception of justice

Special psychologies: which, 87; parties not moved by them, 87, 88, 106–107, 180; of citizens, 88–89, 181, 184, 202

Stability: of principles of justice, 89, 115–117; question of, 103n26; 108n, 110, 181, 183, 184, 186; three requirements for, 115–117, 194; and second fundamental comparison, 124–126; and political legitimacy, 125, 186; idea of, 125–126; and overlapping consensus, 181, 183, 195; and moral psychology, 181, 195–198; not simply a matter of avoiding futility, 185; secured by motivation of the appropriate kind, 185; and good of political society, 198–202

Strains of commitment: and choice of principles in original position, 103–104, 110, 128–129; excessive in utilitarianism, 128–130

Strict compliance theory. *See* Ideal theory

Sunstein, Cass, 146

Taxation, 160–162

Taylor, Charles, 142n8

Teitelman, Michael, 58n24

Tocqueville, Alexis de, 131n49, 144

Toleration, principle of, 1, 192–193

Uncertainty vs. risk, 106

Unreasonable views, 183, 191; not necessarily incorrect, 184

Utilitarianism: as a political conception, 9; 97; as a comprehensive doctrine, 14, 187; and public justification, 28; would require oppressive sanctions of state power, 34; and allocative justice, 50; violates requirements of reciprocity, 63, 117, 122; its idea of society, 95; vs. social contract tradition, 95–96; equality and reciprocity accounted for only indirectly, 96; all pleasures intrinsically good, 100n22; rights restricted for greater good, 100, 102, 104, 110; and reasoning about justice, 107–109; is unstable, 110, 115; and liberty of conscience, 115; and public reason, 116; extreme demands on less advantaged, 127; relies on sympathy, 127; and excessive strains of commitment, 128–130; and satisfaction of desires, 168. *See also* Mill, J. S.; Utility

Utility: average principle of vs. two principles, 95–96, 119; average principle of defined, 96; average principle allows unacceptable outcomes, 100, 104, 110; restricted principle defined, 120; restricted principle vs. difference principle, 120–130; restricted principle lacks idea of reciprocity, 122; indeterminacy of restricted principle, 126; restricted principle and idea of social minimum, 127–128; social minimum in restricted principle vague, 129. *See also* Utilitarianism

Veil of ignorance: defined, 15, 18; and considered judgments, 30; and four-stage sequence, 48; as reasonable condition, 81; and formal equality, 87; removes bargaining advantages, 87; permits knowledge of general facts and circumstances, 87, 101, 121; implies no basis for estimating probabilities, 98, 101, 104–106. *See also* Original position

Virtues: political, 92, 116–118, 142, 190; and public reason, 116–118, 194; constitute a public good, 118; and public political culture, 126; and education, 156, 163, 166; judicial, 170–171; have role in public life, 177, 195; and worker-managed firms, 178. *See also* Civility, duty of

Waldron, Jeremy, 127n47

Wars of Religion, 1

Weber, Max, 154n29

Weitzman, Martin, 72n

Well-ordered society: fundamental idea of as companion idea, 5, 8, 14; three features of, 8, 199; general vs. particular meanings, 9; an idealization, 9; specifies idea of social cooperation, 9; provides mutually recognized point of view, 9, 27; and public justification, 26; regulated by public conception of justice, 31; as just stationary state, 64; position of least ad- vantaged in, 99–100; three levels of publicity (full publicity), 121–122, 146; stability of, 125; and equality at highest level, 132; as a political good, 142, 198–202; vs. Marx's idea of a full communist society, 177; account of in *Theory* based on comprehensive doctrine, 186–187; end of political justice is among citizens' most basic aims, 199; not a private society, 199

Williams, Bernard, 7n

Women: equality of and abortion, 117; equal justice for, 163–165. *See also* Gender